PRIME TIME

SEXUAL HEALTH FOR MEN OVER FIFTY

PRIME TIME

LESLIE R. SCHOVER, Ph.D.

HOLT, RINEHART and WINSTON **NEW YORK**

1984

Published by Holt, Rinehart and Winston,
383 Madison Avenue, New York, New York 10017.
Published simultaneously in Canada by Holt, Rinehart and
Winston of Canada, Limited.

Library of Congress Cataloging in Publication Data
Schover, Leslie R.
Prime time.
Includes bibliographical references and index.
1. Sex.   2. Middle aged men—Sexual behavior.
I. Title.
HQ28.S36   1984   613.9'52   83-18383
ISBN: 0-03-064028-8

First Edition

Designer: Joy Chu
Printed in the United States of America
1 3 5 7 9 10 8 6 4 2

Grateful acknowledgment is made for use of the excerpt on
pages 220–21, taken from the Dear Abby column.
Copyright, 1983, Universal Press Syndicate. Reprinted with
permission. All rights reserved.

ISBN 0-03-064028-8

In memory of
DR. JOSEPH SHEEHAN,
who was my professor,
role model, and friend.

CONTENTS

LIST OF ILLUSTRATIONS

ACKNOWLEDGMENTS

Writing this book has been one of the most enjoyable experiences in my life. A number of people have helped make it so. I want to thank Bobbi Mark, my editor, for making the publishing process so much smoother than I had imagined. I am also grateful to Barbara Reschke of Scientific Publications at M. D. Anderson Hospital and Tumor Institute for editing the first draft, and to Patricia Carlson of our Medical Graphics department for her clear illustrations. My sister, Michal Lawrence, thought of the title. A crucial contributor has been Frances Gange, my speedy and irreplaceable secretary, who rightfully sees this as her book too.

Since *Prime Time* has grown out of my clinical work, I take pleasure in thanking some of the people who shaped my career: Joshua Golden and Anna Heinrich of the UCLA Human Sexuality Program; Paul Abramson and Joseph Sheehan of the Department of Psychology at UCLA; Phil Oderberg and David Wellisch, who enhanced my personal growth and therapy skills; all my friends from the Sex Therapy Center at SUNY Stony

Brook, but especially Jerry Friedman, Julia Heiman, and Stephen Weiler; Ismet Karacan, who provided a rare learning experience at the Sleep Disorders and Research Center, Baylor College of Medicine; and of course my colleagues in the Department of Urology at M. D. Anderson Hospital and Tumor Institute.

Finally, I want to express my appreciation to two friends and mentors, Joseph LoPiccolo and Andrew von Eschenbach. Without knowing Joe and Andy, I not only could never have written this book, but I would not even be the same person.

FOREWORD

Sexuality is important in our lives. Most people in Western society believe not only that they should be sexually active, but that they had better be good at sex. If they are not living up to these expectations—not having lovers, not having orgasms, or not satisfying their partners, they tend to feel inadequate and ashamed.

In just a few decades women's sexual roles have shifted. Instead of being seen as innocent, long-suffering recipients of male lust, women are now asked to be active participants, initiating and enjoying sexual relations, skilled in the art of loving, and multiply orgasmic. Fortunately, medical research has revealed that women are capable, physiologically and psychologically, of living up to these new expectations, although the permission to enjoy sex sometimes becomes more of a demand to enjoy sex.

The sexual revolution has had less of a positive impact on men. We have not given up our expectation that men should always desire sex, always get erections, and always reach orgasm, despite a rapidly accumulating body of research showing that male sexual capacities are more modest than the myths would have it. As men age, it is more likely that they will have physical problems. Their erections and orgasms may be impaired, and often their resulting concern and shame also decreases their desire for sexual relations. Yet older men are often much more capable of enjoyable sexual contact than they realize. Unfortunately, there is an information gap. New medical knowledge about male sexuality has not been made sufficiently available to the public. It is particularly for men over fifty that the facts are so necessary.

Many popular magazines, books, and even video cassettes try to supply that information. Most are more successful in financial terms than they are in providing useful guidance for their male readers. All too many are biased or sleazy in tone. People desperately need clear, up-to-date information, presented in readable fashion by knowledgeable scientists. This brings us to Leslie Schover, Ph.D., and her book, *Prime Time: Sexual Health for Men Over Fifty*.

In the years since I first met Dr. Schover, she has gone from being a bright and innovative graduate student to doing postgraduate work at some of the leading sex research centers in this country. Her most recent job has been with the world-famous M. D. Anderson Hospital and Tumor Institute in Houston, Texas. Thus her early scientific promise has been seasoned and enriched by extensive clinical experience treating patients with sexual concerns. Now she has written a book for the general public. She begins with the question, "Why should you read another book about sex?"

My answer is that her book should be read because it fills a real need. Many other "sex books" are written by professional writers who lack scientific background and clinical experience. Those by scholars in the field are often full of jargon, and nearly impossible to read. Dr. Schover's book is clear, even deceptively simple. She has taken the time to make complicated information understandable. That, as any writer knows, is a very rough task. Although she is still a young psychologist, writing about the concerns of men over fifty, there is a ring of authenticity and a warm, compassionate regard for the men and women in the many clinical vignettes illustrating her points. Yet the scientific content is accurate, carefully selected, and validated, without putting the reader to sleep. The scope and organization of her book is ideally suited for men in the prime years of life, and their partners.

Prime Time: Sexual Health for Men Over Fifty deserves your attention. It should be a great help to anyone interested enough to read this far.

> Joshua S. Golden, M.D.
> Director, Human Sexuality Program, UCLA
> Los Angeles, August 1983

PRIME TIME

1

You as a Lover: Are You Getting Better or Just Older?

Why should you read another book about sex? Men these days are bombarded with advice on how to be better lovers, how to get more out of sex, or just how to get more sex. Yet there might not be as many books, manuals, magazine articles, movies, and TV shows about sex if problems in this area were not at an epidemic level. Perhaps you don't have any sexual problems, but opened this book out of idle curiosity, because you thought it might be titillating, or to see if there was a new trick to learn. But then, maybe you *are* dissatisfied with your sex life.

This book is geared for men over fifty (and their lovers), whether or not their sex lives are entirely satisfying. It is intended for men who are married, single, divorced, or widowed. While this book focuses on heterosexual relationships, homosexuality is also discussed. My goal is to provide commonsense information about the right to sexual health throughout life.

You will not find a chapter on ten easy steps to having intercourse on a trapeze, or a list of the top hundred sexual positions. I cannot suggest a magic pill that will restore your potency, or a way to make orgasms last for an hour. I *can* use my knowledge and experience as a psychologist, sex researcher, and sex therapist to separate some of the facts from the fiction. My hope is that having read this book, you will be able to make informed choices about your sexual health.

IS THERE SEX AFTER FIFTY?

What is our image of a sexual man over fifty? We think of the pot-bellied businessman chasing his young secretary around the desk, or the nasty old geezer goosing women with his cane. The accepted idea is that the way to get older gracefully is to stop feeling desire, or at least not to show it. A sexy old man is a foolish old man. "Normal" people just don't have sexual feelings after a certain age.

For women, the picture is even bleaker. We do not even have a stereotype of a dirty old lady. It is too awful to contemplate. If Mom and Apple Pie are sacred, Grandma is untouchable. Signs of aging in a woman, like gray hairs and laugh lines, are seen as ugly. At least a man with a few wrinkles may be described as "distinguished."

It is a testimony to the strength of the sex drive that in spite of this negative propaganda, older men and women usually keep up active sex lives. Patterns of sexual interest and intercourse are stable throughout adulthood, as long as people stay physically healthy and have a partner. It is always hard to define what is "normal" in sexuality, because there is such a wide range of attitudes, feelings, and practices. Nevertheless, researchers now agree that the average man or woman does not lose desire for sex with age, and that it is healthy, though certainly not always necessary for good health, to keep making love.

We have been taught that erection problems are unavoidable with age. While it is true that erection problems are more common as men grow older, recent studies suggest that they are not part of the "natural" aging process. Rather, diseases such as diabetes and arteriosclerosis, which become more common with age, can also cause erection problems. Many men without these risk factors, or in spite of them, continue to have full erections into their eighties and nineties.

You may have noticed that I do not use the word "impotence" to describe an erection problem. For one thing, "impotence" is a broad and confusing term, which has been used to cover almost any sexual problem, including trouble getting or keeping an erection, not being able to reach an orgasm (climax), reaching orgasm too quickly, or even a loss of desire for sex. Another reason not to use the word "impotent" is that it implies a man is helpless or powerless. The ability to get and sustain a hard erection has become a symbol of manhood, assuming an importance all out of proportion to the percent of our lives spent having sexual intercourse. Sometimes the first step in resolving an erection problem is to shrink it back to size.

THE TROUBLE WITH OLDER MEN

In my work with men over fifty, one problem I often see is the pressure they put on themselves to be sexual performers. "What makes a man a good lover?" I ask them.

"Well, a good lover is always in the mood for sex. He's the one who starts things, and as soon as he feels excited, he gets an erection. He may use a little foreplay to get his wife ready, but she doesn't need to touch him at all. His penis stays hard until it's time for intercourse. Then he makes sure he lasts long enough so his wife has a climax."

This "John Wayne" model of sex is what most men were taught: be strong, silent, and always in control. Unfortunately, there is no room in this script for the realities of sex, such as losing an erection, wanting to ask for a particular kind of caress, not being sure whether your partner had a climax, or suddenly having to sneeze during a romantic moment. When something goes wrong for a sexual hero, he has no way of coping. What can you do if the earth doesn't move?

Sometimes this sexual style works reasonably well in a man's younger, problem-free years. As a man ages, however, he may notice some slowing of his sex responses. If he expects to be a sexual superman, ready for action as soon as he jumps out of the phone booth, he may be disappointed. The first time he has trouble getting or keeping his erection, he may excuse it as just being due to fatigue. The second or third time, however, he panics. Has he lost his magical powers? Maybe he should just stay out of phone booths altogether, and leave the superman game to younger men.

Of course if he could settle for being an ordinary human, he might be able to stay in business. All too often, however, when a man develops an erection problem he stops having any sexual activity at all. If he is dating, he throws away his address book. If he is married, not only does he watch the late-night talk shows and sneak into bed to avoid waking his wife, but he also stops kissing her good morning or cuddling with her on the living room couch. "Why light a fire I can't put out?" he asks. "She'll just get more frustrated than she is now." Meanwhile the woman wonders why her husband or lover no longer finds her attractive. She may even blame the erection problem on her own inadequacy. She then becomes afraid to bring up the topic of the deep freeze on sex and affection. The last thing she wants is to make her partner feel pressured or insecure. He notices her silence and decides that she is no longer interested in sex.

Sexual intercourse, i.e., the moments in which penis meets vagina, is only one of the many ways to express sexual feelings. It is an even smaller fraction of the time that couples in a long-term relationship spend sharing love. Yet in these few words—"Why light a fire I can't put out?"—a man can deprive himself and his partner of all the warmth they have to give each other.

It is not easy to change the sexual habits and beliefs of thirty or forty years. The crucial thing, though, is to take the risk of trying something new. Not only can couples explore, on their own, ways to express sexual and nonsexual caring, but successful, short-term counseling is available for many sexual problems. There are also specific new medical treatments for erection problems, so that no man needs to resign himself to living without sexual intercourse.

AGING WELL

There has been too much talk about a man's sexual prime occurring at age seventeen. While a teenager may be able to have more orgasms in one evening than his father can, stamina is not the only measure of a good lover. Women, in particular, often wish their partners would take more time with foreplay and be more tender and relaxed. This is why making love with an older man can be like drinking vintage wine instead of the cheap table variety. Even beyond the richness of emotion and skill that comes with experience, it almost seems as though the physical changes of aging conspire to make men more sensual lovers.

If you are a healthy man past fifty, you may find that it takes longer for your penis to become fully erect. You also may need to have your penis directly touched and caressed. You may notice that you feel less pressure to have an orgasm each time you have sex. Rather than seeing these changes as a decline in the sexual cycle, you can view them as nature's cue to take your time and be less goal-oriented.

You can compare sex with a train trip to Chicago. Some men spend the whole time being impatient to get there. "When are we due in Chicago? Why is this train so slow? How many more stops do we have to make?" Other men sit back and look out the window, enjoy the scenery, and have a leisurely lunch in the dining car. For them, getting there is half the fun. The older we get, the more aware we often are of the preciousness of time. Each moment of a sexual encounter becomes valuable in itself, rather than being a whistle-stop on the way to the big orgasm.

This awareness of time leads men to reevaluate their priorities. As career goals are met and children grow up, a man may have more energy to devote to relationships. Some men become aware of a lack of warmth and closeness in their lives, while others just want to enjoy to the fullest the intimacy they have always had. Couples promise themselves that they will spend more hours together relaxing, traveling, and having fun after retirement. People who go through a divorce or bereavement in their middle age may look for a new relationship to fill their needs for company and sexual pleasure. Thus sex can become more important and central with age, rather than less so.

A fairly large group of men discover that just when they are finally ready to concentrate on relationships an erection problem develops. In later chapters we will look at some causes of erection problems and some new remedies for "the oldest obsession."

Even if your equipment is in working order, can you enrich your sex life? Many men feel completely satisfied with their sexual relationships, and do not need to change anything. For others, it may be a simple matter of rearranging their schedule to make more time for sex and romance. A number of couples, however, have never felt very comfortable talking about sex. They may have gotten into a sexual routine that is limiting or even boring. This book offers some ways to make sexual communication easier. Being able to ask for what you want and finding out what pleases your partner are the first steps in changing old patterns.

Research on sexuality and aging has made some real advances in the last several years. Every man (and his loving partner as well) has a right to know what he can expect to happen to his sexual function as he gets older and what new treatments are available for some common sexual problems. Unfortunately, even many health professionals are not aware of the latest information. That means you may need to be your own "sex expert." This book makes that task easier by offering some suggestions on what *you* can do to make these the golden years, rather than the retirement era, of your sex life.

2

Is There a Male Menopause?

Bob never had a problem with sex until he was fifty-seven. He and his wife, Annie, always had intercourse two or three times a week. While Bob was usually the one to start things, often by cuddling up to Annie in bed, she was almost always responsive. Gradually, however, Bob noticed that his erections were fading out during intercourse. He started having trouble reaching a climax, and even when he did, his pleasure was less than normal. Finally, Bob's erections stopped getting full enough to allow penetration. One night, when Bob stormed into the bathroom after an unsuccessful attempt to have sex, Annie suggested he see their family doctor. Bob made an appointment for an ordinary checkup. After the physical exam, the doctor told him that all systems appeared to be go. At that point, Bob got up his nerve to explain that he was having a sexual problem. The doctor chuckled, clapped Bob on the back, and told him to go home. "There's nothing wrong with you! You've just hit the male menopause—you know, the change of life. It's time to stop worrying about sex. Maybe you should take up fishing."

Although Bob's physician meant well, his facts were out-of-date. Most experts in sexuality agree that the average man does not go through a "menopause," or "climacteric" as it is sometimes called.

What is this so-called male menopause? The general idea is that a man's desire for sex and his erections naturally decline with age. More specifically, the theory presumes that the testicles stop producing enough of the "male sex hormone," a chemical called testosterone.

Testosterone is manufactured in the testicles and, in smaller amounts in both men and women, by the adrenal glands that sit on top of the kidneys. Testosterone is released into the bloodstream, so that it can do its work in special "receptor cells" in various areas of the body. Testosterone fits into the receptor like a key in its keyhole. One of the most important places that testosterone acts is in the brain, where it promotes sexual desire. Thus a man who does not have enough testosterone circulating in his blood may lose interest in sex and have trouble feeling pleasure and excitement in sexual situations. A man with low testosterone may also have trouble getting erections, partly because he is not even in the mood for sex and partly because testosterone may act directly on the nerves that control erections.

Testosterone is the substance that also acts at puberty to make a boy's genitals grow to adult size and to stimulate the growth of facial, body, underarm, and pubic hair. If a man has abnormally low testosterone, he may notice that he needs to shave less often, or has less body hair than before. He also may find that his testicles have gotten smaller.

How does the male body make sure to produce the right amount of testosterone? Sometimes we joke that a man's thinking is ruled by his sex organs, but actually the testicles are controlled by the brain. A part of the brain called the hypothalamus monitors the amount of testosterone in the bloodstream. Because the hypothalamus is also hooked up to centers controlling emotion and sensation, a man's moods and experiences can affect his hormone balance. When the hypothalamus senses a need for more testosterone, it produces a "releasing hormone." The releasing hormone sends a message to the pituitary gland. The pituitary, which sits at the base of the brain, is often called the master gland. It sends hormones into the bloodstream, to act on various targets. One of the pituitary products, luteinizing hormone, acts on the testicles to start the manufacture of testosterone. This cycle runs in a feedback loop, like a thermostat controlling the temperature in a house (see Figure 1). When circulating testosterone is low (like a house that is too cold), the hypothalamus puts out releaser hormone, switching on the pituitary, which turns on the testicles. If there is enough testosterone (the temperature is in the comfort range), the hypothalamus stays quiet.

One explanation for male menopause supposes that the comfort level on the hypothalamus "thermostat" is reset downwards in older men, for example to sixty instead of seventy-five degrees. Then the amount of testosterone in the blood would be maintained at a much lower level. A more likely theory is that the factory cells in the aging testicles, like a worn out furnace, can no longer respond to the thermostat's call for more testosterone. The hypothalamus keeps sending out releaser hormone, and the pituitary turns out luteinizing hormone, but the testicles just cannot keep up with the demand.

In women, this is essentially what happens at menopause. Their hypothalamus and pituitary hormones act on the ovaries, just as they do on the testicles in men. As women age, however, the ovaries stop responding to the surges of pituitary hormone that create the menstrual cycle. Because of the absence of estrogen and progesterone (hormones produced by the ovaries), eggs stop ripening and the lining of the uterus no longer

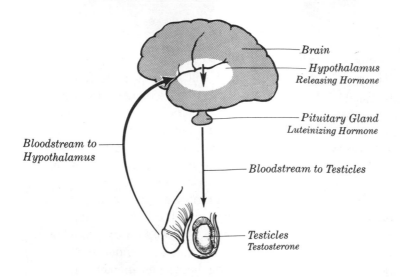

FIGURE 1. THE MALE SEX HORMONE CYCLE

waxes and wanes to produce menstruation. Older women still feel a desire for sex, however, because their adrenal glands are continuing to produce testosterone. In women, as well as men, testosterone is the hormone that seems to produce sexual desire.

Fortunately for men, the testicles, unlike the ovaries, keep functioning throughout life, producing both testosterone and sperm cells. The testicles may slow down, but they rarely come to a complete halt. For example, we have all heard of men becoming fathers at sixty-five or seventy years old, but not too many women have babies after their late forties. This sex difference makes sense in the evolutionary scheme of things. If an older man impregnates his partner, he has one more offspring. A woman, however, would be unlikely to stay healthy through the stress of pregnancy after her middle years. In the early history of humankind, the female menopause probably was a factor in the survival of the fittest. For example, imagine Stone Age Stella, one of the few of her tribe to reach the age of fifty. Her grandchildren were the sturdiest around, since she was available to mind them and gather extra roots and fruit. On Saturday night, Stella could still enjoy a little fun with her mate, Willy the Wanderer, without the danger of getting fatally pregnant. Willy, on the other hand, could take advantage of the young studs' hunting trips, entertaining their wives and perhaps sowing a few last wild oats to ensure his genetic posterity. Thus the women who had a menopause, and the men who did not, were likely to contribute most to the heritage.

It is only in recent years that accurate blood tests for testosterone, luteinizing hormone, and the hypothalamus's releaser hormone have been available. We can now examine hormone levels in older men, to see if there is any evidence of a "menopause." Researchers studying hormones in men of different ages have had conflicting results. The latest thinking is that testosterone levels do not change with age in men who are in good health. Thus there is no natural, universal menopause. Mildly reduced testosterone is found in older men who have health problems, however, such as diabetes or hypertension, or in men suffering the effects of years of overweight, heavy drinking, or heavy smoking.

But even if a man has less testosterone than he did when he was thirty, it may not affect his sex life. The "normal" range for testosterone in a blood test varies by 300 percent. Thus one man can have only a third of his next door neighbor's testosterone level, yet be quite normal. The results of their blood tests will not tell you anything about how much desire each man feels for sex, how often he has sex, or his ability to get erections. The neighbor with higher testosterone would not be more of a "real man." Researchers keep looking for a relationship between testosterone and sexual activity. As long as testosterone is in the normal range, however, the actual amount measured in the blood rarely predicts anything about a man's sex life. One recent study of men over sixty did find that those who had sex more often had slightly higher testosterone. These results could reflect increases in hormone levels caused by having sex, though. They do not necessarily show that high hormone levels generate more desire.

There has been some confusion about hormone levels and homosexuality. Researchers wondered if men who had low testosterone were more likely to prefer men as sexual partners. Modern scientists have not found a relationship between hormones and sexual orientation. Testosterone may control a man's *amount* of sexual desire, but it has no effect on the *object* of his desires. Testosterone works identically in heterosexual and homosexual men.

The great majority of men over fifty still have enough testosterone to maintain normal sexual desire and erections. Testosterone levels may fit what scientists call a "threshold" model. You can cross the threshold in a house by lifting your foot high enough to reach the top of the step. If you raise your foot six inches higher, you can still cross the threshold, though the extra effort would be a waste. As long as a man's testosterone is at the minimum threshold level, there may be no advantage in having more than that.

Scientists, however, do not completely understand the relationship between testosterone and sexual function. For one thing, levels of testosterone in the blood have regular cycles, or "biorhythms" if you will. Testosterone production increases and decreases depending on the time of day, day of the week, and even season of the year. In addition, only some of the testosterone in the bloodstream is in the active or free state. The rest of the testosterone is "bound" to tiny molecules of protein. That means it cannot fit into its keyhole target sites in the body. Finally, the target cells take the testosterone and change its chemical structure before they use it. Perhaps these target cells become less efficient as a man ages, which would account for some changes in his sexual desire. You can see why one blood test gives just a very rough estimate of a man's testosterone level, and why so much confusion remains about the male menopause.

Bob went home after his physical exam and told Annie what the doctor had said. Annie was upset but, after all, doctors know best. Annie's two closest friends confided that their husbands weren't quite the men they used to be, either. One of the women had even read an article on mid-life crises, and said her husband and Bob both fit the pattern to a tee. For Bob's fifty-eighth birthday, Annie bought him a rod and reel. She also treated herself to five romantic novels, a health club membership, and a cold shower.

WHEN IS THE HONEYMOON OVER?

If there is no male menopause, why do older men seem to lose interest in sex or to want sex less often over the years? Ever since Alfred Kinsey's sex studies in the 1940s, scientists have believed that the male desire for sex, as well as sexual activity, steadily decreased after age thirty. At Duke University in North Carolina, a series of interviews with aging men confirmed this observation.

The Duke studies found that both men and women gradually had sex less and less often as they got older. Their sexual interest or desire also decreased, but more slowly. This left a frustration gap between how often people wanted to have sex, and how often they actually did so. Men were always more sexually active than women of the same age. This can be explained by the fact that women often had no opportunity to have sex. Since most women marry older men, and men have a shorter life span on the average, women are more likely to become widows. Among older people, single women far outnumber single men. To make matters worse, many men prefer to date younger partners. Women in the Duke study who had given up sex often were celibate because they lacked a mate. Even in married couples, it was clear that the husband was the one who usually decided when sexual activity would stop. Often this was due to his ill health or to an erection problem.

This research gives the impression that older people just are not very sexual. Fortunately, however, it has recently been pointed out that these studies contain a flaw. Kinsey, as well as the Duke researchers, compared groups of men of different ages rather than observing one group over a period of years. The researchers tried to predict what would happen in twenty years to a man now in his forties, by studying men currently in their sixties or seventies. Considering the changes in our sexual attitudes and practices within this century, it may not be possible to draw a conclusion from such a comparison. The observed decline in sex across age groups may really reflect differing sexual practices in people born in 1890 versus 1920. For example, though they may not speak for your attitudes, or even "typical" ones, let's eavesdrop on a conversation between Earl Smith, aged seventy-two, and his thirty-nine-year-old son, Jack. Jack's wife has just left him, and he is feeling a need for a man-to-man talk.

Jack begins with a little hesitation. "Dad, maybe it's none of my business, but do you and Mom still . . . you know, have sex?"

Earl looks taken aback, and it is a moment before he answers. "Well, Jack, you know your mother is a real lady. Not that we didn't have our good times, but that's bygones now."

"But why, Dad? I can't ever imagine just giving up sex, even now when I'm feeling so down about Marie."

"Well, there was a time when I felt the same way, but sex hasn't worried me for a few years now. Part of it was your mother, of course. When she hit the change of life, she just sort of lost interest, and with her arthritis and all, I felt a gentleman shouldn't push. . . . To tell you the truth, Jack, your mother never has been much on sex, but she's a good woman, and a good wife—good cook, keeps the house spotless, even when she's not feeling well."

"Maybe Marie and I would have been better off if she wasn't so interested in sex. I had a hard time keeping up with her sometimes, especially after she read about multiple orgasms in her magazines."

Earl shakes his head. "I'm not sure your mother usually had even *one*."

"But Dad, didn't that make you feel bad? I mean, did you ever try to help her out, like with foreplay?"

"Jack, your mother didn't hold much with foreplay. And to my mind, there are some things you just don't ask a lady to do. A man and his wife have sex the normal way. If he's not satisfied, he has to find another kind of woman—not that I ever strayed, of course."

"Never, Dad?"

"Nope."

"Well, I wish I could say the same. In fact, I can only think of one or two guys in the office who haven't gotten any on the side at least a few times. . . . Don't worry Dad, I never had anything serious. Just one-nighters on a business trip. Now that Marie's left, I'm not sure what to do. I don't want some woman to get the idea that I'm going to remarry right away. Maybe I should just watch my hard-core videotapes for a while."

Earl looks puzzled. "Won't that just make you feel more frustrated, son?"

"Oh come on, Dad, don't tell me you never masturbate anymore either?"

"That's okay for teenage boys, but I haven't abused myself since I was . . . oh, maybe fifteen. It isn't healthy!"

"Makes you go blind and grow hair on your palms, huh Dad."

"Well now, maybe that's a little too strong. But it probably weakens your blood. Maybe that's why you're looking so stringy."

"Stringy! I lost weight on purpose. I've started to jog too. I'm getting back in shape!"

"Well, you look weedy to me. A man needs some meat on his bones."

"I give up, Dad."

"You'll understand when you get older, Jack. It's just natural for these things to mean less to you."

"Well I'll believe it when I feel it."

When Jack is seventy-two, he may well not be as content as his father to be celibate. Our cultural values are continuing to change, so that sexual health is more and more considered a right of adults of all ages. This can create confusion for men who have watched the "sexual revolution" take place. What is "normal"? Jokes that used to be muttered in the locker room are told on prime-time TV. Lingerie that was only fit for French postcards is advertised in ladies' magazines. Homosexuality is considered an option rather than a perversion. Even doctors have changed their wisdom, advising that sex helps you feel young and active, whereas it used to be something that sapped your strength.

Actually, our recent acceptance of sex as a healthy part of older adulthood is more in line with what the rest of the world has been believing for generations. In 106 cultures, anthropologists asked about sexuality in middle and old age. About 70 percent of the cultures expected their older men to stay sexually active. Only 8 cultures believed that older men should not be sexual.

Many older men want to know how much sexual activity is

normal. A picture is finally beginning to emerge of what happens to sexual feelings and activity as the average man ages. This more balanced view is drawn from examining individual men's lives over a period of years. It is not surprising to find that the best way to predict a man's sexual frequency after fifty is to look at how often he had sex as a younger man. The most common pattern is that sexual interest and activity remains at a stable level, with only mild decreases from the thirties through the seventies, as long as a man is in good physical health and has a willing partner.

Each man has a "comfort level" describing how much sex is satisfying to him. This preference can be seen in his early adulthood and stays true to form for his lifetime. Many men are almost obsessed with sex as teenagers. When they first marry, they may have sex or at least masturbate daily. Even when they are in their seventies, they continue to have many sexual daydreams, to respond with excitement to sexy pictures or to an attractive woman, and to feel frustrated if they go without sex for more than a few days. Another large group of men enjoy sex, but have always been able to take it or leave it. They may or may not enjoy watching an X-rated movie or seeing a pretty woman, and there is less urgency to translate their desire into an actual sex act. These men, especially as they get older, may go through long periods of celibacy without feeling upset. If they begin to have trouble with erections, they often regard the problem as a change that is to be accepted with age.

Most men fall somewhere between these two points, but even the extremes are considered "normal." We do not know whether a man's sexual comfort level is programmed into his genes, or learned as he is growing up. Probably, like most other aspects of a person's character, sexual interest and activity are molded by a combination of heredity and environment.

There is an old myth that a man only has so much sexual "ammunition," i.e., a young man who has sex very frequently will run out of bullets years before the one who sometimes holds his fire. This new research demonstrates that the reality is exactly the opposite: The man who is liberal with his shot is still loaded for bear at age eighty, while his buddy who conserved bullets may have given up hunting.

The crucial point is to know and accept your personal sexual comfort level.

Edward always felt as if there were something wrong with him because he did not see what was so fantastic and wonderful about sex. As a teenager, he was bored and turned off by the other boys' locker-room replays of the previous night's make-out session. When he married Grace, after a short honeymoon period, Edward was content with sex once a week. Grace never complained, and rarely tried to start things herself. Every once in a while she might serve dinner with candles, or put on perfume before they went to bed. On those nights, Edward was glad to take the hint and make love to his wife.

By the time the kids were all in college or off on their own, Edward and Grace had sex about once a month. One Sunday, however, Edward read a newspaper article about sex being important for middle-aged couples. A well-known psychologist was quoted as saying that a sexual frequency of less than once a week was the first warning sign of a marriage on the rocks. Edward stewed about the article for days. He wondered if Grace was secretly frustrated, and even looked through her drawers on her bridge club night, to see if she had a vibrator. After a week had gone by, he asked her if she had seen the article. Grace said that indeed she had read it, and thought the whole thing was ridiculous. "I hope you aren't feeling like we should have sex every night now, are you?" she asked her husband.

Edward heaved a sigh of relief. "No, but how about a week from Thursday?"

A man's amount of desire for sex only becomes a problem if it interferes with his happiness or causes conflict because he and his partner do not match. If a man finds himself getting into risky sexual situations, having sexual activity of a sort that leaves him feeling ashamed, coercing a partner into having sex, or unable to concentrate on his work because of sexual daydreams or the need to masturbate several times a day, then his sexual frustration may be unusually high. If a man is upset and worried because nothing excites him anymore, or if his wife threatens to leave because of his lack of desire for her, then low desire may be a real problem. These are the situations where a thorough medical and psychological evaluation may suggest a remedy.

While stability of sexual interest is the general rule, it is important to remember that every man has some times in his life when he has sex much more or less often than usual. For example, the novelty of starting a sexual relationship often promotes a honeymoon period. This is known as the Coolidge Effect, because of the following story about President Calvin Coolidge:

The President and his wife were touring a poultry farm. Mrs. Coolidge requested in a whisper that their guide point out one particular rooster, who was servicing all the females, to the President. When the guide relayed this message, President Coolidge replied, "Tell my wife that there's more than one hen."

Scientists have produced the Coolidge Effect in the laboratory. They allow a male rat to mate with a female until he stops from exhaustion. If a different female is then put in the cage, the male perks up and goes at it again. (Many a wife, finding lipstick on her tired husband's collar, is convinced that her man bears a strong resemblance to a rat.)

Men may also go on a sexual binge after they have endured

long periods of celibacy. The sailor home from the sea is a classic example. When a couple goes on vacation, the chance for more private time together or the romantic setting may evoke a "second honeymoon." Sometimes sex can even be used to distract oneself from some source of worry or upset:

> Frank was up for promotion to vice-president of the firm. He knew the choice was between him and one other executive, but he would not hear the board's decision for two more weeks. He found himself feeling more passionate than he had in months, until his wife complained that he was wearing her out. The night the company announced that Frank was the new vice-president, the couple broke out a bottle of champagne. Frank's wife went upstairs to put on a negligee, and came down to find him fast asleep in the living room.

There are also a number of situations that interfere with sexual desire and activity. Any major stress or cause for depression can lead to a decrease in sexual feelings. Men often find they have little desire for sex after they have been rejected by a girlfriend or have been divorced or widowed. Losing a job is another factor in many sexual-desire problems. Sometimes even a seemingly happy event can really be a stressful one instead.

> Charlie retired from his job as a factory foreman after twenty-seven years at one company. He had a great time at his farewell dinner, and all of his men made speeches. He showed off his quartz watch to the neighbors and the grandchildren. He had really been looking forward to building a cabinet in his shop in the basement and getting the rose garden in shape.
> Charlie and his wife, Carol, had been having sex at least once a week for years. Even Carol's mastectomy hadn't

changed their habits. Suddenly, however, Charlie stopped snuggling up to Carol in bed, and when she tried to get things started, turned away and said he was tired. He also got irritable and snappy during the day. Finally, Carol realized that Charlie was feeling sad and on edge because he missed his job. He was starting to make remarks about being elderly and useless. Since he no longer saw himself as a complete man, he had a difficult time getting into a sexual mood.

If a man or his partner is ill, his sexual activity may be drastically reduced. He may lose desire as part of a depression, or just feel stressed and fatigued. We will look at the effects of some major illnesses on men's sexual function in Chapter 6, but for now, here is one common example:

George had an episode of chest pain, and was put in the hospital for tests. Luckily, he had not had a heart attack, but he did have to have his gallbladder removed. Even after he had healed and returned to work, however, he felt as if he were just dragging through the day. By the time he got home in the evening, sex was the last thing he wanted. George was also worried about whether it was okay to have sex again. When the doctor had given him his checkup after surgery, he had told George he could go back to work but he didn't mention sex. George was particularly embarrassed to ask, because he was not sure if his doctor realized that George was gay. Things might have stayed this way indefinitely if George's lover had not called the doctor to tell him about the problem. With a little reassurance, the couple was able to get their sex life back to normal and George's stamina gradually returned.

Sex may also go out the window when a man is involved in a large project that uses up most of his energy.

When Warren ran for city council, his fiancée almost called off their engagement. From a joyful sex life of three or four lovemaking sessions a week, they dropped to two half-hearted intercourses a month. Unfortunately for Warren's political ambitions, but fortunately for his home life, he lost the election. Sex went back to its usual level, and a few months later, Warren was married (after he swore an oath to his fiancée not to seek office again).

Thus within each man's characteristic sexual comfort level, there will be ups and downs over the years. It is helpful to pay attention to your own patterns and to be accepting of your body's rhythms and seasons. If you are dissatisfied with your present degree of desire or activity, you might take a few minutes to think about your sexual history. Is the present so different from the past? What is keeping you from seeking your sexual comfort level? Do you really want to have sex so much more (or less) often, or are you responding to what you think you "should" be doing? If you are in a relationship, get your partner's point of view as well. How often would she prefer to have sex? Does she see a big change in your sexual patterns over time?

Sexual desire is one aspect of a man's sexual feelings. In the next chapter we will examine the sexual response cycle as a whole, and see how it changes with age. Although there is not a male menopause, there are physical effects of aging that every man needs to recognize and understand.

3

When Mystery Is Not Romantic: The Sexual Response and Aging

When Mort's wife had a fatal heart attack a month after their silver anniversary, he was devastated. It took him almost two years to feel like dating, and several more months before he tried to have sexual activity.

Mort's new lover was a very attractive woman, whom he was seriously considering as a marriage partner. One evening he began to feel aroused as they were kissing, as they had several times before. Although Mort noticed he was not getting much of an erection, the couple proceeded to the bedroom and got undressed. Mort's wife had always caressed his penis as part of the foreplay, but his woman friend did not take a very active role in touching him. Mort felt too embarrassed to ask her to help him get an erection, or even to guide her hand. "I guess I'm a little nervous," he told her. "Maybe we'd better wait until another night." Mort's lover looked disappointed, but said she understood.

After he got home, Mort sat for a long time, thinking. He had never felt entirely comfortable with masturbation, but he decided to try and see what would happen, particularly since he was still feeling aroused and frustrated. Although Mort was able to get a full erection as he thought about his woman friend and stimulated himself, it seemed to take longer than he remembered in the past. Maybe his memory was starting to fade, because his penis also did not seem quite as hard as it used to be. Even his climax seemed on the weak side. Mort was left puzzled and upset. There was nothing really wrong with his sexual response, but it was not quite right, either.

People complain that studying sex scientifically deprives love of the mystery that makes it truly enjoyable. For Mort, however, mystery did not make sex more romantic. The differences that he noticed were real, but also normal. If he had known more about changes in sexual responsiveness with age, Mort could have avoided a good deal of anxiety.

THE SEXUAL RESPONSE CYCLE

In order to fully understand these changes, you can think of your sexual response as a cycle of desire, arousal, orgasm, and resolution. In the last chapter, we looked at the effects of age on the first phase of the cycle, i.e., desire, or the motivation to have sex. Sexual desire is not really a "drive," like the drive to eat or sleep, but rather a kind of interest in sex. You may experience sexual desire as a thought about how nice it would be to have sex, a feeling of frustration at not having had sex, when you notice an attractive woman, or on becoming aware of a sexual tingle in your body.

Arousal is the second phase of the sexual response cycle. When a man is actually in a sexual situation, or even having a sexual daydream, he may feel mentally aroused. Through any or all of his senses of touch, taste, smell, hearing, and sight he is receiving messages of sexual pleasure. He feels sensations in his genitals that are hard to describe in words, but are undeniably sexy. This is the state we describe as "turned on," or excited. There are also physical signs of arousal: his heartbeat and pulse speed up, blood pressure and muscle tension increase, and sometimes he perspires. The most noticeable sign of arousal in a man is his penis's becoming erect. This happens because the nervous system boosts blood flow into the genital area. Remember, though, that mental and physical signs of arousal do not always go together. Sometimes a man is surprised to find himself with an erection when he is not feeling excited. Other times a man feels tremendously turned on but has little or no erection.

Phase three of the cycle is orgasm. This is the climax of sexual pleasure. The sensation of orgasm is difficult to describe. It involves intense pleasure, often radiating from the genital area in rhythmic waves. After orgasm comes a feeling of release and satisfaction. Many men do not realize that their orgasm has two parts. In the first stage, called *emission*, the internal male organs including the prostate and seminal vesicles (see Figure 2) contract, or squeeze, several times to mix the sperm cells they store with the fluid that makes up the rest of the semen. The semen gathers in the top of the urethra (the tube through which a man urinates and ejaculates). This first stage of orgasm is often felt by a man as the point of no return, when he knows he is about to ejaculate. The second stage, *ejaculation*, occurs when the muscles around the genital area contract rhythmically, forcing the semen through the urethra and out of the penis in spurts.

Each part of the orgasm—pleasure, emission and ejaculation—has some independence. For example, occasionally a man can ejaculate without feeling much pleasure. On the other hand, in some medical conditions emission may not occur, or the body may stop producing semen, but the sensation of orgasm still remains. A man can also have a complete orgasm without

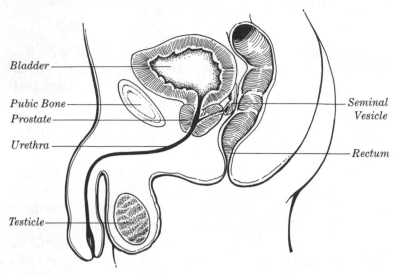

Bladder
Pubic Bone
Prostate
Urethra
Testicle
Seminal Vesicle
Rectum

FIGURE 2. THE MALE SEX ORGANS

an erection—a surprise for people who take it for granted that the penis must be hard before a man can reach climax.

The final phase of the sexual response is resolution, which simply means a rest period during which the body and mind return to their unexcited state. Even if a man gets aroused but does not reach orgasm, his body goes through a resolution phase. His erection fades, his heart and pulse slow down, and he gradually feels less pleasure in his genital area. Our society promotes several myths—that not having an orgasm causes "blue balls," "stops up your tubes," or irritates the prostate. There is actually *nothing* harmful or unhealthy about being aroused and not reaching orgasm. Sometimes it may frustrate you, and you may even feel a slight ache in the area of the testicles and scrotum (sac), but the resolution phase still occurs. The process is just slower than it would be after an orgasm. Conversely, there is nothing unhealthy about having an orgasm. It does not sap a man's strength.

After a man does have an orgasm, he goes through a "refractory period." This is a fancy name for the time it takes before he can become fully aroused and ejaculate again. If he tries to regain his erection too soon, he may be disappointed. Even if he can get an erection and begins intercourse a second time, another ejaculation may not yet be possible. The refractory period can vary from several minutes to several days. The refractory period may be longer if a man is older, is not highly attracted to his partner, or has recently had more sex than usual.

The sexual response cycle, then, is made up of a number of facets. We tend to think of them occurring in a set pattern: desire leads to feelings of arousal and an erection, culminating in orgasm with ejaculation, followed by a return to the unexcited state. Each part of the cycle, however, has some potential for independence from this routine. Just as hormones do not differ between heterosexual and homosexual men, the sexual response cycle works the same way in all sexual situations. It does not matter whether the partner is male or female, or even if the sex act in question is self-stimulation.

EFFECTS OF AGING

No matter what type of sex a man prefers, he may notice changes in his physical responsiveness as he gets older. Masters and Johnson studied thirty-nine healthy men over age fifty in their sex research laboratory. In addition, they interviewed a larger group about their sexual experiences. This research, now almost twenty years old, still provides some of the most detailed information available on sex and aging.

First of all, it may take an older man quite a bit longer to get a full, firm erection. Though a sexy thought or the sight of his wife in a lacy nightgown might have been sufficient stimulation when he was twenty-five or thirty-five, he may now need his penis to be directly stroked for a number of minutes. In fact, his penis may not get completely stiff and full until he is almost at the point of orgasm. If he loses his erection—for example, if he is distracted during foreplay—he may have difficulty regaining it.

Rather than mourning these changes, a man can learn to accept them, and even use them to his advantage. For many couples, their youth was a time of fairly mechanical, routine sex. Often they did not take much time for foreplay, or even bother to learn what kinds of genital caresses were most pleasing to each other. The husband may have been afraid that prolonging foreplay would make him ejaculate too quickly once he began intercourse. With age, couples may have to change this kind of routine to accommodate the husband's slowed arousal time. The bonus, however, is that he may now be moving at a speed more similar to his wife's. Both partners have a chance to enjoy new sensations. They learn to give and to receive as sex becomes more leisurely.

> Mort decided he needed to give sex another try. This time, his lover suggested they cuddle and kiss for a while before trying intercourse. Mort got up his courage and asked her if she would mind stroking his penis. "Of course I don't mind!" she said. "I just thought you were a little shy, and I didn't want to seem pushy." After a few minutes, Mort got a full erection. Though the couple had intercourse for a long time, and Mort's lover had an orgasm, he did not ejaculate. He felt a little frustrated, but his partner pointed out that they had made real progress. As they lay with their arms around each other, Mort found himself relaxed and drowsy.

Again, Mort's experience is a good example of changes an older man may notice in his sexual response. Older men often feel less pressure to reach orgasm. Instead of ejaculating as soon as he approaches high excitement, a man over fifty can often stay on the upper slopes and enjoy them awhile before hitting the peak. A man who ejaculated after only a minute or two of intercourse when he was younger may now attain much better control in delaying his orgasm. Sometimes an older man may not have an orgasm during sex, and yet feels satisfied with the experience. There is not the same urgency and frustration that he used to feel.

The orgasm itself may also change. In older men, the internal contractions of the emission phase are often less strong. The sensation of reaching the point of no return can thus become difficult to identify. The pleasure of orgasm may also seem more gentle. The prostate and seminal vesicles produce less fluid, and it is not expelled with as much force. A man may notice that he ejaculates less semen, or that it does not spurt out as strongly. The orgasm is still a satisfying experience, however. Instead of being very sharp and intense, it just may become less focused and more drawn out.

After ejaculation, an older man's erection may fade much more quickly than he remembers from the past. He may no longer be able to keep his penis inside his partner's vagina once he has ejaculated. This can interfere with some couples' usual routine, in which the husband continued to thrust after his orgasm to help his wife reach hers. Often, however, an older man's improved ability to delay his climax can prolong intercourse, allowing him time to satisfy his partner before he ejaculates.

One of the most noticeable changes in a man's sexual cycle is that his refractory period gets longer as he ages. A teenager may be able to ejaculate, never fully lose his erection, and go on to have a second orgasm almost immediately. By his thirties a man usually loses this ability, and needs some kind of rest period before having sex again. The refractory period often lengthens to several hours, or even a couple of days as men reach their seventies and eighties.

It does no good to get impatient with yourself, or to feel regret for the past. Many men believe they should be able to get an erection and ejaculate whenever they want, and that failure to do so is a sign of weakness. A more healthy attitude is to accept your own desires and needs, rather than comparing yourself to an unrealistic standard. If you are not yet ready for sex, but you feel your partner is dissatisfied, you can always offer to help her reach orgasm through types of caressing other than intercourse. This might include touching or kissing her breasts and genitals, or even stimulating her with a vibrator. You can enjoy her excitement and pleasure without feeling that the favor must be immediately returned.

The changes we have described usually take place gradually. You may even have gone through some of them without really noticing. Many couples just continue with their sex play as before, or automatically make small adjustments. In one large survey of men over sixty, 37 percent said sex felt the same as it always had, and 27 percent said it was better. Only 36 percent reported that sex had become less pleasurable. Often the men who are most surprised and upset by signs of aging are those like Mort who have stopped having sex for some reason and then start up again, often with a new partner. To these men, the differences in their erection and orgasm may come as a shock. As we saw in Chapter 2, however, mild changes in a man's sexual desire or performance do not herald "the beginning of the end." If you know what to expect, there is no need for panic.

SLEEP ERECTIONS

Additional evidence that sexual mechanisms are maintained by the body even into the eighth decade of life comes from research on erections during sleep. Since the early 1960s we have known that erections normally occur several times a night. The technical term for sleep erections is *nocturnal penile tumescence* (NPT). NPT occurs in newborn babies and in healthy octogenarians. Although NPT usually occurs during the same stage of sleep in which a man dreams (Rapid Eye Movement, or REM, sleep), the erections are not the result of a sexual dream, or even of a stimulus such as rubbing against the sheets, or a full bladder. Instead, sleep erections are a reflex controlled by the central nervous system, the brain, and the spinal cord. Unlike erections during waking hours, they do not have much connection with a man's state of mind. Even mental states such as fear and depression do not make much of a dent on NPT (though some controversy remains about the effects of emotion on NPT).

In physical terms such as size and firmness, a good sleep erection is identical to a daytime one. When a man wakes up with an erection, he usually believes it was caused by the need to urinate. In fact, it is probably just due to waking during the stage of sleep where NPT occurs. In one research center, men were awakened during the night and asked to empty their bladders. They then were allowed to go back to sleep until their usual morning waking time. Just as many of these men had erections on waking as did those in a group who slept through the night and hence needed to urinate when they got up.

One confusing thing about a morning erection is that a man usually does not awake feeling sexually excited. Many men, however, noticing they have a full erection, turn over and cuddle up to their partners to have sex. But unless the man's feelings of mental arousal catch up quickly to his reflex erection (and unless his lover is easy to wake!), his penis may get soft before things really get going.

Why does NPT occur? Scientists have no real answer, but perhaps it is a way for the body to exercise the sexual reflexes, keeping them healthy. The nervous and circulatory systems are not the only ones involved in this process. During the sleep erection, the hormone system usually releases a surge of testosterone. Therefore, the amount of testosterone circulating in the blood increases during sleep so that it is highest in the morning.

As we will discuss in Chapter 7, NPT can now be monitored by physicians to determine whether a man's problems in getting or keeping an erection during sex are caused by medical or psychological factors. If the erection problem is the result of fear of failure or anxiety, NPT continues to be normal. If the erection problem is due to poor physical health, however, a man's sleep erections may be totally absent, or at least much less firm or lasting.

If you think in terms of the number of minutes of NPT across a whole night, some changes do take place with age. There are peak amounts of NPT in boys aged three to five and then in adolescence. Between the ages of twenty and fifty, however, the time an average man spends with an erection during the night gradually decreases from a little over three hours to about an hour and a half. Erection time then stays fairly stable through age eighty. This ninety minutes of NPT represents two or three separate periods of erection, occurring at intervals throughout a night. Thus for men over fifty, the penis is still receiving quite a workout. Some of you may have trouble believing that you are actually having two or three half-hour erections every night. Nevertheless, if you still wake up occasionally with full erections, this is probably the case.

In men over seventy, NPT changes in some additional minor ways, even when erections during sexual activity are still normal. The sleep erections may occur more randomly, instead of during one specific stage of sleep. They also may be less firm, and more of the sleep erections may be partial, rather than full, ones. In sum, though, the fact that NPT still occurs to such an extent in older men is much more noteworthy than the decrease in sleep erections with age.

The evidence from sleep research, hormone studies, and observations of the actual sexual responses of older men all suggest that aging is not meant to end your sex life. The scientific data just confirm what older people have been telling us for a long time.

Jim and his wife, Mandy, have four children, ten grandchildren, and even three great-grandchildren. Jim has been retired from his accounting firm for fourteen years. This is what Mandy has to say about their sex life:

"I don't think Jim and I will ever stop feeling like lovers. We may look old and wrinkled to you, but in my eyes, Jim is just as handsome and sexy as the day we met. You may not believe this, but I like our sex life better now than when we were younger. It was never bad, but with the children around, and all the other things to take care of, sometimes sex seemed like just one more thing to get done. Now Jim and I can spend a whole afternoon making love if we want to, and once in a while, we do. Even though we may only have sex every few days, we do a lot of kissing and cuddling. Jim tends to snore very loudly, and so we have separate bedrooms, but he usually comes and lies down with me before we go to sleep. One night I'd turned the lights off, and I heard him coming down the hall. Just to tease him, I decided to hide under the bed. He kept calling, 'Mandy, Mandy? Where are you honey?' until I couldn't keep from laughing. I call him a dirty old man, but he tells me I'm just as scandalous as he is!"

STAYING IN SHAPE FOR SEX

We have seen that the range of sexual activity levels in older men is quite wide. In a recent survey, 80 percent of men and women over sixty felt that staying sexually active has a positive effect on health. You may be wondering if you can do anything special either to keep up your good track record or to get back into shape, sexually speaking. Men often try to spur their flagging desire or erections by buying special mail-order potency "vitamins" or books about secret exercises to strengthen the "sex muscles." The purveyors of these remedies, like the advertisers who sell miracle diets to women, know just how to appeal to our eternal hope for the easy answer. They promise that one week of their regimen will make a man feel seventeen again. Usually, they include testimonials from Albert, a sixty-six-year-old who wears a toupee and claims to be the toast of Manhattan's singles' bars, and Reggie, a spry gentleman of eighty-two whose young wife is begging him to get a mistress because she's too sore to have sex more than twice a night.

Despite all the hoopla, the only part of a man likely to be rejuvenated by these products is his wallet—which will become as light as it used to be when he was in high school. It should not surprise you to find out that sexual function is closely tied to a man's general state of physical health. The same habits that put a man at risk for other medical problems can also damage his sexual vitality. Those risk factors include being overweight, lack of exercise, heavy drinking, and smoking. If you want to improve your general and sexual health, there is no easy substitute for self-discipline and a sensible plan of exercise that has your doctor's approval. (Unfortunately, sexual intercourse is *not* enough of an exercise program!)

Let's take each of these four factors in turn, and examine their effect on your sex life. Excess weight is a problem for many men over fifty who have watched their "love handles" progress to plain old paunches. Feeling fat can have an effect on a man's self-esteem, making him reluctant to approach a woman or even to think about sex. Beyond the psychological impact, a man who is quite overweight may have technical problems finding a position for intercourse that does not exhaust him or smother his spouse. Sometimes the distraction of feeling tired, sweaty, and out of breath can greatly diminish sexual pleasure. Real obesity can even reduce a man's testosterone levels, although usually not by enough to cause a sexual problem. The most important risk is that overweight men are more likely to be diabetic and to have hypertension (high blood pressure), conditions that seriously endanger sexual function.

Keeping your weight down can be an important part of controlling your cholesterol, blood sugar, and blood pressure.

Doing some regular exercise can also be important. Studies have recently shown that at least among young men, the physically fit have higher levels of testosterone circulating in their blood. Army recruits put through a six-month exercise-training program increased their testosterone by 20 percent. Scientists do not know whether athletic men have stronger sexual desires, but it would not be surprising. The glow and sense of relaxation that comes from a regular program of brisk walking, jogging, bicycling, or swimming is very similar to the feeling of sexual excitement. You get the same sensation of quickened pulse and breathing, and the same healthy sweat. Of course if you overdo the exercise, you may feel temporarily too sore and exhausted to think about sex. If you have not been exercising or dieting and would like to start, be sure to consult your doctor and have a physical exam first. You also need to have patience as you build up your stamina gradually.

Another recent study of older men found a relationship between alcohol use and sex. Those who drank an average of more than four ounces of liquor a day were less active sexually than men who were light drinkers. It has been known for some time that heavy alcohol use can damage a man's hormonal balance, actually destroy hormone-producing cells in his testicles, and slowly deaden the nerves in the pelvis that control erection. It is amazing to me how many men coming in with a sexual problem are hard drinkers. "Well, I usually have five or six scotches, if you count lunch and then the cocktail hour," or "Sure I drink a six-pack a day, but it's only beer! I'm not an alcoholic!" Although these drinking habits may not interfere with the man's working ability or family life (or at least not in ways that he realizes), after twenty or thirty years they may effectively destroy his sexual desire or erections. If you think this description fits, try switching from whiskey to wine, or beer to soda, and see if you can cut down on the number of drinks as well. It certainly cannot hurt, and you may find you have more interest in being sexual.

Sometimes men use drinking to cope with feelings of depression or emptiness, or to control tension and worry. Many businesses are now teaching employees more healthy ways of reducing stress. Your company or a local community organization may have a stress-management course available. Men who are retired often have a special need to learn new ways to relax and cope with stress.

There are certainly many techniques around to help men quit smoking. Given how many ill effects of smoking we already know, including cancer, heart disease, and lung problems, no one should be surprised to find that heavy smokers also may have sexual problems. The nicotine in tobacco acts to constrict, or narrow, blood vessels in the body. This interferes with the normal flow of blood, especially to the parts of the body most distant from the heart, such as the fingers and toes. Researchers in the United States and in Scandinavia are finding that smokers may develop erection problems because of reduced blood flow to the penis. In one preliminary study, a group of men with erection problems quit smoking for six weeks. One-third noticed an improvement in their sexual function. Obviously not every smoker has trouble with erections. In older men who already have some arteriosclerosis (blockage of the arteries), however, the additional effects of nicotine may be the coup de grace.

One of my colleagues has begun suggesting that patients who have erection problems resulting from poor circulation quit smoking before considering any other treatment. He is discouraged to find that the usual answer is, "Well, Doc, if it's a choice between smoking or sex, I guess I'll take smoking." These are the same men who send away for miracle vitamins to make their penis stiff as a rod.

A word about vitamins, by the way, while we are on the subject of fitness. As long as you eat a balanced diet, there is no evidence that vitamins will improve your ability to function sexually. If you are really worried, you can always take one decent combination daily vitamin tablet. Dosing yourself with vitamin E, B-12, kelp, ginseng, etc., may contribute to the happiness and well-being of your local pharmacist or health food entrepreneur, but the main effect on you will be to enrich your urine, both in terms of vitamin and financial value. (We will discuss oysters in a future chapter. They also may be overpriced, but at least they taste good.) Your body needs very small amounts of vitamins. The excess gets dumped by the urinary system. In fact, some vitamins can be poisonous in large amounts, so you should never take more than the recommended dose.

What about getting enough sexual exercise? Is celibacy harmful to sexual function? No less an authority than the famous team of Masters and Johnson has warned that older men must "use it or lose it." They believe that long periods without a sexual partner, even if a man keeps on masturbating, will cause a sort of decay of the erection response. Their statements are based on a few case histories, however, rather than on solid research. There are few scientific studies of celibate men. My own research on a group of widowers with erection problems suggested that men who had gone for very long periods of time (an average of four years) without a sexual partner were more likely to have an actual medical basis for their sexual problem. There is some evidence, mainly from work with animals rather than humans, that hormone levels rise after sexual activity. In that case, a long period of celibacy might cause a small decline in a man's amount of testosterone. On the other hand, one group of researchers found normal testosterone levels in nine out of eleven monks.

Going without sex probably does no permanent damage to the hormone, nervous, or circulatory systems responsible for sexual function. As we have seen, the body produces sex hormones and erections during sleep. If a man has gone for a long time without an orgasm, he may even have a nocturnal emission, better known as a wet dream. The body, therefore, can exercise its sexual systems, even in a celibate man.

Sexuality, because it is the way that we continue our species, has been shaped by millennia of evolution. It is a bodily function too crucial to leave to the chance that a willing partner will routinely be available. The body has built-in ways to keep its sexual organs alive and well, regardless of whether we use them voluntarily. A man can abstain from sexual activity, but he cannot ultimately deprive himself of sleep for long, and he cannot prevent his nervous system from producing an erection or orgasm while he dreams.

MASTURBATION

What about the role of masturbation for older men? When we think about sexual activity, often our image only includes touching shared with a partner. Masturbation, however, is an important part of sexuality. By masturbation, I mean a man caressing his own penis, usually to the point of orgasm. Many men think of self-stimulation as shameful, or at least as something only a teenager would do. The Kinsey studies, however, found that over 90 percent of men have masturbated at some point in their lives. The Starr-Weiner survey of men over sixty found that 44 percent still masturbate (and this may be an underestimate). Contrary to the myths about masturbation causing blindness, madness, and general perversion, it is a practice that has no adverse effects on a man's health or well-being. A very fine discussion of masturbation, including some of the negative attitudes men learn about it as well as its positive value, can be found in Bernie Zilbergeld's book *Male Sexuality*.

When I discuss sexuality with older men and couples, I find that masturbation is one of the "touchiest" subjects. Men often are ashamed to admit they masturbate. Women get angry if their men occasionally prefer masturbation over partner sex. Most men do stimulate themselves, at least once in a while. After all, masturbation is a way to attain sexual satisfaction when your partner may not be available (or willing). You can also enjoy a variety of sexual fantasies without acting in a way that could hurt your relationship or get you into too tight a spot! Finally, to paraphrase Woody Allen, "Masturbation is sex with someone I love."

A man who has lost his lover, or is married to a woman who has serious health problems, sometimes tries to ignore his sexual desires completely. While this may seem like a noble solution, it is sad to have to reject a part of yourself. Imagine setting yourself the task of never raising your voice in joy or anger, or never laughing. Suppressing your sexual feelings is just as difficult and unnatural. Masturbation is one way that a man can express his sexuality and yet remain in control of his desires and the way they affect others.

There is no need for an "excuse" to masturbate, although a number of older men feel they have to rationalize it as a tension-reliever or as necessary for proper sexual health. When a man has a sexual problem with a partner, such as trouble keeping an erection or reaching orgasm, he may try masturbation to see if his equipment is still in good working order.

> George was not usually much of a drinker, so half a bottle of champagne turned the opening night of his second honeymoon into a disaster. Edna looked beautiful in the blue nightgown she'd bought especially for the occasion, and the cabin of the cruise ship was romantically lit. George, however, felt more done in than turned on. He tried to play the red hot lover, but his penis was doing an impersonation of Rip van Winkle. Edna finally sighed and dozed off as well. The next afternoon, while she was sunning out on the deck, George decided to try an experiment. Although he had not masturbated since his last business trip, he began to stroke

his penis and think about the last issue of *Penthouse* (which he had confiscated from his twelve-year-old son). Lo and behold, he was back to normal. George decided not to continue to a climax, because his frustration now would just add extra spice to the evening. At dinner, he also made sure to stop after his second glass of wine.

Unfortunately, using masturbation as a test of potency may set a man up for failure. If you put enough pressure on yourself to perform, even masturbation can be spoiled.

Mike, at age fifty-five, was having some prostate trouble. His doctor recommended minor surgery but Mike hated the very thought. He heard from a bowling buddy that regular ejaculation, at least twice a week, was good for the prostate. Since it was hard enough to coax his wife into having sex once a week, Mike took up the slack by masturbating. Rain or shine, whether he felt like it or not, Mike made sure he reached climax twice a week. When his prostate symptoms did not improve, he decided to increase the treatment to every other day. By the second week of this schedule, he found he could not reach orgasm at all, even with his wife. When he became highly aroused, he found himself picturing his prostate as swollen to bursting with semen. This mental image completely took over his thoughts, so that he ended up losing his erection too. Mike went back to his doctor, who explained that ejaculation would not affect his prostate one way or the other. The physician suggested that Mike have sexual activity only when he really was in the mood.

Masturbation does have some clear benefits. For men who have erection problems or premature ejaculation (reaching a climax either before penetration or very soon afterwards), sex therapists often suggest exercises involving some special ways of masturbating. Masturbation gives a man the liberty to focus on his own sensations, without the distraction of pleasing a partner. If you use masturbation as a chance to try out different ways of stimulating yourself, you may be able to discover new ways of touching that give you pleasure. Then you can teach your partner to touch and kiss you in the ways you like best. As a man gets older, the sensitivity of his genital area may decrease slightly. The kinds of touching that are most arousing may then change as well. Masturbation is a chance for you to explore your capacity for pleasure.

Most men masturbate almost exclusively by touching their penis. Men who take great pains to get their lovers ready for intercourse by stroking and kissing different areas of their bodies often do not give themselves the same courtesy. Self-stimulation can be more pleasurable if you start by touching areas of your body besides the genitals. Some men enjoy using a body lotion or lubricant as part of their masturbation. There are even a variety of vibrators available; some that have differently shaped and textured attachments, and others that have "sleeves" that fit over the end of the penis to give the sensation of penetration. Many men find these ideas sexy, but others may see them as too artificial or kinky.

Although masturbation certainly is not harmful, it is also not essential to sexual health. Some self-styled experts in sexuality have a missionary zeal about getting people to "loosen up" and become more sexually "free." On the other hand, some religions teach that masturbation is sinful. (A talk with your clergy may help in providing some guidelines.) My own philosophy is to give men the information they need to make their own decisions about their sex lives. You have a right to your personal choices and to engage in whatever practices feel comfortable to you.

4

What Do Women Really Want?

So far, we have looked only at the male sexual response. One frequent complaint voiced by older men, however, is that they do not understand women's sexual needs. "What do women really want?" they ask. This chapter will try to provide a few answers.

The secrets of female sexual pleasure have eluded not only men, but women themselves. When it comes to sex, women until quite recently have been brought up to conform to the "feminine mystique." According to this model, a woman should enjoy sex, but not too much. She should never ask for sex, but if her husband wants to make love, she should be receptive and even responsive, in a ladylike way. Unfortunately, this leaves the man with more than his fair share of sexual responsibility. It is the husband's duty to teach his virginal bride what sex is all about. For the rest of their marriage, he will be the one who suggests when and where to have sex, as well as deciding the kinds of touching and caressing the couple will use. Needless to say, if the woman fails to reach orgasm it is her husband's fault for not knowing how to overcome her natural "frigidity."

Certainly women have not been taught to enjoy their bodies. Though masturbation and petting are tolerated for male teenagers, women have gotten the message that their genitals are taboo, to be examined or touched only for the purposes of menstrual hygiene, contraception, or childbirth. A surprising number of American women in their middle or later years have never looked at their genitals in a mirror, and cannot identify the various parts of their sexual anatomy. Although many women have tried masturbation, a fairly large percentage, compared to men, have not. Women often begin their sex lives without any idea of how to enjoy genital touching or reach orgasm. Even if a woman knows what kind of caress excites her, the feminine mystique demands that she keep quiet and let her partner be the leader. Otherwise, she may be labeled as "castrating" or a "nymphomaniac." Both women and men are losers in this situation. The woman is frustrated and angry that her lover cannot read her mind, the way men do in romantic novels. The man is left wondering what would satisfy her.

THE FEELING GAP

Men's confusion is partly a result of the different training given to boys and girls about expressing feelings. Females are brought up to cry when they are sad or angry, to yell a little, and to hug and kiss to express affection. Even as small babies, however, males are cuddled less by their mothers. They are expected to "be a man." Big boys don't cry. If they are angry, they "tough it out" and "get even rather than get mad." Many men substitute a stiff handshake for a kiss or a hug. Even if a boy's family expresses feelings more openly than most, he learns these lessons from his friends, from school, and from the media.

When boys and girls grow up and marry, they must learn to communicate caring and anger in effective ways. All too often, a couple ends up like Hal and Roberta, who have been married for thirty-seven years:

INTERVIEWER: How did the two of you meet?

ROBERTA: It was a blind date. Hal was an army buddy of my brother.

INTERVIEWER: Was it love at first sight, or did you take a while to warm up to one another? [*Roberta looks at Hal.*]

HAL (*shrugging*): I guess we dated for a few months before we got engaged.

INTERVIEWER: Hal, what was it about Roberta that made her special to you?

HAL: Oh . . . I thought she was kind of cute, sort of a sweet girl—and she had a lot of friends. I enjoyed her whole group.

ROBERTA: I think I've always been more outgoing. Hal's more of a loner than I am.

INTERVIEWER: What attracted you to Hal back then, when you met?

ROBERTA: Well, he was real serious, and steady. He made the other boys seem sort of immature, I think. I guess I saw him as my white knight, who would carry me off, and take care of me. You know how young girls are.

INTERVIEWER: Are you an affectionate couple, when it comes to things like kissing and hugging, or cuddling in front of the TV?

HAL (*shaking his head*): No.

ROBERTA: Well *I* am. My whole family was like that. We always kissed our parents goodnight, but Hal's brothers and sisters are just like he is—a cold fish!

INTERVIEWER: That's sort of a strong term. Hal, do you see yourself as a cold fish?

HAL: Yup, I guess so. At least I've never liked a lot of sloppy kissing and hanging on each other.

INTERVIEWER: How do you show Roberta that you care

about her? Do you give her compliments, or help around the house, or what?

ROBERTA: Never! He never says I look nice or says, "I love you."

HAL: I tell you I like your cooking.

ROBERTA: You do not! You always say your mother's roast is better than mine. He complains about everything! If I don't do the dishes as soon as we finish dinner, he tells me the house is a mess.

HAL: Well, you don't have anything to do all day. You know you could keep things neater.

ROBERTA: That house is neat as a pin until you come home and drop your things all over.

INTERVIEWER: Hal, how do you think that you express caring to Roberta?

HAL: Well, I've supported her all these years. We have enough money to be very comfortable. I've worked darned hard, and I don't understand what she wants from me. Do I have to say, "I love you" ten times a day? Doesn't she know all that by now?

ROBERTA: Ten times a day? Try once a year! He never even touches me unless he wants sex.

HAL: You aren't going to start with that now, are you? If I didn't love her, why would I put up with this for thirty-seven years?

INTERVIEWER: I did want to ask you a little about your sex life, since it is one important part of marriage. Hal, it sounds as if you're usually the one who starts things sexually.

HAL: I sure am. I could count the times on one hand that Roberta has come to me!

INTERVIEWER: Have you sometimes wished that Roberta would be more forward when it comes to sex?

HAL: Sure. Every man likes to feel wanted once in a while. I always have to pet her and coax her into it.

INTERVIEWER: Roberta, have you been aware of how Hal felt?

ROBERTA: Well, he hinted around a few times, but I was brought up to think that starting sex is the husband's job. And I can tell you I don't get all that much petting, either!

INTERVIEWER: What kinds of kissing and touching do the two of you use before you go on to intercourse?

HAL: The usual.

ROBERTA: That means he wants me to roll over, and we kiss for about two minutes, and he rubs me so hard down there that it hurts!

HAL: Oh come on, Roberta!

ROBERTA: I've told him a hundred times, "That's too rough!" but he never changes. And then before I even get in the mood, he's finished.

INTERVIEWER: Hal, what's your perspective?

HAL: I've tried to please her, but she never says what she wants, just, "Stop that! You're too rough!" So, yeah, it's quick, because I've gotten to feel like she just wants to get it over with.

INTERVIEWER: I can see that both of you have felt frustrated about this for a long time. How do you try to resolve things, as a couple, when you get annoyed with each other?

ROBERTA: We don't really solve anything. I guess I'm the one who yells, when I'm angry, and he sulks.

HAL: I get quiet.

INTERVIEWER: Do you ever leave the house when you're angry?

HAL: Sometimes. Or I walk out of the room.

ROBERTA: And that just infuriates me! Also, he slams doors. [*The couple begins to laugh.*]

HAL: Oh, we get along O.K. Why do we have to bring up all this stuff anyway? Let sleeping dogs lie.

ROBERTA: At least we've stayed together. That's more than young couples do now. We were brought up that marriage is forever.

HAL: Sex isn't that important anymore. We have our children, and next month I'm going to be a grandfather. Now that's my idea of success!

While Hal and Roberta genuinely do care for each other, their relationship has never achieved the emotional richness that each of them deserves. Because of their difficulties in communicating, sex in particular has never been satisfying. Although they have lived together for thirty-seven years, they are not truly intimate. Instead of feeling free to share their inner fears and hopes, they each have tried to fit their picture of a real man, or a good woman.

What do women really want? It is not my intention to foster stereotypes, but in my work with couples, some misperceptions that men have about women keep on appearing, especially when it comes to sexuality. If these next paragraphs do not apply to you, well and good. I think these myths are worth mentioning, however.

OLD HUSBANDS' TALES

There are some sexual notions about women that men have traded with their buddies and handed down to their sons. Most of these locker-room legends portray women as fascinated and enthralled with the penis. When you carry some of these tales to their logical conclusion, it is astonishing that women are not choosing their mates by "short arm inspection." Often legends begin with a kernel of truth—you yourself may even have had an experience that confirmed some of these beliefs about women. By and large, however, these stories are more fantasy than fact, and have done more harm than good.

Locker-Room Legend 1: The thing a woman values most in a lover is the size of his erect penis.

In my years of experience as a sex therapist (and as a participant in "woman talk"), I have rarely heard a woman complain that her lover's penis was too small. I have listened to many men, however, agonize about the size of their penis or blame a sexual problem on their lack of endowment.

How has this misunderstanding come about? Young boys usually compare their penises to those of their peers. In our society, it is more acceptable for boys than girls to see each other in the nude, or even to masturbate in front of each other. These occasions are often marked by a competitive spirit: teammates shower after football or adolescents play games in which the winner is the one who ejaculates the farthest. Here begins the contest for the phallus supreme. Meanwhile, young girls are daydreaming about their hero's blue eyes or broad shoulders. Most still do not know what a penis looks like, or how one works.

The teenager's lack of knowledge becomes adult ignorance. A man often judges his neighbor by the glimpse of his flaccid (soft) penis at the health club. A man who is "well hung" gets a reputation as a real stud. In actuality, differences in penis size quite often tend to disappear with erection. The man whose penis is small in the flaccid state will have a much larger size *increase* with erection than will the man who seems best endowed to start.

Even if one man has a slightly longer or thicker erection than another, variations in penis size have little influence on sexual pleasure for women. The position you use for intercourse and your angle of penetration can be much more important. The vagina, even when a woman is sexually excited, is narrower than the normal erection. During intercourse your partner's vagina stretches just enough to be a snug fit for your particular penis. The areas of the vagina most sensitive to pleasurable friction happen to be the areas within easy access. They include the whole outer third of the vagina closest to the entrance, and possibly a spot on the front wall (the stomach side), about four inches inside. Since the average erection is six inches long, you should have no problem reaching these crucial zones. When a woman is highly aroused, the outer third of her vagina actually swells and becomes firmer as circulation of blood to the area increases, giving even more stimulation to both partners.

If you have had a partner complain about your penis being too small, think back to whether she was angry at you. Women know how vulnerable a man can feel about penis size, making it a tempting weapon to use in a fight. "Well, dear, I *might* have been able to have an orgasm, if you were big enough so I could even *feel* it!" (Men can retaliate by criticizing a woman's breasts or thighs. One woman I know even had a lover complain that her labia were too small to be sexy.)

If you remain convinced that penis size is paramount, take a moment to review your own criteria for a good lover. How crucial are the dimensions of her vagina? When you feel attracted to a woman, do you stop to wonder whether her vagina will be tight enough? If you and your wife have children, was your sex life ruined if her vagina became a little stretched after childbirth? Women and men are not so different in terms of what they value in a mate. You learn to love your partner's genitals because you love all the rest of her or him rather than vice versa.

Locker-Room Legend 2: A woman's favorite part of sex is lots of vigorous, penis-in-vagina intercourse.

This is really an extension of Legend 1, except, as the time-honored saying goes, "It's not the meat—it's the motion." The focus, however, is still on the mighty member. Even if it is large enough, will it stay hard enough, for long enough? A man often fears that his lover will be bitterly disappointed if he ejaculates too quickly, or worse yet, has a problem getting or keeping an erection. Although sexual difficulties can certainly be distressing to both partners, a woman usually takes them in stride, as long as she feels her own needs are being considered.

The problem is that men and women may disagree on what those needs are. On one hand, men believe that women crave long periods of hard penile thrusting. They see foreplay as just the appetizer, while intercourse is the entrée. On the other hand, women most frequently complain that their men are too impatient to spend enough time on foreplay.

Roberta is upset because Hal considers her ready for intercourse the moment her vagina feels moist. Since vaginal lubrication is one of the earliest signs of sexual excitement in a woman, Roberta does not have time to reach the peak of arousal that allows her to enjoy intercourse fully. If Hal then ejaculates quickly, Roberta cannot reach orgasm. She tells Hal that she is tired of "slam-bam, thank-you ma'am" sex.

To be fair, the woman has probably had a part in establishing this kind of sexual pattern. She does not let her partner know that she wants more kissing and touching, but gives him all the responsibility for deciding when penetration will occur. Then she hides her resentment or makes sharp remarks about her husband's sexual clumsiness.

Do women enjoy foreplay more than men? There probably is not an inborn difference between the sexes in this respect. As children, however, girls have many more opportunities than boys to be cuddled and touched. As adults, therefore, women are often more aware than men of the pleasurable sensations that can be evoked by a kiss on the neck, a back rub, or playing "footsie." Sex is one of the only situations in which an adult man in our society is allowed to relax and be caressed. Even then, he is indoctrinated that "a real man" should only be interested in intercourse. Luckily, by the time a man gets to middle age, he has often had a chance to learn that intercourse is not the only worthwhile part of sex.

Women also enjoy foreplay because it stimulates the most sensitive areas of their genitals, i.e., the clitoris and the delicate tissues around and above the entrance to the vagina. Intercourse provides maximum pleasure to a man's most responsive area, the head of the penis. In women, however, the spot supplied with the most nerve endings is the tip of the clitoris. During intercourse the clitoris does not receive much direct friction. Although the vaginal walls are also important sources of sexual pleasure, at least a third of American women have trouble reaching orgasm through intercourse alone; that is, without additional touching of their clitoris.

Foreplay, then, may be a major factor in helping a woman reach orgasm. According to Kinsey, when couples include at least twenty-one minutes of foreplay in their sexual routine, more than 90 percent of women reach orgasm. Few couples, however, especially after years of marriage, permit themselves that luxury. Women also have an easier time reaching orgasm if a man, or even the woman herself, caresses the area around the clitoris during intercourse. Lonnie Barbach, a well-known sex therapist, has called our usual model of sex " 'Look Ma—no hands!' intercourse."

This brings us to the next "Old Husbands' Tale."

Locker-Room Legend 3: The only good orgasm is a coital orgasm.

As far as doctors and researchers know, every physically healthy woman has the potential to reach orgasm. The kinds of sexual stimulation that may lead a woman to orgasm include dreams, fantasies, caressing the breasts, stroking or kissing the areas around the vaginal entrance and clitoris, as well as deep pressure on the walls of the vagina. At the turn of the century, Freud theorized that coital orgasms, those produced during intercourse, were more healthy and mature than orgasms from clitoral stimulation. This idea haunted women for more than fifty years, until Masters and Johnson actually observed women in the sex research laboratory. No physical difference could be measured between orgasms that occur after vaginal stimulation and those following clitoral stimulation. No matter what part of the body was caressed, the woman's orgasm was the same. This may make sense if you compare your sensations when you ejaculate during intercourse with those produced by hand stimulation or oral sex to orgasm. You may prefer one situation to another, or notice some small variations in pleasure or emotional response, but basically an orgasm is an orgasm. Actually, both men and women usually find their orgasms resulting from foreplay or masturbation to be the most intense.

The disproving of Freud's theory has been a relief to women who have trouble reaching orgasm from intercourse alone. Sex therapists now believe that a woman who needs to have her clitoris touched directly to reach orgasm is perfectly normal and should not feel compelled to change. Of course many women reach orgasm easily from intercourse and prefer the experience of penetration to any other caress. These women are also absolutely normal. The key word is "individuality." Women, probably more than men, vary tremendously in the kinds of sexual touching they enjoy. It is no wonder that men are confused. The caress that drove one partner crazy may be too rough, too light, too fast, too slow, or in the wrong place for another.

Perhaps because penetration is a uniquely male kind of loving, many men are still hooked on providing coital orgasms for their partners. For one thing, orgasms during intercourse are romantic. Intercourse is an act in which two people supposedly become one, and through a mystical (or at least mysterious) process, simultaneously reach the peak of delight. Intercourse is also the part of sex in which reproduction occurs, and so is the least "sinful." Orgasms for their own sake may be unacceptable, but if a woman reaches orgasm as a by-product of her wifely duty, it is "natural." Finally, coital orgasms are convenient. When a man has ejaculated, he may feel relaxed and sleepy. It can be annoying to still feel obligated to stimulate a partner to orgasm.

For all these reasons, sex therapy clinics see many couples in which the wife wants to learn to have her orgasm during intercourse. I see the opposite problem, however, in older couples. Both partners may have been routinely orgasmic during intercourse for twenty or thirty years. Now the husband has difficulty with erections, or perhaps the wife has a health problem that interferes with vigorous, intercourse-centered sex. An alternative, of course, is to try a gentler, more prolonged type of sensual caressing. Each partner could help the other reach a climax through touching or kissing the genitals. Unfortunately, since many couples have not included much foreplay in their sexual routine, they have trouble adjusting. Perhaps the wife feels embarrassed and shy about having her genitals touched, or touching her husband. Perhaps neither one knows how to reach orgasm except through intercourse. Even if the couple has found new ways to give each other pleasure, the man may fear that the orgasms he provides are not the "real thing" and doubts that his partner could be satisfied without intercourse. Some women confirm these suspicions, insisting that the penis is a man's only worthwhile sexual "tool." I will suggest techniques for dealing with this situation in Chapter 10. The important point, for now, is that older couples can continue enjoying a sex life together if they are willing to be flexible about helping each other to reach orgasm.

Locker-room legends limit a couple's freedom to experiment during sex because of men's beliefs about the way a woman *should* react.

Locker-Room Legend 4: A good woman will be shocked and disgusted by any sex act except intercourse in the missionary position.

When something is mysterious and confusing, human beings react by trying to simplify it. Given the misunderstandings between the sexes, it is natural that men have tried to divide women into categories. In my clinical experience, men over fifty often see women as either "good" or "bad." A good woman is brought up to be a wife and mother. Her virginity is saved for marriage. Although she may enjoy sex with her husband, she never quite loses the notion that sex is something a woman does for a man, and not for her own pleasure.

Ned and June have sex with the light off, under the covers. Ned generally starts things by a little kissing, and then may stroke his wife's breasts under her nightgown. Most of the time she assents, but once in a while she will push his hand away or say she is too tired. Although June puts her arms around Ned, she does not really do much touching of his body. When Ned guesses that she is ready, he gets on top and guides his penis into her vagina. He thinks she usually has an orgasm. At least she has never complained about not having one.

Ned travels a lot in his business. Every once in a while, he has picked up a woman in a bar. Though they are not prostitutes, Ned sees these women as living in a world apart from his wife. With his casual ladyfriends, Ned tries different positions for intercourse, asks for oral sex, and even whispers sexy things into their ears. Ned's excitement drives him to repeat his encounters, even though he feels terrible the next morning. Ned would never dream of seeking such pleasures in his sexual routine with June. You don't ask a lady to do those things. He feels that an occasional secret affair preserves the dignity of his marriage.

A husband and wife may collaborate in living up to the image of the good woman. Each may feel bored and frustrated by their limited sexual habits, but neither takes the risk of asking for something new. Sometimes, too, the man fears that if passion is unleashed, his good woman will become a bad woman.

Locker-Room Legend 5: Once a woman learns to like sex, she will become insatiable.

A man may want to keep his good woman pure because he suspects that a taste of passionate sex will render her unable to control her desires. After all, it was Eve who tempted Adam to bite into that apple. Women who enjoy sex are usually portrayed on TV and in the movies as unfaithful, slaves to their craving for satisfaction, and generally rotten through and through.

Lois and Matt married right out of high school. Both were sexually inexperienced, but Matt believed that he ought to be able to teach Lois about making love. She was rather shy, and so he took the lead in all aspects of their sex life. After their second child was born, Lois finally began to have orgasms during sex. Feeling more satisfied herself, and wanting to share her pleasure with her husband, she tried coming nude to bed, offering to give Matt back rubs and giving other small hints that she was feeling desire. One night during intercourse, Lois began to caress her husband's buttocks and testicles instead of lying passively. She was shocked when Matt responded by pushing her

roughly away. "What's the matter with you?" he demand-
ed. "You're turning into some kind of slut!"

These ideas can be traced back to teenage years, when
boys told each other that the right kind of kiss or touch could
"drive a girl wild," tempting her to lose control and even "go all
the way." This male power was reserved, if you were a gentleman, for the bad girls who secretly wanted to be corrupted. To
ruin a good girl was shameful (although she probably was a bad
girl at heart, or she would never have given in).

Sometimes a man's sexual experiences strengthen his belief that female desire is uncontrollable. Although he needs a
rest period between orgasms, his partner may be able to have
several climaxes in a row. He may worry about ejaculating before she is really satisfied, even though she already has had two
or three orgasms. Women often are more vocal during sex than
men, moaning with pleasure or saying something loving to their
partner. This does not mean that a woman's pleasure is more
intense. Instead it reflects the fact that women are allowed to
express all kinds of feelings more openly than men.

Men and women are not really so different, in their hearts
or in their genitals. But the image of a woman as either saint or
sinner, Madonna or prostitute, leaves no room for her to be a
real person. In a healthy relationship, sexual passion is an ex-
pression of affection and closeness. Each partner trusts the other to be faithful, if that is a part of their mutual commitment.
Making sexual choices is a part of adulthood, no matter if you
are male or female.

THE FEMALE SEX RESPONSE—A
QUICK TOUR

Earlier in this chapter, I mentioned that many women do
not understand their own genitals. Because the sexual area of a

woman's body is hidden and rather complicated, men also are apt to have a hazy idea of which part is where, and how it all works. In your journey to sexual fulfillment, you might find it helpful to add a quick tour of the female genitals to your itinerary.

The Vulva. The outer female genital area shown in Figure 3 is called the vulva. It is made up of soft tissue that protects the sensitive areas around the vaginal entrance. The tissue forms a set of inner lips and a set of outer lips. The vulva is richly supplied with blood vessels. When a woman becomes aroused, blood flow to the vulva is increased, so that its skin turns a deeper red and the tissues swell gently. This is the female equivalent of an erection.

The Vagina. We tend to think of the vagina as a hole or tunnel. Actually, when a woman is not sexually excited her vaginal walls collapse together. If you could examine the inside of her vagina, it would be pale pink and fairly dry to the touch. When a woman becomes aroused, the deep end of her vagina "balloons" out, getting both longer and wider. As one of the first signs of excitement, the cells lining the vaginal walls produce a lubricating fluid. These changes prepare the vagina for comfortable intercourse.

The part of the vagina most sensitive to a light touch is the outer third, closest to the entrance. A muscle that women can learn to squeeze at will surrounds the entrance. When a woman has an orgasm, the muscle contracts involuntarily in a rhythmic pattern. Recently, researchers have suggested that women have a small zone on the front wall of the vagina, about four inches inside, that is particularly sensitive to pleasure from the penis's thrusting during intercourse. They have named this area the G spot. Some couples have found that rubbing of the G spot helps the woman reach orgasm.

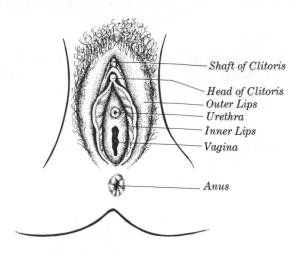

Shaft of Clitoris

Head of Clitoris

Outer Lips

Urethra

Inner Lips

Vagina

Anus

FIGURE 3. THE OUTER FEMALE GENITALS

The Clitoris. When an embryo develops into a female rather than a male, the tissue that would have formed a penis turns into the clitoris instead. The sole job of the clitoris is to send messages of sexual pleasure to the brain. Like the penis, the clitoris has a head and a shaft. The head of the clitoris is usually hidden beneath a hood of skin formed by the top of the inner lips. The tip of the clitoris is so sensitive that women often do not like it to be directly touched. They prefer to be touched at the sides of the clitoris, or along its shaft, which can be felt as a ridge directly above its head. This whole area can become irritated if touched too roughly. A woman may find the touching more pleasurable if her partner uses extra lubrication on his fingers. For this purpose, couples can use the liquid produced by the women's vagina, or a mild, unscented lotion or gel (such as K-Y or Lubrifax). Most women reach orgasm more easily if clitoral stimulation is a part of sexual activity.

Other Areas. The opening of the urethra (the tube that drains urine from the bladder) is a small slit between the vagina and clitoris. It is often hard to spot. An erotic zone for many women is the skin between the vaginal entrance and the anus. Couples may also include some caressing of the anus itself in their sex play. Some enjoy having intercourse with the man's penis in the woman's anus. Though anal intercourse is not unusual, if you include it in your routine there are several important things to remember. One is always to use extra lubricant, since the rectum, unlike the vagina, does not produce its own lubrication. Entrance to the anus should never be forced, because this can result in irritation or tearing of the lining. If the man penetrates very gently and gradually, the muscle around the anus will relax. A finger or penis that has been inside the anus should be washed before being put in the vagina. Otherwise, bacteria from the rectum can be transferred and grow in the vagina, causing an infection.

Orgasm. As we have already seen, orgasm for both men and women is a reflex, consisting of rhythmic contractions of the muscles in the genital area. The resulting sensations travel through the nervous system. The length of time it takes a woman to reach orgasm, and the intensity of the stimulation she needs, vary widely. Some women find that one intense orgasm is totally satisfying, while others prefer to have several orgasms in a row. Furthermore, not only is each woman different from every other, but the same woman may change her pattern of orgasm at different periods of her life. Many women find sex enjoyable and satisfying even if they do not reach orgasm. Sexual problems arise when a woman and her partner try to judge their response by some artificial standard. The best thing you can do is enjoy and explore your pleasure together, without comparing it to the unrealistic ideas in some movies, novels, and sex manuals.

How can you tell if your wife or lover is having an orgasm? Sometimes you cannot. Contrary to popular opinion, most women do not scream and writhe when they have a climax. Instead, they may seem very still and tense. During intercourse, you may be able to feel small contractions of your partner's vagina when she climaxes, but these are not always evident. Some women's nipples feel more prominent or firm after orgasm, but again, not universally. If you are wondering whether your partner reached orgasm, you might ask her. It can be annoying, however, if a man demands to know after each sexual encounter whether a woman climaxed. A better question might be, "Is there anything special you would like me to do right now?" or simply, "How are you feeling?" It then becomes your partner's responsibility to let you know what she would prefer.

It is worth mentioning that women particularly enjoy cuddling, talking, or somehow feeling close to their partner after orgasm. Men seem to be more apt than women to simply turn over and go to sleep. A few extra minutes of contact can help make the entire experience more satisfying for the woman, and perhaps for you as well.

THE GOOD NEWS ABOUT OLDER WOMEN

A recent survey of older men asked them to describe their ideal lover. Contrary to the researchers' expectations, the majority of men who revealed their fantasy lover's age pictured her as over forty-five. Our stereotypes, however, still label a woman past menopause as asexual. Now that we have arrived at a more accurate view of aging and male sexual responses, we need a better understanding of the aging process in women.

Psychologically, menopause frees women to enjoy sex more than ever.

Arlene was not at all sad to reach menopause. She had no symptoms, such as hot flashes or irritability, and she certainly did not miss the cramps and messiness of menstruating. As far as sex was concerned, she could throw away her diaphragm and forget the fears about pregnancy that had always been at the back of her mind.

In Arlene's days as a young mother, she had often been too tired to feel sexy in the evening. Her husband had never understood why she was reluctant to have sex. After all, he had spent a hard day at the office, but was still feeling lusty. He also failed to realize that Arlene was often distracted during sex by worry that the kids might overhear or barge into the bedroom.

Now that the children have households of their own, and Arlene's husband is semiretired, the couple has the leisure and privacy to devote to their sex life. Arlene regards menopause as nature's reward for a lifetime of service.

In addition to having more time for sex, an older woman has had a chance to overcome the sexual inhibitions and taboos of her upbringing. Over the years she has learned to enjoy her body and to ask for the kind of touching she wants. As Kinsey found, the proportion of women able to reach orgasm increases steadily during the first fifteen years of marriage.

It is not only women in long-term relationships who benefit. After a divorce or bereavement, a woman can start a new sexual relationship without the handicap of youthful inexperience. She has the opportunity to avoid any patterns that limited her pleasure in a first marriage. Sometimes an older woman's willingness to communicate in bed surprises her partner. Divorced or widowed men may complain that their female peers are too sexually demanding or aggressive. Men are often bewildered by the changes in the rules of sex since their original dating years. While it is a challenge to adjust to a new lover, or to accept a new assertiveness in your familiar wife, men can profit greatly when women unveil the mystery of what they really want.

The physical aspects of menopause have also received some bad press. In the average woman, menopause occurs between ages forty-eight and fifty-one. The major change is that the ovaries stop working. A fertile egg is no longer produced each month. The ovaries also cease their output of estrogen (the "female hormone"). The most common sexual consequence is that the lining of the vagina takes longer to produce lubrication with excitement. Even after prolonged caressing, the amount of vaginal lubrication may not be sufficient for comfortable intercourse. A woman's vagina may actually shrink in size, and its walls become less elastic. These changes are felt as pain or burning with penetration. A few women experience a painful orgasm which feels like menstrual cramping. This discomfort results from the normal contractions of the uterus during orgasm, acting on tissue that has lost its natural stretchiness.

Although these effects of menopause sound forbidding, they do not have to mean the end of an enjoyable sex life. All of the changes are more pronounced in women who have stopped having sex. Women who stay sexually active notice little change in their physical condition. In one study of women over sixty, only 16 percent had discomfort with intercourse. For unknown reasons, regular intercourse seems to compensate for the loss of estrogen. It is unclear whether other kinds of sexual activity, such as masturbation or caressing of the external genitals, are sufficient to keep a woman's vagina in good shape.

When a woman does have trouble with a dry or tight vagina, replacement estrogens can be prescribed by a physician. Estrogens can be taken as a low-dose pill, or rubbed into the vaginal walls in a cream. These hormones can restore the vagina to its normal state, making intercourse comfortable again. Women often hesitate to use replacement estrogens, since publicity a few years ago suggested a link to cancer of the uterus and breast. Currently, it is known that taking estrogens for more than two years does increase a woman's risk of uterine cancer. The statistics on breast cancer after hormone treatment are still controversial. Estrogen pills may increase the risk of gallstones and high blood pressure, but may actually protect against heart disease, as well as keep an older woman's bones from losing too much calcium. Each woman must make a decision with her physician about the safety of taking estrogens. In recent years, replacement hormones have been made less risky by using lower doses, and alternating the dose of estrogen with progesterone, as in the normal menstrual cycle. Estrogen creams can also rejuvenate the vagina without as much effect on the rest of the body.

If a woman decides that estrogens are unsafe, she can use a water-based lubricant, like K-Y jelly or Lubrifax, to make intercourse more comfortable. After a few minutes these lubricants tend to dry out, so you may have to apply them more than once. They can be spread on the man's penis, or directly inside his partner's vagina. Oil-based lubricants (such as Vaseline) stay slippery for a longer time, but can cause vaginal infections by promoting the growth of yeast or bacteria and are therefore not recommended. It is also wise to avoid body lotions containing artificial coloring or perfume, as the genital skin of both men and women is delicate and prone to irritation by chemicals.

Even though menopause can affect the genital tissue, it does not decrease a woman's capacity to feel sexual desire. Her ovaries stop producing estrogen but, as we saw in Chapter 2, estrogen is not responsible for sexual desire in women. The hormone testosterone, produced in a woman's adrenal glands, promotes her desire as it does a man's. Menopause decreases the estrogens in the bloodstream, but in no way affects testosterone production. If anything, the lack of estrogens to "oppose" the testosterone should result in increased sexual desire in older women. Menopause also does not interfere with a woman's ability to reach orgasm.

If a woman has never learned to enjoy sex, however, menopause can be a welcome excuse to end sexual activity.

Josie had never liked sex very much, but she believed that intercourse was her wifely duty. As she and her husband,

Bert, reached middle age, Josie had more and more head-aches at bedtime. When her periods stopped, Josie was in her element. Each evening she gave Bert a bulletin on her hot flashes. After a few months, she gave their old queen-sized mattress to the Salvation Army, and bought twin beds. Josie had gone through a change of life in more ways than one.

Women are also mistakenly expected to lose interest in sex after a hysterectomy. The term hysterectomy only means re-moving the uterus, which has no effect on a woman's hormones. In older women, however, the surgery we loosely call a hyster-ectomy often removes the ovaries as well, since they stop func-tioning at menopause anyway, and are always at a small risk for developing a cancerous tumor. When the ovaries are re-moved, a surgical menopause is created. The effects on a wom-an's sex life are just the same as at natural menopause. Sometimes a portion of one ovary is left in, and can produce enough estrogen to prevent menopause in a younger woman.

If a diseased condition of the uterus or ovaries had been causing pain during intercourse, a woman may find she can en-joy sex again once she recovers from her surgery. In any case, a woman can still have orgasms, even after the loss of her ova-ries, uterus, and cervix (the entrance to the uterus in the up-permost vagina).

Age is kind to women, in sexual terms. Their capacity for pleasure and orgasm usually remains unchanged or even im-proves. As we will see in the next chapter, however, older men are vulnerable to some frustrating sexual difficulties.

5

Middle Age Is the First Time You Can't Do It Twice. Old Age Is the Second Time You Can't Do It Once!

Nearly every man occasionally has trouble getting an erection, or loses one at a crucial moment. Despite the message of this chapter's title, such difficulties are not legitimate cause for concern unless they happen often. Men are inclined to react strongly, however, to even a temporary erection problem. Erections have a psychological meaning beyond their role in sexual activity. Men tend to see them as proof of youth, vigor, dominance, competence, and manhood itself. This is a large burden for what is in fact a rather delicate reflex.

Ever since recorded history began, men's anguish over erection problems has been discussed and various remedies offered. Suggested cures have included unicorn horn (responsible for the near-extinction of the rhinoceros), ginseng root, oysters, lettuce, a young virgin, Spanish fly, monkey's testicles, a rubber band around the base of the penis, hormone shots, vitamins, psychoanalysis, group sex, sex therapy, and surgery to implant a prosthesis in the penis. A few of these remedies have actually helped men. Some are useless. Others have been posi-

tively harmful. The one thing they have in common is being lucrative for some self-styled healer. Erection problems, like
war, make good business. Therefore, let the buyer beware. If
you are having trouble with erections, or if you are concerned
that you may have sexual problems at some future time, you
need enough knowledge to be an informed consumer when
seeking help.

Erection problems are of special concern to older men because they become more common after age fifty or sixty. It is
hard to get a good estimate of the prevalence of erection problems. Kinsey, interviewing men in the 1940s, found that 2 percent of men aged forty to forty-nine had a major difficulty with
erections. For men in their fifties, the rate climbed to 7 percent. It rose again to 18 percent of men in their sixties, and 27
percent of men in their seventies. A huge 80 percent of men in
their eighties said they no longer had normal erections.

Kinsey's findings may be exaggerated by the sexual climate of his era. Older men may have been reluctant to admit
they were still sexually intact. However more recent research
concurs that a sizable proportion of older men have erection
problems. For example, interviews in the 1970s by Dr. Clyde
Martin with men sixty to seventy-nine years old revealed that
about a third had difficulty with erections. Another 15 percent
were not sexually active at all, and thus unsure of their ability
to function.

Until the past few years, sex therapy and medical text-
books were fond of repeating the statement: "Ninety percent of
erection problems are due to psychological causes." In other
words, men who had trouble with erections were said to be suffering from childhood hang-ups or from simple anxiety and fear
of sexual failure. Often doctors referred men to a psychiatrist,
psychologist, or sexual counselor without even performing a
physical exam. Some physicians took this pronouncement so
much to heart that they merely sent their patient home, telling
him, "Stop worrying. It's all in your head."

Although many sexual problems *are* caused by stress, fears about performing, and relationship conflicts, erection difficulties in men over fifty often have a medical basis. We do not know the exact proportion of erection problems that result from poor physical health, but in older men the figure is probably closer to 50 percent than 10 percent. Evidence from studying sleep erections confirms that medical causes for erection problems become more common as men age.

To the best of our knowledge, however, it is not old age itself that is the culprit. Instead erections are affected by the diseases that accompany aging, such as diabetes, arteriosclerosis (blockages of the arteries), and kidney or lung conditions. Long-term bad health habits, including heavy smoking or drinking, may also damage sexual function. In addition, the treatment for a disease, like surgery to remove a tumor from the pelvis or medication to control high blood pressure or ulcers, may decrease erections.

To understand why these sexual side effects occur, you need a working knowledge of the way an erection is normally produced. We often think of an erection as a hearty, robust reflex, available at a moment's notice. Actually, an erection results from a surprisingly complex coordination of bodily systems.

THE INCREDIBLE ERECTION REFLEX

If television was less heavily censored, the erection reflex would make a great subject for a popular science special. As you read this section, you might picture the erection process in your mind as a cartoon, complete with color and motion.

The brain prepares the way, sending signals of sexual arousal down the spinal cord and through several sets of nerves in the pelvic area. The brain may be reacting to nervous system messages, such as sensations of pleasure from the genital skin, or signals produced by a sexual sight, sound, taste, odor, or touch. The brain can also trigger the erection reflex itself, through a sexual thought, memory, or fantasy.

One of the most important nerve segments that helps produce erections runs along the outside of the prostate gland. When these nerves deliver a message of sexual excitement, the arteries supplying the penis dilate (expand in caliber). As a result, blood flow to the penis speeds up dramatically. (It may help to remember that arteries are the vessels bringing blood *to* an organ, while veins drain blood away, back to the heart.) When the penis is soft, blood flows in at a rate of about two milliliters (three one-hundredths of an ounce) each minute. To create a full, firm erection, the speed of blood flow increases twenty-five to fifty times. No other response in the body calls for such a large *change* in blood flow.

The extra blood is routed into the penis, filling up two spongy cylinders of tissue that run along the right and left sides of the shaft. These cylinders, called the cavernous bodies (see Figure 4), are made up of connective tissue, nerves, tiny blood vessels, and a few muscle fibers. Small blood vessels inside the penis act as passageways from the cavernous bodies. When a man is not sexually aroused, these passages stay open, allowing blood to simply flow in and out of the rest of the penis. When he is excited and blood flow increases, specialized nerves seal the inner tunnels, forcing the cavernous bodies to fill like a sponge soaking up water.

The penis becomes stiff as blood pressure builds inside of the cavernous bodies. The two spongy areas are each surrounded by a tough sheath of tissue that limits their expanding size. Because of the sheaths, the shaft of the penis becomes rigid rather than merely swollen and soft. Though the glans (or head) of the penis also contains spongy tissue, it has no surrounding sheath. The glans remains softer than the shaft, forming a cushion to make intercourse comfortable for the woman.

Once the penis is erect, a much slower flow of blood is suffi-

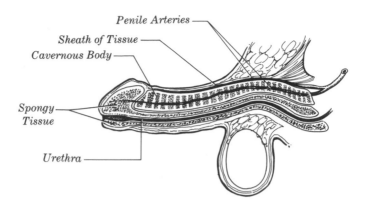

FIGURE 4. A CROSS SECTION OF THE PENIS

cient to maintain the erection. The amount of blood draining out of the penis is also probably less during erection than it is in the resting state, although Japanese and Danish research groups are still arguing on this point. One group says erections result solely from increased inflow of blood. The other laboratory claims that reduced outflow is also necessary. After a man reaches orgasm, blood flow into the penis slowly returns to normal levels, while drainage increases. This also happens when a man loses his erection before reaching orgasm, for example if something distracts him or interferes with his feelings of excitement.

The hormone system, too, plays a role in the erection process. Testosterone, acting on the brain, sets the scene for sexual desire and arousal. It is also possible, but not yet known for certain, that the male hormones act directly on erection-controlling nerves in the spinal cord or penis.

A difficulty in achieving or maintaining erections can occur if there is a problem in any one of the four necessary systems: the emotional state of sexual excitement, the nervous system paths that control blood flow to the penis, the blood vessels involved in circulation to the penis, and the sex hormone cycle.

Rather than being taken aback by an erection problem, we should perhaps be astonished that the reflex usually works!

TEMPORARY ERECTION DIFFICULTIES

Just as TV broadcasts are occasionally disrupted, a man may be annoyed to find that his reliable erection reflex will not turn on or tune in. Most commonly, the kink in the system is an emotional one, or sometimes a temporary physical short-circuit. These erection problems can be resolved with time, a more relaxed attitude toward sex, or, if necessary, short-term sexual counseling. Often the problem starts rather suddenly.

Because he was a tax accountant, Tom hated the months of March and April. The rest of the year he could live like a normal person, but springtime, the season for romance and new beginnings, found Tom working around the clock. Nevertheless, he and his wife, Amy, took a few hours for themselves one Easter weekend. Tom felt that sex would be a good way to relax. While Amy was caressing him, however, the only forms he could visualize were W-2s and 1040s. Predictably, Tom's penis stayed as limp as he felt.

Stress is frequently the source of an erection problem. Job or family problems not only produce fatigue, but can also lead to nagging thoughts that interfere with sexual excitement. Without a mental "turn-on," it is hard to get physically aroused.

Stress is not always the result of external conflicts. A man may put unnecessary pressure on himself to perform sexually. Instead of relaxing and enjoying his sensations or concentrating on a sexual fantasy, he starts focusing on his erection.

Without even realizing it, he begins to think, "Gee, is it hard enough? Maybe I'll lose it if I don't get inside her soon. I'm not getting any younger, either. I wonder how long I'll be able to keep getting it up." Then, if he actually develops a problem with his erection (which is likely, given these distracting thoughts), the internal monologue becomes a self-fulfilling prophecy: "Uh-oh, I wonder if I'll lose my erection tonight like I did last week? How come I don't feel anything when she touches me? I swear I'm getting numb! If I can't satisfy her, maybe she'll have an affair. Oh no, there it goes again." The man begins to watch himself go through the motions of sex, rather than enjoying what he is doing. Masters and Johnson call this "spectatoring."

When we talk about "anxiety" as the cause of an erection problem, we generally think of being afraid or having the jitters. As you can see from the examples I've cited, however, the crucial factor is often not a man's feelings but his thoughts. All of us guide our actions through a continual inner conversation with ourselves. These automatic thoughts, or "self-statements," are our predictions of what will happen if we take a certain course of action. The power of negative thinking on our actions is considerable. What sex therapists call "performance anxiety" or "fear of failure" is really a set of self-statements predicting that sex will be a flop.

Why do I say that sexual anxiety is a matter of self-statements? Isn't anxiety the same as fear? Everyone knows that a man cannot get an erection if he is feeling afraid.

Actually, a recent report on men raped by women reveals that a man threatened with physical harm *can* force himself to have an erection. In addition, some brave men have volunteered to be subjects in a laboratory test of "erections on demand." The subjects were warned that a mild electric shock would be delivered if they failed to get an erection while watching a sexy film. The men threatened with a shock got fuller erections than those who were simply told to enjoy the film and try to get turned on. Anxiety, then, is not simple to define. It seems to be the expectation of failure, rather than fear per se, that causes problems during sex.

How can a man get rid of negative thoughts? Forbidding yourself to think about sexual failure is often futile. Try right now for example, not to think about a pink elephant. Your immediate reaction is probably to picture a huge, rosy, pachyderm in your mind's eye!

The first step in changing your self-statements is to recognize and monitor them. What kinds of thoughts do go through your mind during sex? What scenes do you picture? Once you are aware of any patterns that get in your way, there are several techniques you can use to alter them. Briefly, they include arguing with any irrational beliefs you have about sexual failure, replacing your worries about failure with an image of success, distracting yourself with an erotic fantasy, and focusing on your physical pleasure instead of on your thoughts.

Jerry, at age sixty-one, developed a common type of erection problem. He was able to get an erection fairly easily and to maintain it during foreplay. When he and his wife tried to have intercourse, however, Jerry would almost always lose his erection before he could penetrate. During other kinds of sexual stimulation, such as his own masturbation or oral sex, Jerry's penis stayed hard until he reached orgasm.

When the problem had gone on for three or four months, Jerry decided to seek help. Their family doctor referred the couple to a psychiatrist trained in sex therapy. The sex therapist suggested that Jerry pay attention to what he was saying to himself during sex. Jerry noticed that he concentrated on his wife's reactions or on his own sensations until it was almost time for intercourse. Then he started to think, "Oh come on, we've got to hurry up before I lose it. If I could just get inside, I know I'd be O.K. . . . I think I can feel it getting softer. . . . I guess I'm just not a real man anymore."

The therapist asked Jerry to concentrate on pleasurable sensations during sex. Jerry learned to switch his attention from his thoughts of failure to erotic feelings from the skin of his penis or other areas of his body, and to the texture, warmth, and moistness of his wife's vagina. This strategy increased Jerry's enjoyment of sex, but he still got distracted when he tried to penetrate, and then would lose his erection.

The next suggestion was that Jerry treat his thoughts about failure as a cue to summon up a sexy fantasy instead. The therapist asked Jerry if there was a mental image or fantasy he found particularly exciting. Jerry admitted that when he masturbated, he often remembered a story he'd read about a gorgeous, blonde movie star who could not get enough oral sex. Jerry had always felt guilty about having this fantasy during lovemaking with his wife, however. The therapist reminded Jerry that thoughts do not equal actions. Jerry and his wife were choosing to share pleasure with each other. If Jerry's fantasy increased their mutual enjoyment, surely it was not like being unfaithful. "But my wife is so attractive," Jerry argued. "I should get turned on just by looking at her."

"And you do," the therapist replied, "but when your thoughts about failure start, only the most lusty, exciting mental image can keep you turned on."

Jerry tried the fantasy technique, and was able to penetrate much more often. He still had a mild problem with losing his erection, however, so the therapist decided it was time to work directly on Jerry's self-statements. In the next session, the topic was Jerry's irrational belief that a lasting erection was the hallmark of a "real man," and that his wife would be frustrated unless the couple had successful intercourse twice a week. Jerry's wife told him that she very much enjoyed their sex life, and would be satisfied even if it did not change any further. The therapist helped Jerry to trust that his wife was telling the truth, and not just being kind.

Jerry and the therapist made a list of things to say to himself during sexual activity when he needed to feel more relaxed. Some of the most helpful self-statements were: "Even if I lose my erection, I can get another one and try again"; "My wife enjoys orgasms from oral sex even more than intercourse, so I can always satisfy her"; and "I am a good lover because I care about my wife's pleasure. Having an erection is a lot less important than that."

Over several weeks, Jerry practiced paying attention to his body, using a sexual fantasy, and substituting optimistic thoughts for his negative ones. The erection problem gradually became a thing of the past. If Jerry did occasionally lose an erection, he and his wife returned to nonintercourse kinds of caressing until Jerry felt more relaxed and aroused.

Jerry's case offers some insight into ways a man can work within himself on solving an erection problem. Throughout this process, however, Jerry's wife was an important source of support. A more self-centered woman might have undermined Jerry's efforts with her impatience. A man's relationship with his mate is not always a factor in his fear of sexual failure, but the interaction between partners is at the root of two other causes of erection problems, anger and fear of intimacy.

Anger may have varying effects on a man's sexual feelings. Some find that anger at a partner provokes an upsurge of sexual desire. Couples may even use sex as a way to make up after a fight. For many men, however, angry feelings make sexual arousal difficult or impossible.

Herb and Cecile had waged a twenty-six-year battle about her widowed mother. Herb felt Cecile spent far too much time and energy, not to mention money, taking care of Mom. Cecile's mother lived in the apartment below theirs. As Mom got older and more lonely, Cecile did more and more cooking, cleaning, and visiting. When Herb and Cecile's youngest son left for college, they fought even more about Cecile's mother. One Christmas, Herb wanted to take a cruise to the Bahamas, but Cecile refused to leave Mom. Over the next weeks, Cecile cuddled close to Herb in bed, trying to make it up to him. He had no desire for her, however. Even when Cecile gave him his favorite kind of foot massage, which usually was a prelude to more sexual touching, he felt little pleasure.

A man often expresses anger in indirect ways, such as giving his wife the silent treatment, forgetting her birthday, or making nasty cracks about her in public. Having an erection problem is another terrific way to get revenge on a woman. "Gee, honey, I don't know what's wrong. You just don't seem to do anything for me. Maybe if you lost a few pounds . . ." Sometimes a man may not even realize what he is doing.

If you have been having erection problems recently, especially if they only happen with one particular partner, are there any major sources of anger in your relationship? If so, could you resolve your anger by discussing it more openly with your partner? Have you tried telling her how you feel?

Revealing your inner emotions to a mate takes trust. You need to believe that she cares enough to listen and to try to work things out. The drawback of loving someone is the power you give that person to hurt you. If you deny your loving feelings, you do not risk rejection. By the same token, however, you miss the joy of a close relationship. Men's fears about closeness are another common cause of erection problems.

Drew's story sounded like a cheap novel, except that it was true. After thirty years of marriage, his wife left him for his best friend. Although the people who cared about Drew urged him to try dating as soon as the divorce was final, he sat at home alone for many weekends. Finally Drew decided to join Parents Without Partners. He met several women, one of whom shared his hobby of photography and was also quite attractive. Drew felt like a teenager again, not sure how to get beyond a kiss goodnight. When the couple did attempt to have intercourse, Drew found himself unable to maintain his erection. When his girlfriend voiced some mild frustration with the problem, Drew stopped calling her, afraid to face another sexual failure.

In Drew's case, a bad experience in his marriage affected his ability to relax and enjoy a new relationship. Like a child who has been burned, he was reluctant to try lighting matches again. For many men, the past hurts are not so dramatic. A series of minor rejections or disappointments, however, can be enough to set the scene for a sexual problem. When a man is feeling insecure about his attractiveness or self-worth, he may be distracted from his own sexual pleasure, and, as a result, have difficulty with erections.

In a healthy relationship, each partner is comfortable with the degree of emotional closeness. Sexual problems can occur, however, if one partner wants more intimacy, or more distance, than exists in the status quo.

One reason that Lionel chose his second wife, Sarah, was the sense of peace they found together. In his eight years of widowhood, Lionel dated quite a bit. A number of women made him feel smothered. They wanted to monopolize his free time or coaxed him to confide his troubles to them. Lionel enjoyed spending some evenings alone or out with "the boys." He also liked to be by himself when he felt tired or depressed. At night he was used to some room in bed. He couldn't sleep huddled together with a woman. Often, Lionel found that he lost sexual interest in a woman when she started to be demanding.

On the other hand, the woman he had been dating before he met Sarah was too independent. She only seemed to be free for dinner once a week. Even though she had sex with Lionel, she insisted on going home to sleep afterward. While Sarah had her own career and family, she was willing to share some of Lionel's interests. Perhaps because he was less on his guard, Lionel felt more passionate and had more reliable erections with Sarah than he had in years.

Psychological causes for an erection problem are like broadcast problems at a TV station. On occasion, however, something closer to home can temporarily interrupt your TV show. Turning off an interfering hair-dryer, or just whacking the top of the set will get the picture back in synch. An episode of erection failure, similarly, can result from a temporary mechanical problem with the body's physical response. The best example is trying to have sex after several alcoholic drinks. Because alcohol depresses the central nervous system, it interrupts or weakens the signals that produce an erection. When the alcohol wears off, the erection response should return to normal (unless chronic abuse of alcohol has damaged the sexual response systems, as we will see in Chapter 6). Other medical reasons for temporary erection trouble could include weakness while recovering from an illness; the effect of a short-term medication, such as a tranquilizer or antidepressant; pain from a local condition like a prostate infection or genital herpes; or fatigue due to unusual life stress.

Unfortunately, many men panic if they have trouble with erections even once or twice. If a man believes he is doomed to a sexless old age, he may see any change as the first sign of eventual disintegration. His resulting anxiety takes the form of distracting thoughts, and the vicious cycle of performance pressure is started. The harder the man tries to get erections, the less success he has. A temporary problem becomes a chronic one. Homosexual men may be particularly vulnerable to these worries because of the premium the gay community has placed on youth and sexual skill. Fortunately as gay lifestyles are more accepted, homosexual men are under less pressure to conform to stereotyped images.

As we saw in Chapter 3, the majority of men only experience small alterations in their sexual response with aging. Even if you are in the minority of men who have a more permanent erection problem, medical help is available. If you have begun having difficulty getting or keeping an erection, take a few minutes to review your current life situation. Have you been under unusual stress lately? Have you been ill? Have you been taking any medications that might affect your nervous system? How are you and your partner getting along?

If there is a plausible explanation for your problem, give yourself several weeks before getting concerned. Here are some simple "Do's and Don'ts" in preventing a short-term problem from becoming a long-term one:

ERECTION PROBLEM DO'S AND DON'TS

DO:
* Keep on trying sexual activity, but only when you are in the mood.

DON'T:
* Force yourself to have sex more often than usual.

DO:

- Switch to other kinds of touching, such as mutual caressing of the genitals or a sensual body massage, and enjoy your feelings of pleasure.
- Let your partner know what kinds of touch are exciting for you. You may need more direct caressing of your penis. Many men find oral sex is most arousing. You might also want her to put on perfume or sexy lingerie.
- Let your partner know your problem does not mean that you are tired of her, feel that she is unattractive, or are in love with someone else. A woman tends to blame herself for her lover's trouble with erections.
- Talk about the problem with your partner. Let her know your inner insecurity or hurt. If you are silent, she may think you are angry at her.
- Call your family physician, or a specialist in sexual problems if these tactics do not result in better erections.

DON'T:

- Try to use every erection to have intercourse. Men often put unnecessary pressure on themselves by reacting to each morning erection or erection during sexual play as a demand for intercourse.
- Watch your penis all the time to see whether you have an erection. During foreplay, instead, focus on your pleasure or on a fantasy.
- Rush to penetrate the minute you get an erection. This is a real setup for failure. There is no reason why you must have an erection at all times during sexual caressing. If you lose an erection, the right kind of stimulation can help you regain one.
- Run out and try a new partner. If you think the problem is in your relationship, you need to decide whether it is worth trying to work out. If you usually date several partners, fine.

DON'T:

Often, however, men try someone new to test themselves. Then if they "fail" again, as is likely given the tension of trying to please an unfamiliar partner, they feel even more hopeless.

* Stomp out of the bedroom in a huff, yell at your partner, or turn your back and sulk. This may relieve your feelings, but will create more tension for the next time.

PERMANENT ERECTION PROBLEMS

Sometimes when your TV picture goes on the blink, you find nothing but snow on any channel. You know then that the problem cannot be blamed on the signal—something in your set is broken. In the same way, an erection problem may begin to occur all the time, in every situation, including sex with a partner, masturbation, and waking erections. In men over fifty, a persistent erection problem may well have a medical cause. Thanks to new diagnostic exams and surgical treatments, however, even permanent sexual difficulties can often be remedied. In Chapter 7, you will find some advice on how to seek help from your doctor. Right now, though, let's examine some of the common reasons for a medically based erection problem.

Reduced circulation to the penis is the most common physical cause of erection problems in older men. Because an erection demands such a large increase in blood flow, even minor damage to the circulatory system can interfere. The arteries that supply the penis are very tiny. As a man ages, deposits can build up on their inner walls or scarring can occur, making the blood vessels narrower and less elastic. Mild changes in the arteries may just necessitate a longer stimulation time before a man can attain full erection. With more severe "hardening of the arteries," erections may be only partial or disappear almost immediately.

Even when a man's circulation system remains healthy, damage to his nervous system can prevent his brain's erection signal from reaching the blood vessels in his pelvis. As you recall, this message accelerates the blood flow to the penis. If crucial areas in the brain, spinal cord, or pelvic nerves are damaged, the message may be garbled or cut off entirely. Nerve damage can result from strokes, a severe back or pelvic injury, long-term alcoholism, or a health problem involving the nerves themselves. For example in diabetics, pelvic nerve damage may result from inadequate blood flow in the tiny capillaries. Occasionally, too, the nerves that transmit sensation from the skin of the penis sustain damage. In that case, a light caress may not be enough to spark an erection.

A third possible source of erection problems would be a hormone imbalance. Although a few older men have abnormally low levels of testosterone, hormone problems are less "cut and dried" than disease affecting the circulatory or nervous systems. Some men carry on fairly normal sex lives despite low testosterone levels.

Sometimes it is not a disease itself but its treatment that affects erections. For example, most medications for high blood pressure interfere with the nervous system's control of erections. Other prescription drugs, including some that lessen the chest pain of angina and others that soothe stomach ulcers, upset the hormone system's balance. Although such medications are necessary for health, men often resist taking them because of their sexual side effects. If one of your medications seems to be putting a damper on your sex life, tell your doctor before you give up on sex or, worse yet, throw the pills away. Often a change in the dose or type of medicine can reverse the sexual problem. Since these side effects are not seen in every man who takes a medication, your physician will not know you are having a problem unless you disclose that information.

Most men who suffer from erection problems are anxious to know why. A man may find it comforting to blame his problem on a medical condition, rather than on an emotional or relationship difficulty. While even the strongest and most masculine man occasionally gets sick, "mental" problems are a disgrace. As we have seen, however, the best of men are vulnerable at times to stress, fatigue, pressure to perform sexually, distracting thoughts, anger at a partner, or fears of rejection. At least a psychologically based erection problem can be fixed through counseling, while a medical problem may require a more drastic kind of treatment. In any case, a persistent erection problem in a man past fifty calls for a thorough medical examination. Even if you are not interested in staying sexually active, the loss of erections could be a symptom of a serious health problem.

If you have been having erection problems but are unsure whether to consult a doctor, you might try answering the following questionnaire. If a question does not apply to you, just skip it.

ERECTION PROBLEM QUESTIONNAIRE

1. How did your problem with erections start?
   A. Suddenly   B. Gradually
2. Do you *ever* (even on waking or in nonsexual situations) get an erection firm enough for penetration?
   A. Yes   B. No

3. If you can get a firm erection, do you usually lose it at the moment you try to penetrate for intercourse?
   A. Yes   B. No
4. If you try masturbation, can you get and keep a firm erection?
   A. Yes   B. No
5. Does your erection problem get better with a different partner?
   A. Yes   B. No
6. Do you ever wake from sleep with a full erection?
   A. Yes   B. No
7. During sex, do you usually feel mentally aroused (turned-on) even if you have trouble with erections?
   A. No   B. Yes

Even an expert cannot diagnose the cause of an erection problem without a thorough physical exam. In general, however, if you chose answer "A" to almost all of the questions, your problem is probably not a medical one. If you had mostly "B" answers, a medical cause is likely. The next chapter will discuss some diseases of aging that can be responsible for decreased sexual function.

6

Sexual Health Hazards:
Some Diseases of Aging

The older a man gets, the more likely he is to have some sort of health problem. Many chronic illnesses—or their treatments— can interfere with sexual functioning. In this chapter we take a look at the sexual side effects of arteriosclerosis ("hardening of the arteries"), hypertension (high blood pressure), heart disease, diabetes, cancer, chronic lung disease, alcoholism, prostate enlargement, and Peyronie's disease. If you have experienced any of these health problems, you may want to concentrate on the sections relevant to you and skim the others.

Before focusing on specific diseases though, let's review the general impact that being ill has on a man's sexual feelings and desire. Practically everyone goes through a significant health problem once in a while. Even a bad back, a severe case of the flu, or a broken bone can have a lingering influence on your sexual relationship.

SEX AND ILLNESS: THE PSYCHOLOGICAL EFFECTS

Sex takes energy. Not only the act of intercourse itself, but also the feeling of lust or longing for sex demands a basic sense of physical well-being. When a man is fatigued, in pain, or depressed, his sexual desire is usually one of the first things to fly out the window. If an illness is prolonged, he may crave a kiss, a gentle back rub, or just holding hands, but have little wish for passionate intercourse.

Sometimes this loss of sexual energy feels like insult added to injury: "It's bad enough to be stuck in bed and unable to work or enjoy myself. Now I don't even feel like a man anymore." In the middle of an illness, it may be hard to believe that sexual desire will ever return to normal. As a man's body heals, however, his sexual feelings do come back. If he has to undergo a long-term treatment, like those for diabetes, emphysema, or cancer, a man may not regain his former stamina. Nevertheless, he gradually learns to cope with his daily routine. As he gets used to his physical condition, his interest in sexual activity may reappear.

Besides causing stress, fatigue, and pain, illness can affect a man's image of himself as attractive and sexual. He may lose or gain weight, look pale, or have shadows under his eyes. After an operation, he must adjust to scars and sometimes to the loss of a part of his body. A man who has thought of himself as vigorously middle-aged may start to see himself as old. Under these circumstances, it is difficult to feel desirable as a lover.

Whether a man has something truly contagious such as viral hepatitis or a disease that is not catching, like cancer, he often fears that sex would be dangerous to his partner. Couples also worry that the exertion of intercourse will cause a setback for the patient. Many physicians add to these anxieties by setting ground rules for every activity except sex. Since sex is never mentioned, the couple assumes that it must be forbidden, even when golf, gardening, and going back to work are permitted again.

Illness may also dampen a man's sexual feelings if he sees himself in "macho" terms. Forced to depend on his wife and children, he may feel ashamed or embarrassed, forgetting all the times that he took care of them. Instead of accepting their support, he retreats into despairing helplessness, or lashes out when they try to "baby" him. He may not be able to explain his actions to his family. He just feels and reacts. The wife, in turn, tries not to get angry. She knows he is hurting and wants to help. Her tolerance makes her husband guilty and even more irritable. The more the husband and wife act like a stubborn son and martyred mother, the less they feel like lovers.

Bert and Julie are one of the most popular couples in their Southern town. Bert is a deacon in the church and an avid duck hunter, renowned for the shooting tales he tells whenever he has had a drink or two. Julie has been a successful fund-raiser for the local hospital, as well as a volunteer with emotionally disturbed children. She is always the first to lend a hand when someone is ill or there is family trouble. Although some of their friends do not get along with each other, all the couples include Bert and Julie in social occasions.

About two years ago, Bert began having some vague symptoms that were diagnosed as lymphoma, a form of cancer. Fortunately, his particular illness could be controlled through chemotherapy. Bert had to make frequent trips to a cancer hospital in the next state, however. He lost his hair during the treatments, and often felt weak and tired.

Everyone thought Bert and Julie coped amazingly well. Julie took over much of the running of their furniture store and let her volunteer activities go. In doing so, she discovered she had a flair for business. With Bert laid up, she tried a few of her own ideas about window displays and adding more contemporary furniture to their stock. To her hurt and surprise, Bert was not complimentary about her success. When she showed him the monthly accounts, his comment was, "This is just the novelty. Wait a few months until your cheap goods start falling apart. We'll see how our sales look then and what happens to our reputation in this town."

"But Bert," Julie protested, "the new furniture line is just as sturdy as what we've always carried. It's made by the same company."

"It looks like junk to me. If my father could see his store now, I wouldn't want to hear what he'd say."

When Julie tried to kiss Bert goodbye in the mornings, she got a dry peck on the cheek. He told her he did not need her to come with him to the hospital for his followup visits. The couple had always felt closest when they made love, but Bert rarely moved over to Julie's side of the bed anymore.

Julie reacted by trying to get Bert to talk. "Honey, how was your checkup?"

"Fine. The doctors say everything looks normal." Bert went back to reading the paper.

"Oh, I'm so relieved!" his wife said. She came over to give him a hug. "Are you still worrying a lot about the cancer, Bert?"

He shrugged irritably. "No use worrying about it. Either it will come back or it won't. Hey, I'm trying to read the sports section."

When Bert went out to mow the grass, he had to stop after the front lawn. Swearing at himself, he wondered if he would have the stamina to go on hunting trips again. His back ached, and it suddenly felt frighteningly like the pain when lymphoma was first active. Julie found him slumped at the kitchen table, sweaty and upset. "Are you O.K.?" she asked.

"I'm fine. It's just too hot out. I guess we should hire some kid to cut the grass."

"Let me get you a Coke. Or do you want some iced tea?"

"I don't want anything!" Bert wiped his forehead and slammed out the door. Julie heard the sputter of the mower starting.

That night in bed, Bert took his wife in his arms. Sex was one of his ways of apologizing after a blowup. Julie responded to his kisses, but when he tried to take off her nightgown, she pulled back. "Are you sure you feel up to this?" she whispered. "I don't want you to tire yourself out. You know, I'd love you even if we never had sex again."

Bert did not reply, but turned over with his back to his wife. Julie felt his body trembling, but it took her several moments to realize that Bert was crying.

How can a couple minimize the impact of illness on their intimacy? From my work with cancer patients I can make several suggestions:

1. While you are ill, maintain as much of your normal routine as possible. If you usually balance the checkbook, do the dishes, and wash the car, accomplish as many of those tasks as you can. Even if you can only reach the pitcher by your bedside, pour your own water rather than letting your wife do it.
2. If you feel scared or angry about your illness, talk about it. If you try to hide your feelings, they will come out somehow, often as anger at your loved ones, since a wife or girlfriend is a safer target than your physician or your religious faith.

3. If important family decisions such as a tax problem or a crisis with one of your children come up while you are ill, be as active as you can in making necessary choices. If you can tell your mate your opinion, she will not have to risk making a decision without your input—even though she may have to carry out your agreed course of action on her own.

4. Even if you do not feel up to sex, keep on kissing, cuddling, holding hands, etc. You may need physical affection more than usual. Men often worry that their wives will be frustrated by touching that does not lead to sexual intercourse. The great majority of women are far more upset, however, if their husband stops being affectionate than if he feels too ill to have intercourse. The cuddling may reassure your partner that you need and want her.

5. If you do feel like having sex, and if there is no medical barrier, let your partner know. If either one of you has fears that sex will jeopardize your recovery, or that your illness is contagious, schedule a joint visit with your doctor to get his or her opinion.

6. During sex, you may need to change your lovemaking routine. Perhaps you will feel more relaxed if you extend your foreplay. On the other hand, maybe you have only enough energy for a very short session of lovemaking. If you find the man-on-top position for intercourse too strenuous, your partner may need to be more active in caressing you than usual. Ask her to let you lean back and enjoy it! As I keep repeating, communication is the key to a satisfying sexual relationship.

These suggestions can apply to any illness.

ARTERIOSCLEROSIS

One feature of the aging process, at least in modern Western cultures, is arteriosclerosis. Often called "hardening of the arteries," arteriosclerosis occurs when deposits and fibrous changes in the arteries make these blood vessels narrower and less elastic. If arteriosclerosis takes place in the arteries leading to the heart, it can lead to angina pain or a heart attack. Arteriosclerosis in arteries bringing blood to the legs can result in cold feet or pain with walking. If arteriosclerosis is present in the arteries that carry blood to the penis, an erection problem often occurs.

In men over fifty, arteriosclerosis is probably the most common medical cause of erection problems. The penile arteries are quite small to begin with. If they are narrowed by scarring or deposits, the blood cannot flow in fast enough to create and maintain a full erection. Since changes in blood flow are so extreme in the erection response, even mild arteriosclerosis can cause an erection problem. Physicians now regard such erection problems as an "early warning sign" of circulatory system disease. New exams to test blood pressure and flow in the penis can often determine whether arteriosclerosis is responsible for an erection problem. We will look closely at these tests in the next chapter.

Most commonly, arteriosclerosis damages the small arteries just above and inside the penis. A man who has diabetes or has been a heavy smoker is at higher risk for this condition. His symptoms typically start with a gradual increase in the time it takes to get a full erection. Over the course of months, or even several years, the problem gets worse. His erections may only get partially firm or quickly lose the stiffness needed for intercourse. He has few or no waking erections and can no longer get an erection from seeing an attractive woman or watching an X-rated movie, even though his desire for sex and ability to reach orgasm remain normal.

Sometimes the large arteries in the upper pelvis are partially blocked. In that case, a man may have circulation problems in his legs, often accompanied by an erection problem. When his symptoms become severe, they can be corrected surgically (through aortoiliac revascularization). These operations used to create erection and ejaculation problems, even if none existed before. With recent improvements in technique though, surgeons can sometimes improve a man's erections along with repairing the circulation to his legs (see Chapter 8).

Occasionally, partial blockage of a central pelvic artery (distal aorta or common iliac artery) can cause a "pelvic steal syndrome." In this condition, a man can get a full erection but loses it when he begins to move his hips or legs during intercourse. If he stays still, stands up, or lies on his back, he has better erections than he does in the missionary position. When he thrusts during intercourse, he may also feel a cramping pain in his buttocks. These strange symptoms occur when the circulation to the legs is just barely enough to take care of the body's resting needs. When the leg muscles move, they need more blood. This blood is "stolen" from the arteries feeding the penis and the erection is lost. Doctors often mistake the pelvic steal syndrome for a psychological problem, because it only happens during intercourse. It can be diagnosed, however, by testing blood pressure in the penis before and after a man does a series of "toe lifts" or "bicycle" exercises (see Chapter 7). In normal men, blood pressure stays constant. If a man has a pelvic steal, however, his penile blood pressure drops radically after leg movements.

Erection problems caused by arteriosclerosis can be treated in several different ways. If the sexual problem is mild, a longer period of foreplay with more direct caressing of a man's penis can result in satisfactory erections. Scientists are also experimenting with drugs called "vasodilators" which open the small arteries wider, letting blood flow through more easily.

For smokers, eliminating tobacco use may accomplish the same result.

If the erection problem is severe, surgery to improve blood flow to the penis or to implant a silicone penile prosthesis may be the only cure (see Chapter 8).

HYPERTENSION

Hypertension (high blood pressure) rarely interferes with sex in itself—though some hypertensive men have arteriosclerosis with its associated problems. Unfortunately, however, the medicines used to control hypertension often interfere with erections, ejaculation, or sexual desire. Most antihypertensive drugs (blood pressure medicines) work by affecting the way the nervous system controls blood circulation. As a byproduct, they may weaken the signals for erection that the nervous system sends. Even some diuretics (medicines that reduce fluid retention in the body) seem to interfere with erection. Some blood pressure drugs can also prevent a man from reaching orgasm or at least cut down the intensity of his pleasure and the amount of semen he ejaculates. A few drugs even diminish sexual desire, either because they are mild tranquilizers or because they affect the hormone system.

Walt was astonished when his annual checkup revealed high blood pressure. He had never felt better in his life, and in fact had recently won a tennis tournament in the over-sixty-five category. Walt, who had been divorced five years before, was almost as proud of his hit rate with women as he was of his tennis score. He cultivated a reputation for bringing a good-looking, young date to parties. Walt also prided himself on his skill as a lover. He liked to think that he had never left a woman unsatisfied.

Walt's doctor put him on a diuretic plus a blood pressure pill. After a couple of weeks of medication, Walt noticed that he felt sluggish on the court and for the first time, could not return a serve in bed. When he skipped his pills for a few days, his erections and energy returned to normal.

Walt decided that the cure for hypertension was worse than the disease. He pushed his prescription to the back of the medicine chest, and went about his daily business. Several months later, Walt began to have severe headaches. When he returned to his doctor, Walt's blood pressure was at such a dangerous level that he had to stay in the hospital for a week to get it under control.

Although practically every blood pressure medication affects sexual function in some percentage of men, many patients do not notice any change. If your doctor tells you it is necessary to take medication to control your blood pressure, there is no reason to panic. Your sex life may remain at its status quo. Even if you are one of the unlucky men who have sexual side effects, do *not* stop taking the drug without consulting your physician. Tell the doctor about your problem, and ask if the dose or type of medication can be changed. With some experimenting, the physician often can find a drug that controls your blood pressure without destroying your sex life. Of course if you had problems with sex before you began the blood pressure medicine, you cannot blame the problem on your pills. You may remember the old joke about the patient who asks his surgeon, "Doc, will I be able to play the piano after my operation?" When the doctor replies, "Yes, of course," the patient is delighted. "Gee," he says, "that's great, Doc, because I never could play the piano before!"

High blood pressure, although it is a major threat to health, often has few symptoms. If you do not feel sick, it is hard to believe you need medication that may bring down the curtain on your sexual performance. Many men, like Walt, throw their blood pressure medicine in the garbage because they dislike sexual side effects. Not only can untreated hypertension lead to strokes and kidney failure, but it can also make sexual intercourse dangerous. A group of British researchers monitored blood pressure during the daily activities, including sexual intercourse, of eight hypertensive men. At the time of orgasm, their blood pressure reached unusually high levels (an average of 237/133 mm Hg). Such peaks in blood pressure can lead to angina pain, a heart attack, or a stroke. Antihypertensive medication should lessen these peaks in blood pressure, making sexual activity safer.

HEART DISEASE

For men who have had a heart attack, angina pain, or cardiac bypass surgery, sexuality is often a worrisome issue. In one group of men interviewed after a heart attack, over half said their physician had not mentioned whether it was safe to resume sexual activity. This lack of communication is really unfortunate. Men with heart disease often have low sexual desire or trouble with erections. Researchers estimate that 50 to 75 percent of cardiac patients have some disruption of their sex lives. While a minority of these problems are caused by arteriosclerosis or necessary medication, much of the sexual inactivity arises from fears that intercourse is too strenuous or risky.

When *is* it safe to have sex? This is always an individual matter, to be decided with your physician's advice. There are some general guidelines, however. For one thing, as far as we know, "dying in the saddle," i.e., having a heart attack during intercourse, is a very rare event. When such a death does occur, it is sensationalized by gossip (and even in the media, if the person in question is famous). The only really extensive study of death during sexual activity was based on coroners' reports from Japan in the early 1960s. Out of more than 5000 cases of sudden death, less than 1 percent occurred during sexual activity. In most of these, the man was with a woman other than his wife, and in an unfamiliar setting. Before you conclude that intercourse is totally safe, however, or even that death is the wages of sin for adultery, you must realize that this research has flaws. If a man died in the midst of sex with his wife in his own bed in Japan in the 1960s, would the coroner have been called, and would the wife reveal that sex had been in progress? If marital deaths went unreported, the estimate of total deaths during intercourse may be conservative, and unfairly biased toward men with extramarital partners.

To better understand the risks of sex, researchers have asked cardiac patients to wear a portable heart-rate monitor during sexual activity. At least for the middle-class men in one study, during sex at home with their wives peak heart rates are around 120 beats per minute. The heart does a similar amount of work when a man walks briskly up two flights of stairs. Most of these men attained heart rates during their normal working day that equalled those during sexual intercourse. Men taking a medicine called a beta-blocker, which dampens the nervous system's response to stress, have had peak heart rates measured during sex of only 82 beats per minute, on the average. Men who get into better shape through a program of aerobic exercise, such as walking, jogging, bicycling, or swimming, also average lower heart rates during sex. Normally, sex just does not take all that much exertion. Some physicians have counseled heart patients to avoid the missionary position for intercourse, but researchers have found little change in heart rate whether the man is on top or on the bottom.

If a man experiences angina pain during sexual activity, a beta-blocking drug (such as propranolol) may help. A physician can also prescribe a nitrate pill to be melted under the tongue a few minutes before starting sexual activity. These medicines keep a man's heart from working too hard during sex. One drawback, however, is that these same drugs may cause low sexual desire or erection problems in a small percentage of men.

If sexual activity poses a special risk to patients with heart disease, it is probably not from increased heart rates, but rather from disturbances in the heart's rhythm. When the nervous system is activated by orgasm, these "arrhythmias" may be more likely to occur. We still do not know as much as we should about the risks of sexual activity to the heart.

If you have had heart disease, you may enhance your sex life by following these simple steps, modified from the Cardiac Rehabilitation Program of the University of Texas Medical Branch at Galveston:

1. Ask your physician whether sexual activity is risky for you. Include your partner in this discussion. Even if a man is comfortable resuming sex, his wife or lover may object because she is afraid it will harm him.
2. Start slowly, and do not get discouraged if you have some problems the first few times. You might try starting with a sensate focus exercise (see Chapter 10).
3. Avoid having sex when you have had a big meal or more than one or two drinks. Make love in a place that is comfortable, and not too hot or cold.
4. If you are with a new partner, let her know you need to take things slowly. Reassure her that it is safe for you to have sex, but enlist her support in keeping the activity relaxed and unpressured.
5. If you have persistent problems getting your sex life back on track, consider trying some brief sexual counseling (see Chapter 9).
6. If your sexual desire and orgasms are normal, but you have a medically caused erection problem, you may want to consider corrective surgery (see Chapter 8).

DIABETES

Diabetes is a notorious cause of sexual problems in men. The best available estimate is that about 50 percent of diabetic men have trouble with erections. In diabetic men over age fifty, the rate may be even higher. Although this is the most common problem, men with diabetes also may lose their desire for sex.

Diabetes, like other chronic illnesses, can have a psychological impact on sexual function. Some men, knowing that diabetes has potential sexual side effects, start watching their own responses, dreading the first sign of a problem. Their fears then become a self-fulfilling prophecy.

Grant's diabetes was first diagnosed when he was fifty-two. He was able to keep it under control by diet and oral medication for several years, and he and his wife continued to have a satisfying sex life.

Grant's blood sugar eventually began climbing, despite his usual medication. The doctor told Grant it was time to start using insulin. He also warned that Grant might develop some erection problems. The next week, Grant noticed he did not get an erection right away in response to his wife's touch. He started paying more attention to the state of his penis. He saw a beautiful teenager in a bikini at the beach, and had no erection. He woke up from sleep without an erection. He tried masturbating, and lost the partial erection he was able to produce. Within a month, Grant was rarely able to get erections with his wife, even though his diabetes was in better control than before and he had no other symptoms.

Dr. Domeena Renshaw, a sex therapist in Chicago, has successfully used counseling to treat diabetic men with erection problems. She believes that the stress of being ill and the fears of sexual side effects are responsible for many diabetics' sexual difficulties. Grant's problem, for example, might improve considerably with sex therapy.

In some men, however, diabetes clearly damages the nervous system or aspects of the sexual response related to circulation. We used to think that diabetic men had sex-hormone imbalances, such as a low level of testosterone. Physicians now agree that a hormonal cause for diabetic sexual problems is rare. The next theory was that diabetes damages the nervous system in the genital areas. In a recent study of forty-seven diabetic men who had erection problems, however, only about a third showed nervous-system abnormalities that could account for their difficulty. Instead, the most frequent culprit was reduced blood flow to the penis. Circulation was abnormal in 72 percent of the men, and appeared suspiciously low in another 23 percent. The researchers believe that diabetes damages the small arteries that feed the penis. When nervous-system or circulatory disease is severe, the only way to restore erections may be through a penile prosthesis (see Chapter 8).

A few diabetic men notice a decrease in sensation on the skin of the penis. This is often part of a more general neuropathy (tingling or numbness due to nerve damage, particularly common in the legs and feet). In a small percentage of diabetics, nerve damage causes retrograde ejaculation, a condition where the semen is pushed back into the bladder rather than out through the penis at orgasm (see the section later in this chapter on benign prostate overgrowth). Although this sounds painful, it is not, and the man's pleasure at orgasm may just be mildly reduced. He may be surprised or upset, however, when his ejaculation does not produce semen.

It is hard to predict which diabetic men will experience sexual problems. Many men who have been diabetic for decades have normal sexual function, while others more recently diagnosed have no erections. If a man's blood sugar gets temporarily out of control he may experience erection problems, but these decrease again when his medication and diet are regulated. This explains why some men have trouble with erections when their diabetes is first found, but improve sexually once diabetes treatment begins. In fact, an erection problem is often the symptom of diabetes that drives a man to seek medical help. The need for insulin therapy also has no direct relationship to sexual function. However, men whose diabetes produces side effects, such as neuropathies, changes in the retina of the eye, or disturbances in the nervous-system control of breathing and heart rate are also more likely to have erection problems. Since these men usually are taking insulin, it may seem as if the insulin itself is at fault.

CANCER

Ruthie and the other women in her bridge club liked to talk about sex. In fact, if their husbands or lovers ever realized how much was revealed during those evening card parties, they would probably have died of embarrassment. Ruthie even took credit for encouraging her friend Joan to try oral sex for the first time. The women described their men's little foibles and oddities in bed—albeit humorously—and often swapped ideas on how to reach orgasm, in the same time-honored way that their mothers had traded recipes for pie. It was a way for the women to blow off steam and feel understood, sometimes more easily than they could be at home.

When Ruthie's husband was put in the hospital for cancer of the colon, the bridge club took turns visiting and making casseroles for Ruthie's freezer. They got together one week without her, although it didn't feel the same. Joan had just seen Ruthie that morning, and reported that the husband had come home to recuperate. "He looks really gray and thin," Joan told them, "but they say they got it all. Of course you know he has a colostomy now."

"Poor Ruthie," one of the women murmured.

"Oh, it isn't so bad," Joan said. "You can't even tell with his clothes on."

"But they were always so *close*, I mean they seemed to have such a good sex life," one of the others sighed.

"Well, if it was my husband, I think I could deal with it," said Joan, who was divorced. "I mean if a man loved me the way Ruthie's husband loves her, I could put up with anything."

"But Joan, don't you *know*?" the first woman exclaimed. "Men are impotent after that operation. And besides, who even knows how long he'll be around?"

The bridge club illustrates some common attitudes about cancer and sex. Not only is cancer seen as a stigma, but there are many myths about cancer and sexuality. For example, the surgery to remove the rectum and create a colostomy does not invariably lead to erection failure.

When we hear the word *cancer*, our fears of death sometimes overwhelm our common sense. Since one out of four Americans will have a cancer at some time in life, most of us have some first- or secondhand contact with the disease. As cancer treatments improve, and the life expectancy of cancer patients increases, we need to regard cancer as another chronic illness, much like heart disease or diabetes. The quality of life during and after cancer treatment becomes a much more important issue. Part of that quality of life involves preserving a normal capacity for sexual pleasure.

Cancer takes so many different forms, each with its own treatment, that talking in generalities is difficult. People with cancer have several common worries, however. For example, it is surprising how many people still regard cancer as contagious, particularly through sexual activity. In actuality, a cancer cell from one person's body cannot take root and grow in someone else's body. This protection is due to the fact that each human is genetically unique (except for identical twins). Finding two people whose cells match would be like locating two snowflakes that are exactly alike. Even if a tumor is in the prostate or penis, sexual contact (including swallowing semen during oral sex) cannot transmit cancer cells that will harm a partner.

One of the few associations between sex and cancer is that both cancer of the penis and cervical cancer occur more often in people exposed to the genital herpes virus, type II. Though the cancers are not transmitted through sexual contact, the viruses promoting them may be. In homosexual men with weakened immune systems, a recent outbreak of the rare cancer Kaposi's sarcoma has been seen. Researchers are speculating that acquired immune deficiency syndrome (AIDS) is contagious through sex, again perhaps by means of a virus. No one yet knows why AIDS has been more common in the homosexual community. With the sudden increase in cases of AIDS and Kaposi's sarcoma, however, many gay men have decided to find out more about their partner's health before starting a sexual relationship.

Even if a cancer does not affect the genital area, many men regard it as a punishment for something in their past. Often that "something" is sexual, such as an affair, contact with a prostitute, or even too "strong" a sex drive. Sometimes men bargain with themselves, resolving to stop being sexual if that will somehow cure their cancer. At a time when a couple needs to be free to touch, talk, and support each other, these sexual fears may make a man withdraw from his mate.

Many cancer treatments are even more destructive to sexuality than is the disease itself. Radical surgery to remove the prostate, bladder, or rectum frequently results in erection problems because the operation damages the nerves and blood vessels around the prostate. The most tragic consequence, however, is that many men do not even attempt to have sex after cancer surgery. They may not realize that they have at least a small (15 percent) chance for sexual recovery. It may take several months for erections to return after pelvic surgery. Even without erections or semen production, a man's desire for sex, sensation on the skin of his penis, and ability to experience the sensation of orgasm usually remain intact. A man who loses the ability to get or keep erections can still enjoy sexual caressing, and is a good candidate for a penile prosthesis.

Some cancer surgery involves creation of an "ostomy," i.e., a passageway through the skin of the belly for eliminating urine or stool. The body wastes are collected in an opaque plastic pouch, which is sealed to the skin around the ostomy with special adhesives. When cared for correctly, ostomy appliances are clean and odor-free. Men with ostomies usually start out with some feelings of insecurity, however, about being accepted as a lover. The United Ostomy Association, Inc., (2001 W. Beverly Blvd., Los Angeles, California 90057), publishes some excellent booklets about sexuality and the male ostomate and coping with life as a single man with an ostomy. They even give some technical hints on how to minimize interference from the appliance during sex. Homosexual men who lose their rectum to cancer surgery may have some special concerns about finding alternate techniques for sexual pleasuring.

Cancer patients may also go through periods of radiation therapy or chemotherapy. Unless their immune defenses are severely weakened by these treatments, however, men can safely continue to have sex even during the weeks of therapy. Actually, we know very little about the effects of chemotherapy or radiation on sexual function. Hormone production may decrease during treatment, but the testosterone level usually returns to normal when therapy is over. Radiation to the pelvis, sometimes used to treat prostate or bladder cancer, may cause scarring of the arteries important to erection. This scarring progresses over several months after treatment, sometimes causing a gradual loss of erections. However, the majority of men continue to have good sexual function after radiation therapy.

When prostate cancer has spread beyond the gland itself, men are often treated with estrogen, the "female" hormone. Their testicles may also be surgically removed (orchiectomy). The purpose of these procedures is to decrease the testosterone available in the body, since testosterone feeds the cancer cells, keeping them alive and growing. Most men have a less frequent desire for sex after these treatments, but a number of patients do continue to have erections and orgasms.

The Department of Urology at The University of Texas M. D. Anderson Hospital and Tumor Institute at Houston has a program of sexual rehabilitation for cancer patients. Hopefully, this type of service will soon become available to cancer patients in other areas of the country.

CHRONIC OBSTRUCTIVE LUNG DISEASE

Another set of illnesses that become more common with age are chronic obstructive lung diseases, including emphysema and chronic bronchitis. Many lung disease patients lose their desire for sex and have problems getting erections. Estimates of the number of men in this group with sexual difficulties range from 17 to 83 percent. Most studies agree that the more severe the breathlessness and other lung symptoms, the more they interfere with a man's sex life.

The sexual problems have several possible causes. Chronic lung disease often restricts a man's daily activities. If he feels trapped and depressed, his sexual desire may decrease. During sex he may get out of breath, and even have a panicky feeling of suffocation. A number of men lose their erection at such a point during intercourse.

A man can cope with breathlessness by finding a more comfortable position for intercourse and letting his partner do more of the active movement. Since our traditional notion is that the male should be "on top," these changes are sometimes easier to suggest than to accomplish. When twenty lung patients at the University of Oklahoma Health Sciences Center were interviewed, seven revealed that they had stopped having sex altogether, and the other thirteen reported that sex occurred at less than a quarter of its former frequency. This same research suggests that men with chronic obstructive lung disease often sustain damage to the genital nervous system, causing erection failure.

ALCOHOLISM

Most men are aware that drinking too much alcohol on any given occasion can interfere with erections and the ability to reach orgasm. What you may not know is the relationship between long-term heavy drinking and sexual function.

Anywhere from 50 to 80 percent of alcoholics lose their desire for sex or have difficulty with erections. Unfortunately, even after many months of sobriety, only about half of them seem to recover good sexual function. Alcohol abuse over a period of years often damages the genital nerves and hence the erection reflex. A large percentage (65 to 80 percent) of long-term alcoholics also have atrophy (shrinkage) of the testicles, a visible clue that their testosterone-producing cells are not working well. Alcohol also disrupts the hormone feedback cycle, particularly if drinking damages a man's liver. Although some of these effects are reversible, others are permanent, which can be frustrating for the man who has invested so much energy in staying sober. If a recovered alcoholic feels his life has stablized but is still experiencing sexual problems, he may want to seek some counseling. If medical problems are interfering with his enjoyment of sex, hormonal or surgical treatment can help.

BENIGN PROSTATE OVERGROWTH

Some physicians believe that if every man lived long enough, his prostate would become enlarged and cause difficulties with urination. Certainly by the time men are in their eighties, at least half have "benign prostatic hypertrophy" (BPH). In BPH, the inner core of the prostate gland literally becomes overgrown. Since the urethra (the tube carrying urine from the bladder) passes right through the middle of the prostate, BPH can cause such symptoms as having to urinate very urgently or frequently, having trouble starting the flow of urine, having a very narrow stream, or, in extreme cases, inability to urinate.

The solution is usually for a surgeon to "core out" the prostate, reducing the pressure on the urethra. This surgery, called a TURP (trans-urethral resection of the prostate), involves passing an instrument through the urethra and scooping out the overgrown prostate tissue. You may have heard some myths about the effect of a TURP on sexual function, since many men believe a TURP destroys the capacity for erections, but actually a TURP has no medical effect on the erection response. The surgeon does not touch the nerves that control erection, because they run along the *outside* of the prostate.

A TURP does affect ejaculation in about 80 percent of men, however, since the surgeon usually has to stretch out the opening of the bladder where it joins the urethra. This opening normally shuts tight at the time of orgasm, so the semen is forced down and out of the urethra when the surrounding muscles contract. After a TURP, the bladder remains slightly open so that ejaculation is often "retrograde," i.e., the semen takes the path of least resistance back into the bladder. Control over urination is not lost, however. The semen simply mingles with the urine stored in the bladder. When the man urinates after an orgasm, he may notice the semen clouding his urine.

Most men do not find that retrograde ejaculation changes

their sensation at orgasm. The climax is still pleasurable, though it may feel a little less intense. Women also can tell little or no difference during intercourse. Contrary to what you read in novels, a woman can hardly ever feel semen spurting into her vagina.

A surgeon should always warn a man to expect retrograde ejaculation after a TURP. If the patient is taken by surprise, he may panic when there is no visible semen at orgasm, and imagine that something is terribly wrong. It is often these uninformed men who develop an erection problem as a result of their anxiety.

PEYRONIE'S DISEASE (CURVED ERECTION)

A few men, usually over forty years old, notice a puzzling change in their erections. In its soft or flaccid state, the penis looks normal. With erection, however, the shaft of the penis starts to develop a curve, bend, or "knot," instead of being straight. Often erection causes pain, especially during the first several months as the bend is becoming noticeable. Sometimes the bending and pain gradually lessen. Often the bend stabilizes, and the pain disappears, but the erection no longer gets really firm, especially at the tip of the penis. If the penis bends at a severe angle, or if the erection is not rigid, penetration for intercourse becomes a problem. Some men are so embarrassed by their odd symptoms that they do not consult a doctor.

These symptoms are typical of Peyronie's disease, a scarring of the tissues inside the shaft of the penis. This scarring usually starts in the sheath around the cavernous bodies (see Chapter 5), causing the curvature and pain when the spongy tissue inside fills with blood. If the scarring spreads into the spongy tissue itself, it blocks the tip of the penis from filling with blood during erection, even though the base gets firm.

Nobody is sure what causes Peyronie's disease. It seems to be more common in men with diabetes or high blood pressure. Perhaps it is also more likely in men who take phenytoin (Dilantin), a drug that prevents epileptic seizures, or beta-blockers, drugs used to treat high blood pressure and heart disease. Physicians have tried to treat Peyronie's disease with vitamin E or low doses of radiation to the penis. Today, men with severe Peyronie's disease are usually advised to wait until it stabilizes and then have an operation to remove the scar and insert a prosthesis in the penis (see Chapter 8).

If you have noticed an unusual curve or bend in your penis, ask a urologist to examine you for scarring. Peyronie's disease causes a lot of pain and worry, some of which can be avoided.

I have suggested many times in this chapter that a man needs to ask his physician for advice about a sexual difficulty. Both doctors and patients are often reluctant to discuss sex, however. Each waits for the other to mention it, and somehow the conversation never takes place. In the next chapter you will find some tips on how you can increase your chances of getting high-quality sexual health care.

7

You and Your Doctor: Your Right to Sexual Health

Jake was somewhat miffed when his internist, Dr. Steinman, took a young partner into the office. He was even more upset when that new partner, younger than Jake's son, walked in the examining room to give Jake his annual physical. "I've been coming to this office for fifteen years," Jake warned. "I don't want some intern practicing on me."

The young doctor just smiled and asked Jake to lie down on the table. Jake was surprised at the thoroughness of the exam. The new partner even took a few minutes to ask Jake about his daily life—how many hours Jake still spent in the store, what his hobbies were, how many grandchildren he had. "How do you and your wife get along?" the doctor asked.

"After forty-five years? What's left to fight about?"

"And how is your sex life? Are you and your wife still active together?"

"Funny you should mention that," said Jake. "Dr. Steinman never asked, and I never brought it up, but I've been having a little trouble."

The doctor then asked about the details of Jake's problem, which involved difficulty getting erections and reaching a climax. He suggested that Jake return the next week for some specialized tests to try to locate the cause of the sexual difficulties. Jake protested a little, insisting that sex was unimportant at his age, but made the appointment.

This is a medical fairy tale worthy of Dr. Kildare. Although I hope a few readers have had such an experience, most physicians do not take the initiative to inquire about a patient's sexual health. Yet you have as much right to get help for a sexual problem as you have to get advice on dieting, allergies, bowel habits, or failing eyesight. Sadly enough, however, most doctors have little or no training in sexual medicine. If your physician was trained before 1965, he or she probably was taught nothing at all about sexual function in medical school or a residency program. Even today, most medical schools do not require a course in sexuality, and the elective courses available are not always of top quality. I have heard doctors remark, "Oh yes, they came in and showed us some dirty movies!"

Because physicians, after all, have been raised in the same society as everyone else, they are often uncomfortable discussing sex. Rather than reveal their embarrassment, they may ignore a question about sex or answer it with a dismissive joke. Physicians are also reluctant to meddle in sexual problems because there is rarely a simple cure to offer. Medical knowledge of sexual function lags far behind our understanding of other bodily functions. Many recently discovered facts are still buried in specialized journals instead of being at the fingertips of the practicing physician. Doctors have to keep up with so much new and crucial medical information that staying expert on sexual problems may take a low priority on their list.

Their other problem is time. Most physicians have a very limited amount of time to spend with each patient. In a general or internal medicine practice, patients often confide their emotional difficulties to their physician. Doctors struggle to balance the need to treat the whole person with the demand to see all the patients who want appointments that day. They often end up dismayed and overwhelmed by patients' psychological needs—treating physical pain and disease is stressful enough! Despite our stereotype of the physician who spends half the week playing golf or tennis, most doctors work so many hours that they can barely find time or energy to attend to their own well-being and that of their families. When a patient brings up a sexual problem, the physician's first thought may be, "Oh no, this can of worms is going to take twenty minutes just to open, and then I won't know what to do with it!" This sense of helplessness, compounded by lack of knowledge, too little time, and inadequate counseling skills is the feeling a physician dreads most.

So where does that leave you? You have a sexual question or problem, and you want some guidance. You *can* get the help you need if you approach your physician in the right way:

1. Bring up the topic of sex yourself, rather than waiting for a cue from your doctor. With most doctors, you will wait forever. Even when a medical illness or treatment is likely to affect your sexual function, many physicians will not mention that fact.
2. When you do seek help for a sexual concern, be explicit and to the point. If you beat around the bush, you may never get a chance to ask your question. For example, if you have been having pain when you ejaculate, but you tell your doctor, "I've been a little tired lately, and I think something is wrong 'down there,' " he or she will have trouble guessing what on earth you mean, let alone finding the cause of your pain.

3. Before your appointment, sit down for a few minutes and write some notes describing your problem.

    a. What is the problem? Be specific.

    Example: I can only get about 50 percent of an erection, not enough to penetrate for intercourse.

    b. When did the problem start? Was it gradual or sudden?

    Example: I first noticed a change six months ago, on our trip to Canada, and it has been slowly getting worse.

    c. Does the problem occur in all situations? Be honest!

    Example: It almost always happens with my wife. I tried masturbating and looking at a men's magazine, but I still could not get a good erection. I have many fewer erections when I wake up, and they too are only about half or three-quarters full. Last month I got desperate and tried having sex with a secretary from work. The erections were even poorer with her.

    d. Do you have any ideas about the cause of the problem? What was happening in your life when it started? Any unusual stress or changes in your health?

    Example: It started a couple of weeks after you gave me that new pill for my ulcer. I also was working on an emergency project at work.

    e. Have you tried anything to solve the problem?

    Example: I sent away for some potency vitamins, but they didn't work. Then I saw a psychiatrist for one session, but she was only interested in asking about my childhood. I called the sex clinic over at the medical school, but they wanted to see me with my wife. I'm afraid she'll find out about that secretary if we talk to someone together.

    Take your notes with you when you see your physician. Use them to give a quick but accurate description of the sexual difficulties. Remember to focus on the problem, rather than telling your life story.

If you have an illness that may affect your sex life, you have a right to know what to expect. Your physician may not know all the answers, but here are some helpful questions to ask:

1. What percentage of men have a sexual problem as a result of this illness (or surgery or medication, etc.)?
2. What kinds of sexual side effects are common? Does it affect sexual desire, erections, ejaculation, or a man's sensations of pleasure and orgasm?
3. If I do develop a sexual problem, what can be done about it?

If you are dissatisfied with your physician's ability to help, you can ask to be referred to a specialist. Often your family doctor will suggest a referral without your requesting it. When a man has a sexual problem with a suspected physical cause, the most common referral is to a urologist, a surgeon who is expert on diseases of the genitals and urinary tract. Most urologists are action-oriented and not too interested in the psychological side of a sexual problem. Many urologists, however, have equipment to do specialized tests to find the cause of an erection problem. They are also familiar with surgical techniques for correcting erection problems.

An endocrinologist may be the appropriate choice if screening blood tests reveal abnormal hormone levels, or if you have noticed one or more of these symptoms—a loss of all sexual desire, reduced beard and body hair growth, or pronounced shrinkage of your testicles. Otherwise, you probably will do better by starting with a urologist or sexual medicine specialist.

At the present time there is no such thing as a residency training program in sexual medicine. However, some physicians do specialize in treating sexual problems. Most of them are psychiatrists, urologists, or gynecologists who took the initiative on their own to learn about sexual counseling as well as medical treatments for sexual problems. You are most likely to find a sexual medicine specialist in a sexual dysfunction clinic within a medical school department of psychiatry, family medicine, urology, or gynecology. Such clinics are more common in urban areas. Look for a clinic that offers specialized physical exams as well as sex therapy. Some have their own laboratory to monitor sleep erections or a staff that includes surgeons who perform penile prosthesis or revascularization operations (see Chapter 8). An excellent referral guide to medical school sex clinics is published each December by the magazine *Sexual Medicine Today* (a supplement to *Medical Tribune*, 257 Park Avenue South, New York, New York 10010).

If your sexual problem is clearly not related to your medical health, it is appropriate to see a specialist in psychotherapy, usually a psychiatrist or psychologist. If you have any suspicion that your problem results from physical causes, however, insist on a complete medical evaluation first.

Since this array of specialists can be bewildering, you will find your way around more easily if you know something about the types of examinations currently in use. Knowledge is a good antidote for helplessness in patients, as well as in doctors. If you are familiar with the most up-to-date procedures, you can evaluate the quality of your own medical care.

PHYSICAL EXAMINATIONS FOR SEXUAL PROBLEMS

Any medical evaluation of a problem with erections or low sexual desire should start with a general physical examination.

It should include routine blood tests, especially a fasting glucose value, since sexual symptoms occasionally are an early sign of diabetes, or of multiple sclerosis, poor circulation, or various other medical conditions. Examinations of the penis, testicles, and prostate should also be included. In addition, a urologist or sexual medicine specialist may test several genital area reflexes that indicate a healthy nervous system. For example, when the head of the penis is lightly squeezed, the muscle just inside the rectum normally contracts. The doctor also may press along the shaft of the penis to detect scarring inside, or test the skin of the penis to see whether it has lost sensitivity to light touch. All too often I hear men say, "I have been to three different doctors about this erection problem. Not one of them ever asked me to take my pants off!"

Depending on your symptoms and the results of the general exam, some specialized tests, developed within the past few years, may be in order.

Blood Tests for Hormones. Although hormone levels fluctuate quite a bit (see Chapter 2), a screening blood test can be useful. The most common is the test for testosterone. The blood sample is usually drawn before 10:00 A.M., when the hormone concentration is at its peak. If the laboratory results look unusual, two or three samples, drawn at the same hour a few days apart, can be compared. The laboratory may also test the amount of testosterone that is "free" to act rather than being bound to proteins in the blood.

Most physicians send blood samples for hormone tests to a special laboratory for analysis by "radioimmune assay." This type of test accurately measures tiny amounts of hormone. It detects the hormone's reaction with other chemicals, which have been tagged with radioactivity. Since the tests are expensive, a doctor often measures just testosterone at first. If the testosterone level is low, the doctor usually orders blood tests of other hormones, such as prolactin, luteinizing hormone (LH), follicle-stimulating hormone (FSH), and the thyroid hormones, to see which part of the hormone system is malfunctioning.

Measuring Blood Pressure or Pulse in the Penis. If an erection problem is caused by poor circulation to the penis, some painless exams can often tell the story. Blood pressure in the penis can be compared to blood pressure in the arm. If penile blood pressure is greatly reduced (less than 80 percent of the general blood pressure), the large or small pelvic arteries may be partially blocked. In this test, the physician inflates a tiny blood pressure cuff around the patient's penis, just like the kind used on your arm. The physician listens to the pulses in the arteries of the penis through a special Doppler stethoscope.

Similar equipment (all painless, with no needles involved) is used to record the penile pulse as a wavy line on a strip of paper. Some physicians also measure blood flow in the penis with a little sensor called a photoplethysmograph, which reacts to changes in skin color reflecting the circulation underneath. In another helpful test, the doctor leaves the small blood-pressure cuff on the penis for four to five minutes, restricting the blood flow. The cuff is then deflated, and the pulse recorded again, to see how efficiently the blood flow rebounds and then returns to its normal levels. This exam measures the health of the nervous system that controls penile blood flow.

X Rays of the Pelvic Circulatory System. If the studies just described suggest that the penis has poor circulation, it is sometimes helpful to discover exactly where the arteries are blocked. To determine if a penile artery is blocked by blood clots or cholesterol deposits (occlusion) or is narrowed by scarring (stenosis), the physician can use a special procedure called selective arteriography. Under a general anesthetic, the physician threads a tiny tube or "catheter" through the artery system into the blood vessels close to the penis. He then injects a dye through the catheter. The dye makes the arteries visible on an X ray, revealing any abnormal areas.

In an additional X ray, called a cavernosogram, dye is pumped through a needle directly into the spongy tissue of the penis, creating an artificial erection. The cavernosogram, which is sometimes performed right after the selective arteriogram, allows the doctor to see the smallest penile arteries, examine the cavernous bodies themselves, and test for abnormal leaks in the veins draining the penis.

These specialized X ray tests are used more frequently in Europe than in the United States. They are particularly helpful as guides for a vascular surgeon who is considering repairing the penile circulation system (see Chapter 8). Otherwise, the test is really not worth the risks of the anesthesia and the X ray procedure.

Examination of the Genital Nervous System. Besides testing sensation on the skin of the penis and looking for the presence of good genital reflexes, some physicians use special equipment to see if the nerves controlling erection are healthy. The bulbo-cavernosus muscles, which surround the root of the penis, are controlled by the same nerves involved in erection. Stimulating these nerves produces the bulbocavernosus reflex (BCR). The speed of the BCR can be tested with a machine called an elec-tromyograph. If the reflex is very slow, or in extreme cases absent, the nervous system's control of erection is probably damaged.

The BCR test is somewhat uncomfortable. Usually a thin needle electrode is placed into the muscle, which lies behind the scrotum (sac holding the testicles) but in front of the rectum. Since this area has a lot of nerve endings, it stings when the needle is slipped in. Sometimes a surface electrode can instead be glued onto the patient's skin. This is less bothersome to the patient, but not as accurate a test. A mild electrical current is then delivered to the tip of the penis, and the electrode records the time it takes the muscle to react—normally less than 42 milliseconds (42 thousandths of a second). The electrical current itself is not painful like a shock, but can tingle uncomfortably for a moment.

Monitoring Sleep Erections—Stamp Test to Sleep Lab. As we saw in Chapter 3, reflex erections during sleep (NPT) can be monitored to find out if an erection problem has a medical basis. Theoretically, if an erection problem is caused by thoughts about sexual failure or by relationship conflict, a man continues to have normal erections during his sleep. If, in contrast, the problem results from a hormone imbalance, nervous system disease, or poor circulation to the penis, sleep erections are just as abnormal as waking ones. Some researchers, however, argue that if a man is severely depressed or highly nervous, his sleep erections may be temporarily poor, even though nothing is permanently damaged in his sexual response systems.

Even the technical aspects of measuring NPT are controversial. For one thing, if a man's sleep is disturbed, erections may be absent because the necessary sleep stage (REM sleep) does not occur. NPT monitoring is done most thoroughly in a sleep laboratory—a specialized clinic set up to treat insomnia and other sleep-related problems. Most sleep laboratories also offer NPT testing. In a sleep laboratory, electrodes glued to a man's scalp are used to measure his brain waves and eye movements while he sleeps. Even his breathing and heart rate may be monitored to make sure all systems are working correctly. A sleep laboratory evaluation usually lasts for two or three nights in a row, since it is hard to relax in unfamiliar surroundings while attached to a bunch of electrodes and wires, and a man's sleep on the first night may be restless, reducing his amount of NPT. The second and third nights, once a man is used to the laboratory, give a more accurate estimate of the best erections his body can produce.

You are probably wondering how your erections would be measured during sleep. Would someone sit and watch your penis all night? You may be relieved to know that you would have some privacy, because the erections are monitored by a machine. Two loops called strain gauges are placed around the penis, one at the base, and one just under the ridge at the tip. The strain gauges stretch as the penis changes in size during the night. These size changes are recorded by a machine called a polygraph, the same equipment used as a lie detector—really just a specialized recorder that can measure electrical signals produced by a variety of processes in the body.

Most sleep labs let the patient sleep in a private room, while a technician outside watches the signals from the polygraph. During one of the patient's sleep erections, the technician may come in the room to actually observe how stiff the penis has become. The physician's judgment that sleep erections are normal is based on how many erections occur during the night, how long each erection lasts, whether the penis gets fully rigid, and whether the erection is normally shaped (no Peyronie's disease).

Since a complete sleep laboratory exam is quite expensive, and may not be covered by a man's insurance, some shortcuts have been tried. Doctors can send a man home with a simplified, portable machine that records penis size from a single strain gauge that the patient wears at night. Unfortunately, the home monitor results have been disappointing. Few or no recorded erections may be a sign that the man slept poorly. Since no measure of his sleep is available, the test is inconclusive. If a good recording *is* obtained, the doctor still does not know if the erections were completely firm and normal.

Similar criticisms apply to some new erection gauges made to work at home. These are strips of plastic with a Velcro closing. The man fastens the strip around the middle of his penis before going to sleep. If he has a firm erection during the night, two small plastic snaps break. A partial erection breaks one snap, and if no erections occur, both snaps remain closed. This test cannot measure the shape or duration of the erections. Since the gauges are fairly inexpensive, though, they can be useful as a first screening step, before you invest in a full sleep lab evaluation.

Finally, one proposed do-it-yourself method of testing your sleep erections is to fasten a single ring of postage stamps closely around the mid-shaft of the penis before you go to sleep. You connect the stamps on the ends by moistening their edges. If you wake up with the stamp ring torn open, your manhood is supposedly intact. If the stamps are unbroken, you might consider using them to mail yourself to the nearest urologist!

KEEPING YOUR EXPECTATIONS REASONABLE

Most of us go to the doctor expecting a cure for whatever health problem we have. With a sexual difficulty, however, an immediate remedy is not always available. Treatments usually involve at least a few weeks of sexual counseling or may entail a surgical operation. When given these choices, a man often feels disappointed. "Isn't there a pill I can take?" he asks.

The hope for a magic pill is nourished by advertisements and magazine articles. Unfortunately, in the long history of medicine, no true aphrodisiac—a substance that produces desire or erections—has ever been found. If an aphrodisiac were discovered, you can be sure it would not remain secret for long. The drug company owning the patent would be a blue-chip investment. The only substance currently known to be a sexual stimulant is testosterone—which has major effects only on men who had abnormally low hormone levels in the first place.

Some physicians, aware that erection problems often disappear if a man can regain his sexual self-confidence, prescribe a placebo. A placebo, or "sugar pill," is a substance without known physical effects on the body. The physician counts on the power of positive thinking, i.e., the patient's belief that his erection will return to normal. One respected urologist advocates telling an older man with an erection problem that a congested prostate gland may be the cause. He then gives the patient some harmless medicine (which actually makes the patient's urine more acid, to fight bacteria) and has him abstain from sex for a week. The doctor also mentions the need for an optimistic sexual attitude. At the next visit, the urologist reports that the patient's prostate fluid and urine contain less bacteria, and suggests that the patient gradually return to having nonpressured sex.

While such treatments have undoubtedly helped some men, I personally do not believe in giving placebos. If an erection problem has a medical cause, the "sugar pill" will not help. If the source of the difficulty is an emotional or relationship problem, brief counseling is more effective than a sugar pill. Sex therapy (see Chapter 9) teaches a man self-control in solving his problem. If he ever encounters a sexual difficulty again, he will have the skills to nip it in the bud. Using a placebo leaves all the control in the doctor's hands and is less likely to create a lasting change for the better. It also gives the patient a false impression about the cause of his problem.

One very common practice is for a physician to prescribe replacement testosterone to treat an erection problem, even if the patient already has a normal level of the hormone in his blood. In fact, doctors often give a hormone shot or pills without even ordering a blood test to see if treatment is necessary. These doctors are banking on a combination of the placebo effect and the mildly stimulating effect of the hormone. A German research group studied the reaction. They observed twenty-nine men who had erection problems but normal testosterone levels. Each man was either given a placebo or testosterone. Neither the patient nor the doctor interviewing him knew which kind of capsule had been taken. That information was kept secret by the researcher until the end of the experiment. About 45 percent of the men noticed an improvement in their erections, no matter whether they had received testosterone or the placebo. The hormones, therefore, were not of any *more* value than a sugar pill (though they are considerably more expensive).

Hormone treatments also carry some risks, both psychological and physical. Men often complain that the testosterone increases their desire for sex without having any positive effect on their erections, resulting in more frustration than ever. Physically, the most serious side effect is that the hormone treatment could activate an early, undiagnosed prostate cancer. Testosterone nourishes the cancer cells, making the tumor grow. Men over fifty are already at high risk for prostate cancer and should never receive testosterone unless their natural hormone values are below normal. A further risk of unnecessary hormone therapy concerns the hormone feedback cycle. When a man is given extra testosterone, his hormone feedback cycle is short-circuited so that his testicles reduce their output of the hormone. When the replacement testosterone is discontinued, the testicles do not always turn back on. Hormone therapy can thus produce a testosterone deficit where none existed before. And finally, some forms of replacement testosterone can damage the liver. All these are potent reasons to avoid testosterone pills or shots unless blood tests prove they are needed.

The only other "pills" that may improve erections are a couple of drugs that doctors hope will improve blood flow to the penis. One, yohimbine, is distilled from an African plant and has been used for many years to treat erection problems. So far there is no evidence that it is any better than a placebo. A research group in Canada, however, is testing it further, hoping it will stimulate the nerves that direct blood into the cavernous bodies of the penis. Other groups are experimenting with a vasodilator, i.e., a pill that increases blood flow to the more distant parts of the body (hands, feet, or penis). Early reports suggest that taking vasodilators can improve erections in men with poor circulation. Larger studies comparing the vasodilator to a placebo are needed, however, before it is proved effective.

As you can see, it is probable that your doctor will not have an astounding new prescription for you. Nevertheless, some exciting developments are taking place in the treatment of medically caused erection problems. In the next chapter, we will examine these techniques in detail. Because of them, living without erections has, for most men today, become a choice rather than a necessity.

8

Medical Treatments for Sexual Problems

The most exciting developments in sexual medicine have been the new treatments for problems with erection and low sexual desire. Our "medicine chest" now includes hormone therapy to correct imbalances, surgeries to repair damage to the blood vessels supplying the penis, and operations to place a prosthesis (implant) in the penis.

The causes of a sexual problem—including fear of failure, relationship conflict, hormone imbalance, reduced circulation to the penis, or nervous system damage—determine the type of treatment most likely to work. However since most sexual problems result from a combination of factors, effective treatment usually involves a double-barreled approach.

Gordon was diagnosed as having low testosterone. Though he was given shots that brought his hormones back to a normal level, he did not feel his sex life was as good as new. Gordon did notice himself having more thoughts about sex, and was even able to masturbate to orgasm with a firm erection.

With his wife, however, Gordon still had to push himself to start the kissing and touching and often did not get aroused enough to reach orgasm. Gordon and his wife were referred for some short-term sex therapy designed to help them increase the variety of the sexual caresses they used together and enhance their sexual desire. After several months of treatment, Gordon was enjoying sex more than he had since his early marriage.

The sophisticated medical exams described in the last chapter allow you and your health care team to make intelligent treatment choices. In the next few sections, we will take a look at the medically oriented treatments currently used. None is a cure-all in itself, but the potential benefits, compared to the risks, are steadily growing. I hope to provide you with a realistic idea of what each remedy can and cannot do for your sex life.

WHEN DO HORMONES REALLY HELP?

As I have stressed before, hormone therapy for a sexual problem helps only when something is actually wrong with the hormone cycle. Because this chemical system of checks and balances is so complex, there is some art as well as science to deciding when hormone treatment is indicated.

Normal levels of circulating testosterone in adult men vary between 300 and 1200 millionths of a gram for each tenth of a liter of blood. When a radioimmune assay of a blood sample shows a testosterone value below 300, most physicians believe that the patient needs testosterone replacement therapy.

If a low testosterone level is the main problem, replacement testosterone can be given in a pill or a shot. These replacement hormones, prescription drugs that must be ordered by a physician, are not identical to the testosterone manufactured by the testicles. Their chemical makeup has been changed slightly so that the replacement hormone can be used effectively by the body's cells. Physicians prescribe testosterone shots more often than pills, since the latter are more likely to affect the liver, causing jaundice, and, at least in some men, are not absorbed as easily by the body. Although having a shot is "a pain," most men, thanks to long-acting forms of testosterone now on the market, need the shot only once or twice a month. Sometimes it takes a couple of months to find the best hormone dose.

Occasionally a man's pituitary gland produces too much of the hormone prolactin. Although a low testosterone level usually results, the problem cannot be corrected by merely boosting the testosterone. The high levels of prolactin must also be reduced before sexual desire and erections improve. A medication called bromocriptine, which has only recently been available, is often given to reduce prolactin output. High prolactin may be caused by drugs used to treat schizophrenia, severe anxiety, ulcers, or high blood pressure, or by a noncancerous tumor in the pituitary. In the latter case, the patient may need surgery to remove the tumor.

Either too much or too little thyroid gland activity can also affect the sex hormone cycle. Again, the thyroid problem should be corrected with appropriate medications (or occasionally surgery).

When hormone therapy is really needed, the results are good. In one recent report from Harvard Medical School, thirty-three out of thirty-seven patients had an increased desire for sex and better erections after a hormonal imbalance was corrected. In Germany, fourteen out of sixteen men reported improved sex lives after they were treated for low testosterone levels. Some of these cures, however, may be explained by the man's expectations that the hormones would help. The German researchers pointed out that at least two patients whose testosterone values were below 200 had already had active sex lives, including adequate desire for sex, and normal erections and orgasms. Other men whose testosterone was in the low normal range (300–450) benefited from replacement hormones. Guidelines for hormone treatment are obviously still unclear.

SURGERY TO REPAIR CIRCULATION TO THE PENIS

In efforts to correct erection problems caused by poor blood flow to the penis, surgeons have been experimenting with the bypass techniques developed to repair circulation to the heart or legs. These operations, called penile revascularizations, are becoming more common in the United States, though they originated in Czechoslovakia, France, Denmark, and Argentina. Because the percentage of long-term successes is still low, revascularization surgery is controversial. Right now, you might regard it as a long shot, although in five years the techniques may be considerably more effective.

The most important thing to remember about surgery on the pelvic blood vessels is that erections will be restored only if the problem was caused entirely by blocked circulation. It is especially important for the doctor to rule out nervous-system disease before trying to repair circulation. Most revascularization operations make more blood flow *available* to the penis but without the nerve message to direct that flow into the cavernous bodies and create an erection, the penis will remain soft.

Surgery may also fail if there is a psychological aspect to the erection problem. A man's sexual thoughts and feelings spark the nervous system signals. If he is still anxious or uncomfortable about sex, his brain will not send the erection-producing message to the newly repaired blood vessels. For this reason, a combination of sex therapy and surgery is sometimes necessary.

The most successful revascularization operation restores good blood flow to the penis as part of a repair job on the circulation to the legs. This is called aortoiliac surgery because it involves either removing blockages in the central aorta and iliac pelvic arteries or installing bypasses around the blocked areas. Until recently, aortoiliac surgery often created an erection problem, even if one did not exist beforehand. The surgeons would divert blood flow *away* from the penis and to the legs, offering their patients the choice between intercourse and comfortable walking. Surgeons also routinely cut through nerves important to erection and ejaculation. With better surgical techniques and more awareness of the importance of sexuality, surgeons now are usually able to avoid this damage, and, in fact, improve erections. In one recent series of 110 patients, about a third of the men who started out with an erection problem noticed an improvement after surgery. No new erection problems were created.

The sexual benefits of aortoiliac surgery are a bonus from an operation made necessary by nonsexual symptoms. But what if loss of erections is caused by blockages in the *smaller* arteries branching off to supply the penis, and is the sole health problem? Indeed, this is the most common situation. The potential risks of major surgery must then be weighed carefully against the anticipated benefit. These new erection-restoring operations are the ones most hotly debated.

If an arteriogram shows that the arteries deep in the pelvis, just above the penis, are narrowed or blocked shut, the surgeon goes in and "steals" an artery that normally brings blood to the stomach. The surgeon disconnects this artery from the area it usually serves and resews it directly into one of the cavernous bodies of the penis, or (using a microscope) into one of the tiny arteries that run along the length of the penis. Some surgeons vary the operation by taking a piece of vein from the ankle and using it as the connecting segment between a pelvic artery and the blood vessels in the penis. The result is an increase in the resting blood flow to the penis. When the nervous system signals for an erection, there is enough circulation to supply the accelerated flow that makes the penis hard.

This all sounds pretty miraculous. Unfortunately, there are reasons why this surgery is not being performed in every hospital in America. For one thing, the techniques are very delicate and hard to learn. Only a few surgeons have been trained to do them. Another difficulty is knowing just the right amount of blood flow to add to the penis. If the new connection provides too much blood, the patient ends up with an erection that will not quit, forcing the surgeon to reoperate and shut off the rebuilt system. The biggest drawback, however, is the tendency for the new connections to scar shut on their own. This often happens almost immediately or sometimes within a year or two. The most reliable estimates are that only a quarter to a third of the men end up with their erections permanently improved.

Even more recent and more debatable are operations to correct problems in the drainage system of veins from the penis. Some physicians believe that the veins play no role in erection—that the increased blood pressure in the penis is all due to inflow through the arteries. Others think that during erection the outflow of blood through the veins is also reduced. If this is true, too much venous drainage could interfere with getting or keeping erections. Surgeons in Denmark have found that a few men have abnormal openings in the sheaths around the cavernous bodies, allowing some of the blood to drain out during erection. They report good results after closing these holes. Some French surgeons believe that the veins themselves are sometimes at fault and need repairing. We must wait for the test of time to see whether such operations are anything but experimental.

The lure of revascularization surgery is the chance of restoring fully "natural" erections. Another type of surgery implants a penile prosthesis; a procedure far more reliable, but one that adds something manmade to the sexual system.

PENILE PROSTHESES—THE BIONIC
MAN HITS THE BEDROOM

Penile prosthesis surgery is the closest thing yet to a sure cure for erection problems. These operations, which involve placing a silicone implant inside the penis, are technically successful in more than 90 percent of cases.

There are several types of penile prosthesis, but they all have some common features:

1. A penile prosthesis can mechanically stiffen the penis, no matter what originally caused the erection problem.
2. A penile prosthesis is not designed to cure any other sexual problem, including low sexual desire, premature ejaculation, or difficulty reaching orgasm.
3. A penile prosthesis does not make the skin on the penis more or less sensitive to touch.
4. A penile prosthesis does not have any direct effect on orgasm or ejaculation.
5. A penile prosthesis has no effect on urination.

Man's earliest attempts to artificially stiffen the penis involved slipping a rodlike object into the urethra (urinary tube) through the opening at the tip of the penis. Not only is this apt to be a painful practice, but it can damage the delicate tissues lining the urethra. To add insult to injury, it does not create an erection. Even nowadays, emergency rooms are not astonished to see men who have unwisely inserted pencils, sticks, spoons, or even birthday candles into their urethra. These supposed "stiffeners" then slip back into the bladder where they can cause serious infections and complications.

Another primitive concept was to enclose the penis in some type of splint, to hold it rigid from the outside. Unfortunately, this cuts down on sensation for the man since his skin is covered by the device. Today the sex shops still sell strap-on dildos; artificial plastic penises hollowed out to fit over a man's own organ. Men complain that having intercourse wearing a condom is like taking a shower in a raincoat. If so, making love from inside a dildo must be like taking a shower in a Sherman tank! Another option is a "cage" to stiffen the shaft of the penis, leaving the glans (head) free. This tends to wobble, however, making intercourse less than satisfactory.

Other Rube Goldberg inventions set up a vacuum around the shaft of the penis that supposedly keeps it stiff. This is a deluxe version of the old trick in which a man puts a rubber band or elastic ring around the base of his penis. The idea is to keep blood from draining out of the penis, maintaining its erect state. Since the great majority of erection problems are caused by lack of blood inflow, rather than too much outflow, this is like trying to dam a riverbed in the desert. In addition, blocking the normal drainage in the penis can actually cause gangrene (so please save your rubber bands for your slingshot!).

My favorite story is of a resourceful engineer who came to a clinic to get a penile prosthesis installed. He was still a bit reluctant to undergo the surgery, especially since he had invented a metal framework that fit around the shaft of his penis to keep it erect without an operation. One ring encircled the base, and the other fit just below the head, stretching the organ to its erect length. Iron strips connected the two rings into a cylindrical cage. The patient swore that he enjoyed sex just as much, while wearing his invention, as he had in his virile youth. "My sensation is perfect!" he exclaimed. Unfortunately, the patient's wife enjoyed the experience about as much as a session of medieval torture.

The modern penile prosthesis is a silicone device surgically installed to fill and stiffen the spongy areas of the penis. Two basic types of implants are used. The simpler type creates a permanent, semirigid erection. The more complicated kind of prosthesis is inflatable, so that the penis has both an erect and a soft position. Each prosthesis has its pros and cons. If you are interested in having implant surgery, you need to know about the different alternatives. Even if you cannot ever foresee having a penile prosthesis, you may be curious about how they work.

The Basic Semirigid Prosthesis. The simplest type of implant, named the Small-Carrion Prosthesis after its inventors, has been available since 1975. It consists of two separate silicone rods. The surgical procedure used to insert them is considered minor. It is even less of an operation than an appendectomy or a hernia repair. The operation usually takes only thirty to sixty minutes, and is occasionally even performed under a local anesthetic.

To reach the spot where the cavernous bodies begin, the surgeon must get back to the root of the penis. The visible part of the penis, the part that hangs down from the body, is actually only its outer half. The inner half extends into the body, above the area where the testicles hang (see Figure 4 in Chapter 5, page 70). A small incision is made, usually at the point where the underside of the penis meets the scrotum (sac), though some surgeons prefer an incision in the area between the scrotum and anus. The surgeon opens the innermost ends of the cavernous bodies, and then uses an instrument called a dilator to push aside some of the soft tissue, making a tunnel through each spongy area. No tissue is actually removed or "carved out" of the penis. The end result is two tunnels running inside the upper left and right sides of the shaft of the penis. The surgeon slips a silicone rod into each tunnel, and closes the incision.

Figure 5 shows how the rods look. They come in several lengths and diameters, and curve at the end to follow the shape of the root of the penis. The surgeon measures the patient's penis and tries to pick the size closest to its natural erect dimensions. (To many men's disappointment, the surgeon cannot make the penis a couple of sizes larger!) The erection after sur-

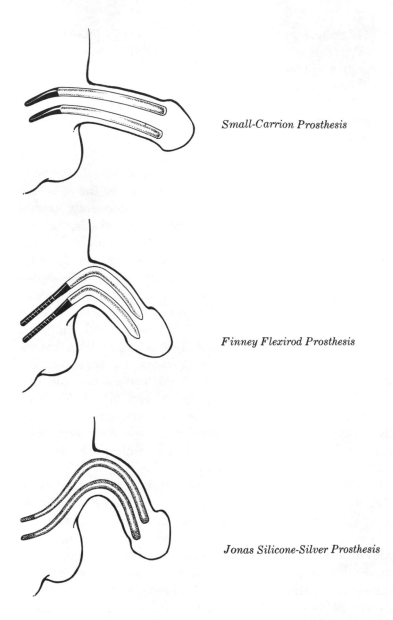

Small-Carrion Prosthesis

Finney Flexirod Prosthesis

Jonas Silicone-Silver Prosthesis

FIGURE 5. TYPES OF SEMIRIGID PENILE PROSTHESES

gery is about 80 percent as large as the man's fullest natural one. Thus it is somewhat shorter, and definitely somewhat narrower around than in the days of his youth.

Women, however, usually find the erection large enough to make intercourse pleasurable. Although some women notice the size difference, it rarely stops them from reaching orgasm. The rods have a spongy texture that is close to the firmness of a natural erection.

Although the penis is stiff and stable enough for intercourse, it is flexible enough to be hidden during the nonsexual 99 percent of a man's waking hours. Men frequently express misgivings about concealing the semirigid prosthesis. Actually the situation is not as difficult as it sounds. Because the erection is not completely full, the penis does not stick out at a ninety degree angle. Instead it hangs at about forty-five degrees from the body, and is flexible enough to bend upwards. Most men switch to wearing Jockey briefs made for athletics that are heavily elasticized at the crotch. These shorts hold the penis closely against the man's stomach, preventing an embarrassing silhouette from showing through his slacks. (Of course if he prefers to "advertise," who could stop him?) The main occasions for attracting funny looks occur in a health club locker room, at a nude beach, or at the urinal in a men's room. Men who like active sports, such as tennis or running, or who prefer tight, knitted bathing trunks may also find the semirigid implant too springy for comfort.

What about the practical aspects of the surgery itself? Usually the hospital stay is about three or four days. Though most insurance policies, including Medicare, pay at least 80 percent of these bills, it is wise to check with your insurance company beforehand. If a medical cause for the erection problem can be demonstrated, the insurance company is more likely to pay, since surgery is then considered rehabilitation rather than a cosmetic operation like a face-lift. If the patient has a health condition known to cause erection problems, i.e., diabetes, a history of pelvic cancer surgery, or a spinal cord injury, a doctor's report on the source of the sexual difficulty may be accepted. If the cause is less clear-cut, the insurance company may require some special exams, particularly monitoring of sleep erections.

Patients have a fair amount of pain during the healing period, because the genitals are well supplied with nerve-endings. Although the penis and testicles are very tender and swollen at first, the worst pain is usually over by the time a man goes home from the hospital. Soreness often lasts up to six weeks after surgery, however. Men most often complain of tenderness at the tip of their penis, or of an ache in the area behind the scrotum. It generally takes four to six weeks before a man is ready to use his prosthesis for sexual intercourse.

Hank had been a diabetic for a decade and suffered from erection problems for four of those years before hearing about penile prostheses from a friend of his. Hank was divorced, but, in his frustration over being a sexual "washout," had practically stopped dating. Hank and his urologist decided that a semirigid prosthesis might improve Hank's self-image and social life.

Although the surgeon had warned Hank that his penis would be swollen, Hank did a double take when the dressings were removed. His poor phallus looked as if it had been through the wars—black-and-blue and lopsided. To Hank's relief, the erection appeared almost normal by the day he was sent home. It still felt uncomfortable, however, to wear the tight Jockey shorts the doctor had recommended. Hank wished he was an Arab sheikh, so that he could wear flowing robes for the next few days.

As his pain subsided, Hank began to get impatient to try out his renovated penis. Never again would he have to worry about losing an erection at the wrong moment. Three weeks after his surgery, Hank was invited to dinner at the house of some old friends. A single woman had also been included as his dinner partner. When Hank met his date, he could not believe his luck. She was not only the best-looking woman he had ever met on a blind date, but she was easy to talk to as well. He invited her to go to a movie the following evening. After the show, she suggested they have a drink at her apartment. Predictably, one thing led to another. Hank knew he was not supposed to have sex until he got his doctor's O.K., but how could he explain about his implant to such a new acquaintance? She might get scared or disgusted and decide he was not worth her trouble. Besides, Hank was feeling pretty excited himself. He decided to go full speed ahead, and hope his woman friend would fail to notice his little scar, especially since she would have to take off her glasses to make love. He was sick and tired of excuses. Wasn't that what his surgery was designed to prevent?

Hank usually liked to have a light on during sex, but this time he was just as glad when his partner turned off the bedside lamp. He also was relieved when she had a quick climax, because his penis was still more tender than he had realized. For the first time in his life, Hank faked an orgasm. When his partner asked if sex had been good for him, Hank said, "Oh, of course! It was terrific!"

The next day he called his surgeon, who predictably gave Hank a good scolding. Though no permanent damage had been done, Hank certainly had not made his recovery period any easier.

Although men are often tempted to jump the gun and try out the prosthesis before healing is completed, the results can be disappointing. In fact, even after the doctor gives the go-ahead, it often takes a number of practice sessions before sex becomes fully satisfying. One followup study suggests that it takes six months, on the average, before a man is totally comfortable using his prosthesis. If a man had partial erections before surgery, he may still get some blood flow to the spongy tissue surrounding the rods and also to the head of the penis. The result is a more complete erection when he is sexually aroused. Men who do get a little natural erection are more likely to be satisfied with their prosthesis. Surgery does disturb the blood vessels inside the cavernous bodies, however, so no surgeon can guarantee that partial erections will still occur. It is *crucial* to remember that once any type of penile prosthesis is installed, a man will never be able to have a full, natural erection without the implant. Although the prosthesis could be removed, he would have even less of a capacity for erections than before the surgery ever took place.

Complications are also possible, even with the simple Small-Carrion implant. Any surgery involves a risk from anesthesia as well as a chance of infection in the area of the operation before it heals. An infection after prosthesis surgery, however, can be a mess. Although silicone does not provoke allergies in the body, it *can* provide a hiding place for bacteria. If an infection gets started in the incision or tissue around the implant, the presence of silicone makes it very difficult to cure. Only one or two percent of men have an infection from penile prosthesis surgery, but if this complication does occur, the implant often must be removed. The infection can then be cured and after a rest of several months, the rods are replaced into the penis.

Another one or two percent of men can have a problem months or years after the surgery with a rod "eroding" through the cavernous body. If the wrong size of rod was used, or if a man's penile tissue is weakened from disease, the rod rubs through the spongy area and gets displaced inside the penis. If erosion occurs, the rod must be removed. Again, it can often be replaced after the area has healed.

A few men with the implant complain of pain during sexual activity even after their incision has healed. This complication is rare. More common is some minor discomfort because the tip of the penis is cold, since it is stretched to its erect length without any extra circulation. Sometimes women complain that the penis is startlingly cool at penetration. Occasionally a man is annoyed because he notices the cold tip during his daily routine. A couple may also notice that the head of the penis is less full and swollen during sexual activity than it was when natural erections took place. This small difference in penis shape does not usually affect either partner's pleasure.

Because the surgery involves only the cavernous bodies, the urethra and bladder are not touched, and urination remains normal. If a man has ever had bladder infections or tumors that need to be checked with cystoscopy (an exam in which the doctor looks into the bladder through a special scope inserted into the urethra), the semirigid prosthesis may not be a good choice, since the scope is not long enough to reach the bladder through an erect penis. For a man with bladder disease, the inflatable penile prosthesis is more practical.

The surgery also does not involve the nerves supplying the penis. Therefore, skin sensation, orgasm, and ejaculation do not change. Men with erection problems often have trouble reaching orgasm or find that their ejaculation is weak and unsatisfying. There is no guarantee that a penile prosthesis will take care of these problems. If the pleasure of intercourse was the missing ingredient, a prosthesis may help, but if the disturbance of orgasm had a medical cause (such as nervous-system damage), the surgery may not improve things.

What are the statistics on success of the Small-Carrion prosthesis? From the surgeon's perspective, Dr. Small reports that 152 out of one recent series of 160 men ended up with an erection that looked natural and allowed them to have intercourse. Only 3 patients had a poor result (the other 5 had an acceptable result). Another gauge of success is a patient's own satisfaction with the prosthesis. In general, about 80 percent of men express satisfaction with the results of their surgery. The rate of all complications combined (infection, rod breakage, rod eroding out of position) is usually around 10 percent for semirigid prostheses.

The Flexirod Prosthesis.   One variation on the basic semirigid implant is a hinged model, invented by Dr. Roy Finney of Tampa, Florida. His Flexirod implant has been in use since 1977. Its two silicone rods are similar in shape to the Small-Carrion implant (see Figure 5). The middle of the rod, however, contains a flexible section, allowing the penis to hang freely, with less springiness than the Small-Carrion version. This feature does not change the quality of sexual intercourse, but does make the erection easier to hide under clothes. Surgery procedures and complication rates are very similar to those already described.

The Jonas Silicone-Silver Prosthesis.   The newest type of semirigid implant was introduced in 1979. Again, the prosthesis consists of two silicone rods, but in this version a core of silver wire runs down the center of each rod. When the penis is bent into a position, the wire ensures that it stays curved, rather than springing back (Figure 5). This modification is designed to improve the concealment of a prosthesis, rather than to aid sexual enjoyment. Yet about half of the patients surveyed after their silicone-silver implant surgery said they still had to wear special underwear to keep the erection hidden. There was an 89 percent rate of patient satisfaction, though, along with the typical 10 percent complication rate. One disadvantage of this model is that the silver makes it more than twice as expensive as the Small-Carrion implant.

The Inflatable Penile Prosthesis.   The inflatable type of penile prosthesis has been in use since the early 1970s. Invented by the Houston surgeon, Dr. F. Brantley Scott, it is known to my patients as the "Cadillac." The inflatable implant has the advantage of being closer to nature in the way it works. It has the disadvantages, however, of being more complicated and expensive than the semirigid models.

The inflatable prosthesis is shown in Figure 6. This operation, too, is most often done through a small incision where the penis meets the scrotum. All the necessary equipment can be placed in the body through this opening, with surgery taking from half an hour to two hours, depending on the complications encountered. As for the semirigid prosthesis, the surgeon makes a tunnel through each cavernous body. Instead of implanting silicone rods, however, the surgeon slips two silicone inflatable cylinders into the spaces created. The cylinders are durable balloons that can be filled with fluid to increase both their length and width. They inflate the cavernous bodies in very much the same way as blood fills them during the natural erection process. The rear ends of the cylinders are solid silicone, providing a stable base in the root of the penis.

Inside the body, the cylinders are connected with tubing to a small pump and a reservoir (storage container). The surgeon installs the pump inside the man's scrotum, in the empty space above one of his testicles. Although the pump can be felt through the skin, it is not easily seen. The reservoir, which looks like a round balloon, gets tucked behind some of the muscles in the groin (where men often get hernias). The whole system is filled with a saline (saltwater) solution mixed with some X-ray dye. Normally, all of the solution is in the reservoir, and the cylinders in the penis are empty. From the outside, the penis is in its normal, soft state. Unless you looked for the scar, you would not guess that the man had a penile prosthesis.

When a man wants to have an erection, he can squeeze the pump with his fingers, through the skin of his scrotum. The pump works by a pressure system, so that a battery or other power source is not necessary. Ten to fifteen squeezes force enough fluid into the cylinders to create a full erection. The squeezing motion is not painful, but does take a little time and

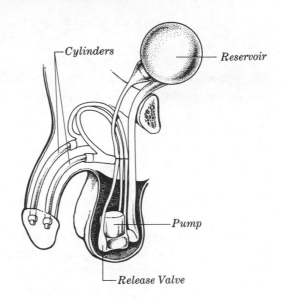

Cylinders

Reservoir

Pump

Release Valve

SOFT PENIS

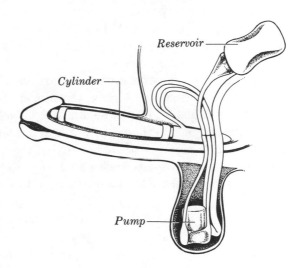

Reservoir

Cylinder

Pump

ERECT PENIS

FIGURE 6. THE INFLATABLE PENILE PROSTHESIS

skill to learn. The fully inflated prosthesis is closer in size to a 100 percent natural erection than is a semirigid prosthesis, though the penis will still be somewhat shortened in erect length.

After a man ejaculates, his penis will not automatically become soft. Instead, it stays erect until he presses a release valve at the bottom of the pump. A few seconds of finger pressure on the valve allow the fluid to return to the reservoir. When the cylinders are emptied, the penis reverts to its soft shape.

Since the inflatable prosthesis is a simple machine, it sometimes needs a surgical repair job, or "revision." In the early 1970s, at least a third of patients eventually had to have a second operation to replace a broken part. The rate of revisions is now under 10 percent, at least according to publications from the major clinics where expert surgeons do several hundred prosthesis operations a year. In talking to urologists familiar with the operation, however, my impression is that revisions are still a troublesome issue.

The most common malfunctions are caused by pinhole leaks in the cylinders or a kink in the tubing. These problems do not affect a man's general health, but his inflated erection will be lopsided or less than full. If a leak does occur, the fluid will not harm a man's tissues. The dye in the fluid allows the problem to be easily located with an X ray. Repairs can often be accomplished under a local anesthetic, with a very short hospital stay.

Surgery for the inflatable prosthesis carries the same risks of infection as for the semirigid implant. There is no chance however, of the cylinders wearing away the cavernous body tissue, like the rod erosion that can occur with the semirigid models.

The healing process is especially important with the inflatable implant. Scar tissue forms around the cylinders and reservoir. In order to make sure the scarring allows enough room for full inflation and deflation, the penis must spend some time in both the erect and soft positions during recovery from surgery. While the patient is still in the hospital, the surgeon begins to inflate the prosthesis daily, so that tight scar tissue does not form. In the first several weeks at home, the patient must continue to follow instructions on inflating his prosthesis regularly.

Usually the hospital stay is five to seven days. Total costs for an inflatable prosthesis operation range from $6,000 to $10,000, depending on the type of anesthesia and the number of days in the hospital. The rate of ultimate surgical success (after revisions, etc.) in most followup studies is around 90 percent. The proportion of satisfied patients is similar to that after semi-rigid implant surgery—80 to 90 percent.

You can expect penile implants to become more reliable and simple in the next few years. In 1983, both Dr. Finney and Dr. Scott announced new inflatable models. Further developments will undoubtedly follow, since there is a lucrative market for this surgery.

Who Should Have a Prosthesis Operation?

What type of a man is likely to be happy with a penile prosthesis? Specialists in sexual medicine are striving to answer this question. As a patient, you might feel that any man who wants prosthesis surgery has a right to get it. Imagine for a minute, however, that you are the surgeon. How would you feel if some of the following patients came to you? Would you operate on them? I think you will find that the answers do not come easily.

John, a healthy, fifty-four-year-old engineer, has been having erection problems for six months. He is divorced and has a number of casual sexual partners. Once in a while he is able to have successful intercourse. Most of the time, however, his erections fade and he feels too humiliated to ever call the woman again.

John's doctor put him through a series of exams, including a sleep lab evaluation, but could find no physical reason for the erection problem. The doctor explained that many divorced men feel pressured to perform sexually. He suggested that John see a sex therapist. John replied that he was unaware of any anxiety or pressure during sex. His body simply was not obeying his mind. He certainly was not about to see some psychiatrist when the problem was with his penis.

He heard about the inflatable prosthesis on TV, and it made sense to him as an engineer. If a system is not working, you fix it or invent something new to replace it. John knows that the surgery will destroy his physical capacity to have an erection, but he thinks the prosthesis is an improvement on nature.

Do you think John will be satisfied with his prosthesis? Would you, as a surgeon, be acting ethically to operate?

Raoul, a sixty-one-year-old administrator, no longer feels any sexual desire for his wife. He still enjoys masturbation once in a while, and gets erections while watching X-rated movies, but rarely can attain a hard erection during lovemaking. Raoul cannot really explain his feelings, though he knows that the problem is emotional rather than physical. The loss of desire began when the couple's only daughter and their grandson were killed in a car accident. Raoul's wife has had a great deal of difficulty getting over her grief and shock. She continues to wear black, two years after the tragedy. She also has gained thirty pounds.

Raoul loves his wife dearly, and feels he has failed her by leaving her sexually frustrated. Without telling her, he has sought a consultation with a penile prosthesis surgeon.

Raoul cannot imagine how he could renew his desire for his wife, but with an implant he could at least have erections and satisfy her.

Do you think Raoul should have a penile prosthesis?

Pete's sex life was never very complicated. Usually on Saturday night, he and his wife would kiss and touch for a few minutes, have intercourse, and go to sleep. At age seventy, Pete had a heart attack. His erections had been slowing down a bit even before his illness, and the medication he took when he got home from the hospital seemed to finish things off. After a few foreplay sessions with no results, Pete's wife told her husband to stop trying. She said that sex was not important anymore at their age, not to mention the danger of another heart attack. Pete took to spending long sessions in the bathroom with sexy novels, but his wife said nothing. Even in his own masturbation, Pete could not get much of an erection.

When Pete announced he had an appointment to see a surgeon about having an implant put in his penis, his wife had a fit. "You old fool!" she yelled. "You're going to have an operation just so we can have sex? At your age? You'd better start looking for some alley cat to use that thing on, because you're sure not going to use it on me!"

Pete told this story to the surgeon, but said he was sure his wife would come around. When he returned home with his prosthesis, their sex life would just go back to normal.

Should Pete's wife have veto power over his surgery? Do you think his wife will "come around" if he does have a prosthesis?

Lenny's life had been dominated for years by pain and illness, since he had been in an accident on his job at a manufacturing plant. Although Lenny complained of persistent low back pain, the company doctors refused to grant him the large disability settlement due for a permanently handicapping injury. Lenny hired an attorney and many months of frustrating lawsuits began.

During this period, Lenny developed a problem with erections. The cause was obvious: tests showed that his penile blood flow was very reduced. Though the doctors could not relate this finding to Lenny's back pain, Lenny suspected a connection. His lawyer suggested they bring the erection problem into the legal case as another result of the injury.

Meanwhile, Lenny decided to get a penile prosthesis. He expressed some fears, however, about pain after the surgery. He wondered how many men had long-term pain, and if this complication often resulted from a surgeon's mistake.

Do you think Lenny will have a good recovery from prosthesis surgery? As the surgeon, are you at all worried about a future malpractice suit?

Because the surgeon needs to make such difficult choices, most clinics have set up evaluation procedures to decide whether a man can really be expected to benefit from prosthesis surgery. If you take a cynical view, you might say the surgeon has three major concerns: He or she will not want to operate on a man who will (1) go crazy, (2) commit suicide, or (3) sue the surgeon. Of course surgeons are also eager for the operation to truly make the patient's life better. Otherwise all that effort would be futile. Because resources are limited, however, the presurgery evaluation usually focuses on preventing bad outcomes, rather than on ensuring a really enriching result.

Most surgeons want to know the cause of an erection problem before they operate. Men whose problem is psychological, rather than medical, sometimes have the surgery, though doctors are reluctant to destroy a healthy erection reflex. Insurance companies, too, may refuse to cover the surgery under these conditions. Often, the surgeon suggests starting with a course of sex therapy (see Chapter 9). If psychological treatment is unsuccessful, a prosthesis can be installed. Personally, I think this is a good option. The cost of ten to fifteen weekly sessions of sex therapy is less than the price of most sleep lab evaluations, much less the surgery itself. Even if sex therapy does not restore full erections, it can teach some helpful sexual communication skills. If a man feels coerced into the treatment, however, chances are slim that he will learn anything. He may even be determined to show that sex therapy cannot help. The decision to try sexual counseling should be made with an open mind, rather than to "prove" that surgery is needed.

Some surgeons may also hesitate to operate on a man with a homosexual lifestyle. Since homosexuality is a preference for one type of partner, and not an illness, I see no reason why a homosexual man should be treated differently from a heterosexual one. Although gay men enjoy a variety of sexual activities, only some involving penetration, they are just as likely as other men to be concerned about an erection problem. A homosexual man can, therefore, be just as good a candidate for a penile prosthesis as a heterosexual man.

If you seek a prosthesis operation, your surgeon will probably have you fill out some questionnaires that measure your emotional strengths and weaknesses. You may also be required to talk to a psychiatrist or psychologist who will ask about your past and current life and about why you want the surgery. These evaluations protect you, as well as your surgeon, from rushing impulsively into an operation that might have a negative effect on your life.

In my view, however, more should be included in a decision to have a penile prosthesis. This presurgery period is an ideal time to look honestly at your sexual relationship. Are there some changes that could add intimacy and zest? Having good erections again may be one such improvement. Chances are, however, that other aspects of your sex life could use some work. Perhaps you would enjoy more variety in your caresses, or would like to be able to discuss sex more freely with your mate. The prosthesis evaluation can open up these topics.

Making the Penile Prosthesis a Natural for You

One crucial piece of advice, if you are in a committed relationship, is to include your partner in your decision to have penile prosthesis surgery. When a couple is married (unless the husband is sexually active only outside of the marriage), it makes sense for the wife to be present when the surgery is explained. I also think a fiancée or a woman who is living with her lover should participate in his decision-making process.

Women have some common fears about a penile prosthesis, as the following interview illustrates:

Rhonda's husband was being evaluated for a semirigid penile prosthesis. Clyde was diabetic and had recently developed an erection problem. Rhonda had left her first husband after she found him with another woman. Clyde had been widowed for several years before meeting Rhonda, who worked as a secretary in the industrial company where he was a factory foreman. The couple had been married for only six years. After Rhonda and her husband met with the surgeon and a psychiatrist together, the psychiatrist asked to spend a few minutes alone with each partner. Rhonda's interview gave her a chance to say a few things that she was reluctant to reveal to Clyde.

PSYCHIATRIST: I wanted a chance to ask you if you have any particular worries about Clyde having this operation.

RHONDA: Well, I guess my worst fear is that he'll have complications from it, but the doctor makes the whole thing sound pretty safe.

PSYCHIATRIST: Do you have any concern about how it will affect your marriage?

RHONDA: It couldn't hurt, I guess. It would be nice to have sex again.

PSYCHIATRIST: You still sound a little doubtful.

RHONDA: It's just that . . . that Clyde's always been a good man. I could trust him, you know. And I'm sure I shouldn't doubt him now, but I hear him joking about this with his friends, and you know how guys brag. I guess I'm worried that he'll start running around on me, now that he can have an erection whenever he wants.

PSYCHIATRIST: Have you told your husband how you feel?

RHONDA: Oh, I tease him about being jealous, but I haven't really made a big deal out of it. I think he knows. The only other worry I had, come to think of it, the doctor answered today. Until I had a chance to see the rods, I thought they were made out of some kind of plastic. I was afraid they'd break if I touched Clyde's penis too hard.

PSYCHIATRIST: Some wives worry that the implant will be very fragile, but once the penis heals, you can use the same kinds of touching as you would with a natural erection. Did you also get a chance to really touch the sample rods, and bend them?

RHONDA: Yes. They felt pretty reasonable. That was another thing I worried about. I was afraid the erection would be too stiff, so intercourse would hurt.

PSYCHIATRIST: Are you comfortable with the thought of something artificial in Clyde's penis?

RHONDA: Oh that never bothered me. I figure it's like wearing contact lenses, or having a pacemaker for your heart. I don't think of it like making love with a what-do-you-call-it . . . a dildo, or a vibrator. It's still Clyde's erection. But I am a little worried that Clyde will have sex just to please me. I mean, now he doesn't even have to feel excited to have an erection. How am I going to know if he's really in the mood for sex?

PSYCHIATRIST: It sounds like you feel a little insecure about your own sexiness.

RHONDA: Well, I think that's always a wife's thought when her husband has a problem in sex. Is it me? Is he tired of me? Is he seeing someone else? I hate to say it, but I was a little relieved to find out it's part of his diabetes.

PSYCHIATRIST: I think those feelings are pretty natural.

RHONDA: Actually, I sort of hope he doesn't feel *too* sexy after the operation. Sex is nice, but not every night.

PSYCHIATRIST: A lot of couples go through a kind of honeymoon period, where they have intercourse much more often than usual. After a few weeks, though, things settle down.

RHONDA: I bet it's like a kid who gets a new toy for Christmas. By January it's gathering dust. Well, hopefully we can work things out so we don't go to extremes. It's helped me just to hear about what it really will be like. I'm looking forward to about two months from now, when we can find out for ourselves!

Including your partner gives her a chance to express her opinion and to get accurate information about the prosthesis. Women's biggest fears are usually about the risks of the surgery and the pain that their lover will have to endure. Every now and then, I see a wife or lover who pressures her partner to have the prosthesis. More commonly, however, the woman takes a neutral "whatever he wants" stance, or is against the surgery. Particularly when couples are older, the wife feels embarrassed that her sex life is being discussed, or ashamed that her husband wants erections "at his age." She may feel relieved that their sex life has ended, rather than eager to get back to sex again. A sensitive doctor or counselor can help the couple hold a more open dialogue about their feelings. I will never forget one wife who was initially opposed to her seventy-five-year-old husband's operation. After we talked about it she told him, "If it will make you get up and go, instead of sitting like an old granny in a rocking chair all day, I'm for it!" That couple went on to enjoy intercourse together. Occasionally, a partner remains adamant that she will never have sex with her husband or lover if he has a prosthesis. If the man hears and accepts her message, but still wants surgery, the final decision must be his, since it is his body.

The more flexible a couple is in their sexual routine, and the better their communication, the more likely they are to be happy with a penile prosthesis. Many men who have the operation, however, are like Roger:

Roger, a sixty-four-year-old salesman, was scheduled to get an inflatable prosthesis. He did not bring his wife with him, since the surgeon practiced several hundred miles from their hometown.

Roger had had his erection problem for eight years before he found out about the prosthesis. During that time, he and his wife had essentially stopped having sex. When questioned about how he expressed affection, Roger realized that the couple also had decreased nonsexual touching. For example, Roger did not hug his wife in bed, because he feared she would think he wanted sex. When, on rare occasions, Roger coaxed her into a little foreplay, the couple gave up after a few minutes of only partial erections. They never said much to one another at these times, but usually just turned over and went to sleep.

When asked what his wife thought about the erection problem, Roger said, "She tells me she'll stick by me even without sex, but I can tell she's frustrated." Roger could not really explain how he got this impression, however. Roger's wife also had expressed little curiosity about the prosthesis surgery. She told him to make his own decision, though she felt surgery was a little drastic. "What do you think will happen when you come home with your prosthesis?" the interviewer asked.

"Oh, I'm sure it will be great!" replied Roger. "It will be right back to the old days."

Roger is a good example of a patient with unrealistic expectations about what the prosthesis can do for his sex life. If a man's sexuality is only defined by the stiffness of his penis, having a better erection is all he needs. If sex includes feelings of closeness, laughter, affection, touching and kissing, and being able to fantasize and play together, a prosthesis is just one part of a much greater whole. If your sex life has ranged from humdrum to nonexistent for twenty years, a silicone implant cannot act as a magic wand to transform your lovemaking into an orgy of passion. If a man has lost his desire for sex or is having weak orgasms, a prosthesis will not solve his problems. If two lovers have never learned the special ways and places that the other likes to be touched, a half-hour of surgery will not transform them into Romeo and Juliet.

In my observation, couples who hide unresolved anger under the surface of their relationship are often disappointed with a prosthesis. The husband or wife focuses on small deficiencies in the size or shape of the erection that a more tolerant lover could easily overlook. The frequency of intercourse then drops back to zero. As one man related:

"My wife says my erection is so thin now that she can barely feel it. She never has an orgasm from intercourse anymore. I have to spend about half an hour rubbing her clitoris before she climaxes.

"I know it's not all me, though, because last year I ran

into an old girlfriend while I was out of town on business. We spent the night together, and she told me my erection was perfectly fine. She enjoyed the prosthesis, too, because we could keep on for as long as we wanted."

If you have an erection problem and are wondering whether your sex life would be better with a penile prosthesis, try asking yourself these questions:

1. *Have you and your partner discussed your feelings about the sexual problem?*

If not, this is a good time to bring up the subject. Try to choose an occasion when you are both feeling relaxed and you have some privacy. (The moments after an unsuccessful sexual experience are not always a good time!) You might even let your partner know that there is something you need to discuss, so you can schedule a special hour together.

Start by saying how you *feel* about the erection problem. I do not suggest that you give her a lecture on the causes, i.e., "I suspect this problem is due to poor circulation in my penis. I have all the symptoms." Rather, let her know some of your vulnerabilities and ask for her support and understanding. "When I lose my erection, I feel so frustrated. It's like being half a man." "I feel so excited when I'm with you, but somehow my body isn't responding to my mind." "Sometimes, when sex doesn't work, I just want to break down, but I'm ashamed for you to see me so upset." "Even though you say it doesn't bother you, I feel like you're frustrated." "The other night when I got so mad at you, I was really angry at myself for being such a failure. And I felt jealous because you can have sex even if you aren't that excited, and I have to depend on these lousy erections."

Try to avoid putting the blame on your partner: "You know, if you would use oral sex on me like my first wife, I might get better erections!" or "Why don't you ever come to bed without those darned curlers?" If you put her on the defensive, she will not be able to listen to you. In fact, it helps if you can honestly let your partner know that her attractiveness or skill in bed is not the cause of the problem. If she has been patient and responsive to your needs, tell her how much you appreciate her help. If you fear you and your partner will end up blaming each other instead of listening, it may be better to have this talk in a sexual counselor's office.

Ask your partner for her reactions to your erection problem. "How do you feel when we can't have intercourse?" "Have you ever wished I would help you reach your climax by hand stimulation if intercourse doesn't work?" "Would you be willing to work on solving this with me?" If she does not know much about the penile prosthesis, you might give her this chapter to read or ask her to go with you to see your doctor for an explanation of the surgery.

If you do not have one particular partner, you may want to bounce some of your feelings off a good friend who can help you come to a decision about having a prosthesis.

2. *How well do you and your partner know each other's sexual likes and dislikes?*

Many couples are too shy to let each other know what they like in bed. In Chapter 10 we will look at some ways to improve your sexual communication. For now, remember how you learned to please each other. Did you ever directly tell your mate how and where you like to be touched? Have you asked her to try a sexual activity you especially enjoy but worried that she might dislike, such as oral or anal caressing, or acting out a fantasy? Are you confident that you know what she likes in bed? Did she tell you herself, or did you have to guess by watching her reactions?

A penile prosthesis is not an exact duplicate of a natural erection. The kinds of caresses that helped you reach orgasm before surgery may need to be modified to work with the implant. In adjusting to the slightly changed size and shape of your erection, you might also want to experiment with different positions for intercourse. If you are unable to reveal your desires to your mate, you may be disappointed with your post-surgery sex life. Couples whose communication needs a refresher course may want to practice before the operation. Chapter 10 will give you some hints on how to begin. Some brief sexual counseling, too, can be of help with communication skills. Single men can get some good advice from individual or group therapy on how to approach a new partner.

3. *When you have trouble getting or keeping your erection, how do you cope?*

Couples have a variety of reactions to an erection problem. Some stop touching each other after a few minutes of unsuccessful foreplay. Others have long talks about the problem, or try to make their sexual routine more exciting. When the erection problem becomes chronic, some couples stop all sexual activity, while others keep on using hand or oral stimulation to reach mutual orgasm.

Research suggests that lovers who remain sexually active, even without erections, will be more satisfied with a penile prosthesis than a couple who quit having any sex life. This may be just another indication that a man and woman who talk to each other about sex and are flexible in giving each other pleasure can adjust to a new dimension in their sex life. Also, a couple who give up on sex if they cannot have intercourse are more apt to focus on the minor differences between a natural erection and an erection with a penile prosthesis.

If you are single, the premise about staying active may not apply. Men in casual dating relationships are more likely to get uncooperative responses when their erections flop. After a couple of negative encounters, they may decide to give up on sex until they meet a woman to whom they feel closer, or until the erection problem has been corrected.

If it has been a while since your last sexual activity, and you are going to have prosthesis surgery, consider adding some sexual counseling to your agenda.

Taking Your Prosthesis for Its First Spin

When your surgeon gives you the nod to have sex after a prosthesis operation, you might want to take some time to explore. Before you try out your bionic penis with your partner, experiment on your own. Try touching the different areas of your penis, with light caresses and with stroking. (If you have the inflatable prosthesis, try self-stimulation in both the soft and erect positions.) You might want to use some extra lubrication on your fingers. Have your sensitive zones changed at all? Does the tip of your penis feel cooler than usual? Are there any areas that still feel tender? Do you notice the scar from your incision? If you are comfortable with masturbation, see if you can reach orgasm. Do your usual techniques still work well? Did you discover anything new that you want to tell your partner? Do not be upset if your orgasm feels weak. Men often find that their ejaculation becomes stronger and more normal after several experiences with the prosthesis.

With a partner, you may be tempted to go straight to penetration. After all, that was the goal of surgery! If you take your time, however, you may get more out of sex. Many men use their erections as the barometer of excitement. "If it's hard, I'm ready." Now that you can have an erection without being mentally aroused, you may have to pay more attention to your feelings and sensations. If you just dive into intercourse before you are fully excited, sex can be a disappointing experience. In this respect, men who have a prosthesis are more like women—physically capable of intercourse before they are really at a peak of arousal.

During the kissing and touching, you may want to guide your partner's hand away from any tender spots on your penis, and show her the kinds of caresses that feel the best. Expect that intercourse, when you do get there, will be a little awkward. You have to get used to the "angle of the dangle."

You also have the new option of keeping on with intercourse as long as you want, even after you ejaculate. How will you decide when to quit? For some couples, the stopping point is obvious. Both partners reach orgasm after a reasonable length of time and let each other know they are satisfied. Many women, however, take a long time to reach orgasm during intercourse or can have several orgasms if thrusting continues after their first climax. If you feel tired, or are one of the many men whose penis gets tender and sensitive after ejaculation, stop. If you continue out of a sense of duty, your partner will probably just end up feeling guilty. Flesh and blood can make love for only so long, even though silicone can last forever! The first time you try penetration, you may want to set some limits on intercourse, just to take the pressure off. You and your partner could agree to stay joined for a minute or two, and then help each other reach orgasm through nonintercourse types of sexual activity.

If your partner is past menopause and has not had intercourse for quite some time, she may notice burning or pain when you resume sex. Her vagina may have gotten smaller and drier, especially if she was not using any replacement estrogens. To minimize her chance of discomfort, spread some water-based lubricant on your penis or in her vagina before you penetrate. This can be part of your love play. It also will help if she is highly excited and ready for intercourse.

With a little forethought, your first experiences with your prosthesis can be the introduction to the best chapter yet of your sex life.

9

Sex Therapy: Or It's Not So Crazy to Get Some Counseling

The director of the sleep laboratory calls a patient, Mr. Jones, into her office. She wants to tell him the results of a complete medical evaluation of his erection problem. "Hey, I have good news for you!" the doctor says. "All the exams were normal. There is nothing physically wrong with your erections."

The patient shakes his head. "No, Doc, there must be something you didn't find."

"But, Mr. Jones, you saw the good erection you had last night. Don't you remember when the technician woke you up?"

"I don't know. I guess. But it must have been some kind of fluke. I sure don't get them like that during the day."

"But you could. The ability is there. You just need to overcome whatever is holding you back in your emotions or your relationship. We have a very expert sex therapist on our staff who can help you."

"You mean you think it's all in my mind, and you want me to see a headshrinker."

"Mr. Jones, I think you have some negative ideas about sex therapy. It's not like the cartoons where a psychiatrist with a little goatee just says, 'Mm hmm.' Sex therapy is a short-term treatment that works directly and actively on a sexual problem."

"No way. Isn't there a pill you can give me?"

"There are no pills that work on this type of erection problem. I wish there were, Mr. Jones. But aren't you glad you can cure the problem by unlearning some bad habits, instead of going through surgery?"

"Are you telling me I can't have an implant?" Mr. Jones's face is getting red.

"Mr. Jones, our surgeons don't like to use a penile prosthesis in a man who doesn't have a medical problem—unless the man has really tried some good psychological treatment, and it hasn't worked. You know that the operation would destroy your natural ability to get erections."

"How can it wreck something that's already broken?"

"But, Mr. Jones . . ."

"Doctor, I can see I've wasted my good money. But I'm not throwing any more of it away on some little guy in a white coat. If your people won't cut on me, I'll find a surgeon who will. I hear there are hundreds of them who put in these implants." Mr. Jones puts on his jacket and walks out.

The director slumps in her chair. This is not the first time a patient has been disappointed by her "good news." She wishes she could think of a way to make them understand what sex therapy is all about.

Why are men often so reluctant to try counseling for a sexual problem? Although a man can accept the news that a medical problem is interfering with his sexual powers, he may have a hard time believing that his mind is preventing him from enjoying sex. Acknowledging a "mental problem" is even more shameful than admitting a physical weakness. A stigma is also attached to psychotherapy. A "real man" does not need any help to control his emotions. Only women and crazy people see psychiatrists. These attitudes have been strengthened by our stereotypes of mental health professionals. Who could imagine that lying on a couch and delivering a monologue about your toilet training would cure an erection problem that developed at age sixty-two? (Indeed, old-fashioned psychoanalysis rarely did help sexual problems.)

A man's skepticism about the worth of counseling can prevent him from trying sex therapy. Even if he does begin treatment, it is with the preconceived notion that it will fail. Unfortunately, sex therapy is not a kind of treatment that can be "performed" on a pessimistic patient. Rather, a man has to take an active role in changing his sexual beliefs and practices if therapy is to be successful.

Sexual medicine specialists at the University of Chicago have documented the way that men's attitudes about psychotherapy keep them from seeking helpful treatment. Their evaluation of a man's erection problem had two parts: an examination by a urologist and an interview with a psychiatrist/sex therapist. Most patients, however—64 percent—first contacted the urology department rather than the psychiatry service. Of those men who did see the psychiatrist first, 98 percent then made an appointment with the urologist. In contrast, only 62 percent of the men who first saw the urologist followed up by going to the psychiatrist.

Men at the Chicago clinic whose problems were not medically caused were offered sex therapy. Most of the men who had first sought help from a urologist—57 percent—refused this treatment. Even a good many of the men who had initially called the psychiatrist—27 percent—refused. Almost all of the psychiatrist-referred men stayed in sex therapy once they had started, though, with many successful outcomes. Half of the urologist-referred men dropped out of sex therapy after only a few sessions. This study implies, then, that men who are willing to see a psychiatrist are more likely to overcome their sexual problems.

I am not suggesting that sex therapy is a panacea. For men over age fifty, its success rate in permanently reversing a sexual problem is probably around 50 percent. I am convinced, however, that treatment with an experienced and well-trained sex therapist is one of the more inexpensive and effective ways of increasing a man's satisfaction with his sex life.

Men often have some misunderstandings about sex therapy:

1. *That kind of treatment is for crazy people. I'm normal.*

Sex therapy is actually designed for people without major mental health problems. Most sex therapists will not start treatment with someone who is severely depressed or actively schizophrenic. Problems like these must be treated first so that both patient and therapist are free to focus on the sexual problem.

2. *Counseling can take years! I want my problem solved now.*

Most sexual problems can be treated in ten to twenty weekly sessions. If the therapy lasts longer, it is generally because the patient's other conflicts, such as severe marital conflict or long-term emotional difficulties, get in the way of sex therapy. Sometimes therapist and patient agree to deal with these areas, rather than working strictly on the sexual problem. The "contract" at the start of sex therapy, however, is usually to concentrate directly on changing the sexual relationship.

3. *I'll probably have to talk about my childhood. What does that have to do with my sexual problem?*

Sex therapy, unlike traditional treatments, focuses on the present. Many sex therapists do set aside the first or second session to take a "sexual history," asking the patient to describe his life as a sexual person, including early childhood memories of his family's attitudes, his reactions to reaching puberty, and his sexual experiences as an adolescent and then as an adult. The therapist gets a chance to identify all the strands that weave into the patient's current situation. If the therapist is working with a couple, each partner's sexual history is taken separately. The rest of the treatment, however, deals with day-to-day events in the patient's sex life. Information from the history is mainly brought in as needed to explain a patient's current belief or feeling about sex.

4. *Therapy is just talking. How can talking about a sex problem make it better?*

Sex therapy is not a "talking cure." It is a treatment that depends on action: *You* do the "homework" suggested by the therapist. The idea is that the hour a week you spend in therapy sessions has a limited power to change your life. The important arena for change is in your real-life behavior. Every week, the therapist suggests several new experiences to try at home. Usually these include exercises designed to take the worry and pressure out of sex. Other goals are learning more about your body's capacity to experience pleasure and passing this new information along to your partner. The homework is then discussed in the therapy sessions. Any difficulties are explored, and a strategy is devised so that they do not reoccur the next week.

If a couple is working together on solving a sexual problem, they usually are assigned sessions in which they take turns giving and receiving a sensual, all-over body massage. The therapist also suggests ways to make sexual communication clearer and more open. Specialized treatment programs have been developed for men who have trouble with erections or with reaching orgasm too quickly, or for women who do not get aroused or reach orgasm. When one partner has lost his or her desire for sex, additional homework exercises are included. Depending on the sexual problem and on a man's comfort with masturbation, his homework may involve first trying a new technique during self-stimulation and then adding it to his partner sessions.

The basic theory behind sex therapy is that sexuality is learned. It is not merely an inborn instinct, but rather results from your unique history. A sexual problem, unless caused by ill health, is a kind of bad habit. What has been learned can be unlearned, so that a new, more gratifying habit can replace it.

Since the most powerful way to learn is to try out a new experience, sex therapists assign homework. If you can change what you *do*, chances are that your feelings and thoughts will change as well. A good example is starting on a jogging program. If you manage to jog for a whole mile, without stopping, you feel proud of your achievement. The next time you are tempted to sleep for an extra hour instead of getting up early to run, you remember how good you felt, and jump out of bed. You may also recall the example in Chapter 5 of a man learning to change the pessimistic self-statements that contributed to his erection problem. Once your actions begin to influence your thoughts, your new positive self-image may inspire you to be more adventurous.

5. *Only couples can have sex therapy, and I don't have a partner to go with me.*

It is true that sex therapy was first designed for couples. Even though one person "owns" the problem, such as an erection that will not stay up or a lack of desire for sex, the trouble developed out of an interaction between two people. Unless masturbation is a man's only sexual outlet, he will at some point need to deal with a partner. Sex therapists have discovered that the easiest way to solve a sexual difficulty is for both partners to work together. The problem really belongs to their relationship, rather than to one person alone.

When Masters and Johnson first began using sex therapy in their St. Louis clinic, they accepted only couples. As the field of sex therapy developed, however, this practice changed. If a man is not in a committed relationship, he can be treated either on his own or in a group of men with similar problems. He is still given homework, but he tries out new techniques through self-stimulation. If he has a lover who is willing to work with him, he can also do homework exercises with her, even if she does not attend the therapy sessions. If a man is dating casually, or not at all, he may want to learn how to begin a comfortable relationship that has good sexual communication from the word go. Sex therapy techniques have also been used successfully with homosexual men or gay couples who have a sexual dysfunction.

A male therapy group is especially useful for men who have been divorced or widowed and are trying to get back into dating again. Group members can help each other by sharing their experiences. A good therapist quickly nips in the bud any attempts to turn the group into a locker-room bragging session. Since every man in the group has a sexual problem, there is no need for anyone to feel competitive or inadequate.

Ben joined a group for men who experienced premature ejaculation. There were seven in the group, ranging in age from twenty-three to fifty-eight. Ben was the oldest, but, like most of the others, he had been quick on the trigger as long as he could remember. After a long, unhappy marriage, Ben got divorced and began to date. Several women complained when he reached his climax almost immediately after penetrating. It hadn't been a problem with his wife. She didn't like intercourse and always seemed glad to get it over with. Since their sex life was unexciting, Ben had also lasted longer with her than he could with his dates.

Ben was nervous about discussing his sexuality with a bunch of strangers, but it wasn't so bad. They all had similar experiences, and it was actually fun to compare notes. At first, Ben found himself taking a fatherly role with the youngest men, but there came a time when he asked their advice on the new rules of dating. Things had certainly changed since he was in his twenties!

When the therapist gave them all an assignment to try masturbation at home, Ben was upset. He had always felt that playing with yourself was for kids. A man goes out and finds a woman, or he has to do without. Ben was able to tell the group how he felt, and several men recalled boyhood horror stories about masturbation. The therapist explained that it was easiest to learn how to delay ejaculation by caressing your own penis until you felt close to orgasm, and then stopping to let the excitement die down before you started again. He also showed a film explaining a "squeeze technique" in which the man squeezes his penis in a particular way to temporarily reduce his excitement and erection. Ben could see the payoff of learning to delay ejaculation on his own before he tackled the problem with a new lover. Besides, if masturbation was "prescribed" by the doctor, how unhealthy could it be?

Later on, Ben and the other group members talked about the pressure they felt to have sex early in a relationship. The group agreed that men have a right to say no to sex if they are not yet ready to trust the woman. Ben remembered this discussion when he started dating again.

After the ten weeks of group sessions, Ben could stimulate himself, without pausing, for twenty minutes before he ejaculated. When he tried sex with a partner, he found a woman who was willing to take things slowly. They had to go back a few steps and try the squeeze and stop-start exercises, but within several dates, Ben was lasting as long as he wanted during intercourse.

6. *I know about those "sex therapists." They have sex with you in their office. If I want to pay for sex, I'll try a prostitute. They're cheaper.*

There has been considerable controversy about what "sex therapists" do, and the kind of credentials they should have. When I use the term *sex therapist*, I am speaking of a mental health professional (psychologist, social worker, or psychiatrist) with special training in the treatment of sexual and marital problems. An ethical sex therapist *never* has sexual contact with a patient. Sex between therapist and patient is not only forbidden in the ethical codes of the American Psychiatric Association, the American Psychological Association, and the Association of Sex Educators, Counselors, and Therapists, but is grounds for a malpractice suit as well. A reputable sex therapist will certainly discuss your sex life and suggest sexual activities to try with a partner. Because the job of a professional is to focus on your needs rather than on her or his own desires, however, the therapist can never *be* that sexual partner.

A mental health professional sees people at their most vulnerable. To seduce a patient would be an abuse of trust tantamount to rape. This holds true even if the sex therapist is a woman and the patient a man—although the great majority of these unethical relationships occur between a male therapist and his female patients.

Some confusion has arisen from the use of sexual surrogates. When Masters and Johnson pioneered the use of sex therapy, and felt it was necessary to work with a couple, they provided a "surrogate" partner for a man who wanted treatment but could not persuade his wife or lover to participate. Surrogates were volunteers carefully chosen for their supportive attitudes and lack of sexual hang-ups. They were not prostitutes, but rather middle-class women who felt they were contributing to science.

Masters and Johnson discontinued their use of surrogates after a lawsuit regarding this practice was settled out of court. Today, very few sex therapists provide surrogate partners for their patients. In most states, a therapist who used surrogates could be charged with procurement. If either the surrogate or patient is married, the therapist can also be sued for promoting adultery.

A drawback more crucial than these legal issues, however, is that sex with a surrogate is quite different from most men's reality. The surrogate is paid to put the man's needs above her own, and never to be sexually demanding. She is trained to provide relaxed, sensual caressing, and to communicate clearly and openly about sex. A man knows that his surrogate knows he has a problem. He does not have to prove himself to her. He does not have to make an effort to please her, or even to attract her. Suppose a man has successful sex with a surrogate. Will he feel as relaxed with the woman he has admired at the local singles' dance? Will she be as practiced and understanding? There is quite a leap to make from surrogate sex to real-life sex.

7. *There is a medical reason for my sexual problem. I don't need sex therapy, because that's just for men who have psychological problems.*

Sex therapy can be helpful even if a sexual problem has a medical cause. The way that a man reacts to a health problem still is a function of his personality. Counseling can be useful in teaching him more effective strategies for coping with sex.

When there is a medical reason for a man's sexual problem,

the goals of sex therapy may shift toward adapting to the problem, rather than "curing" it.

Neal has mildly reduced circulation to the penis. He still has some erections, but they take a longer time to become full, and are easily lost. Sex therapy with Neal and his lover will focus on making sex more relaxed, with more foreplay, better communication about what each partner likes, and less pressure to go on to intercourse. The therapist cannot promise, however, that Neal will always get erections firm enough for penetration.

Guy and his wife have a more severe problem. Guy has had his penis amputated to stop the spread of a penile cancer. He still is able to reach orgasm, however, and even ejaculates through a new urinary opening created behind his scrotum. So far, Guy has been able to reach orgasm only in a "wet dream." He and his wife had always had their climaxes during sexual intercourse. Now they want to get more comfortable and skillful in bringing each other to orgasm through alternate types of caresses, such as through genital touching, kissing, or vibrator stimulation. The sex therapist will take them through a step-by-step series of exercises to reach this goal.

Sometimes medical treatment is just not sufficient to take care of the problem, so that some counseling needs to be combined with it.

David had semirigid penile prosthesis surgery, but he and his wife were not happy with the results. They told their doctor that David's penis was too small and flexible to make sex enjoyable. Neither partner was able to reach orgasm during intercourse. Through further questioning, the doctor discovered that David and his wife had a good deal of trouble talking about sex. They were spending only a couple of minutes on kissing and stroking before going right into intercourse, which was always in the missionary position. The doctor referred them to a sex therapist who could suggest ways to enrich their sex life. Perhaps delaying intercourse until each partner was more excited or experimenting with different sexual positions would render the size of David's penis less important.

In one clinic, 140 men with erection problems were offered sex therapy, even though half of them had a medical cause for their sexual difficulty. About 44 percent agreed to try the sexual counseling. In the end, 52 percent of men whose problem had a medical cause were satisfied with sex therapy and wanted no further treatment. In contrast, only 43 percent of the men with purely psychological problems were satisfied with the counseling. Sex therapy, then, was *more* successful when health factors contributed to an erection problem. Although the satisfied men may not have ended up with perfect, push-button erections, they felt more content with their sexual relationships.

What kinds of problems can be helped with sex therapy? Most sex therapists are trained to work with the following sexual difficulties:

Lack of desire for sex
Difficulty getting or keeping erections
Premature ejaculation
Trouble reaching orgasm, for men or women
Lack of excitement or vaginal lubrication for women
Involuntary tightening of the vaginal muscles, making penetration difficult
Pain during sexual activity (when there is no curable cause)

Couple disagreements on how often to have sex, or which
  activities to include
Coping with medically based sexual problems

FINDING A GOOD SEX THERAPIST

Sex therapy may sound like a simple treatment, and the
homework exercises easy to learn. (In fact, in the next chapter
I will describe some beginning sex therapy techniques that you
can try at home.) Many sexual problems are complex and stubborn, however, so that sex therapy is one of the most difficult
kinds of counseling to do well.

A competent sex therapist should be trained in psychotherapy for individuals, couples, and groups. Knowledge of the
body's sexual systems, and the effects of disease, medications,
and aging on the sexual response is also a prerequisite. A sex
therapist must be familiar with medical exams and treatments
for sexual problems, relaxed in talking about sex, and very
aware of his or her own "blind spots" and sexual prejudices. A
sex therapist should be an expert in observing and changing the
way that couples communicate.

Unfortunately, many people who call themselves sex therapists lack these qualifications. Few states have laws specify-
ing who is allowed to use the title of "sex therapist." Many sex
therapists are not mental health professionals (social workers,
psychiatrists, or psychologists) and so have never had supervised training in psychotherapy. Some who do have good credentials in a mental health field have had little special
coursework in sex therapy. After reading a textbook or attend-
ing a weekend workshop, a therapist may decide to add sex
therapy to his "bag of tricks." Depending on his experience in
marriage therapy or in other action-focused treatments, he
may be quite competent. Even a professional degree, however,
is no guarantee of skill in treating sexual problems.

The lack of regulation of sex therapy practice is particularly unfortunate because people are so distressed when they have a sexual problem. Patients are emotionally and financially vulnerable to quacks who offer an easy answer. I think there are more charlatans calling themselves healers in the sexuality field than in any other area of health care, except possibly the diet racket.

If you have contact with a sex therapist who seems to be acting unethically, stop your sessions. Sometimes unethical acts are blatant, like a therapist trying to seduce a patient or guaranteeing a cure. Other violations of trust are more subtle, such as pressuring patients to participate in nude encounter groups, giving the hard sell to an expensive, electronic gadget invented by the therapist to improve your sex life, or encouraging patients in a group to date each other. I recently heard a therapist describe a clinic in which he provided male or female sex partners for his patients. He did not call these partners surrogates, because they did not actually have "penis-in-vagina" intercourse with patients. All sexual activity took place in the clinic, sometimes with the therapist observing (with the patient's permission) through a one-way mirror. While none of these treatments is in clear violation of ethics, their use is questionable. I do not think it is necessary or helpful to intrude on a patient's privacy in such a manner, and I would never refer someone to such a clinic.

If you have a run-in with an unethical therapist, please lodge a formal complaint with the state licensing board for his or her specific profession. You will be protecting others from sexual mistreatment.

So how do you find a trustworthy sex therapist? If you are lucky, you live near a large city, a university with a training program in clinical psychology, or a medical school. Professionals who are well trained in sexual counseling cluster in these settings. If you do not have such resources nearby, you may need to do more sleuthing, be less choosy, or if you can afford it, get short-term treatment at a clinic out of town. Some sex-therapy clinics telescope fifteen weeks of treatment into fifteen consecutive daily sessions, for patients who do not live in commuting distance. A concentrated treatment program can be quite effective, especially for couples who have a basically happy partnership.

Clues for Locating a Sex Therapist

No matter where you live, here are some suggestions on finding a competent sex therapist:

1. Ask a family physician, urologist, or gynecologist for the name of a mental health professional who specializes in treating sexual problems. Often doctors in private practice know who has a good reputation.
2. Call the information number of the nearest medical school. Ask if they have a sexual dysfunction clinic. If they do not, call their department of psychiatry and ask if anyone on the faculty specializes in behavioral sex therapy. Even if they have no specialist on staff, they may know who is available in the community. If those calls fail, try the departments of urology and gynecology. Professionals who work at a medical school or university are usually highly trained in their area of expertise. Since they work closely with other faculty, they are less likely to violate professional ethics. Their fees are often lower, since you may be treated in a university clinic rather than in a private practice. Also, as already mentioned in Chapter 7, page 114, *Sexual Medicine Today*, a magazine for physicians, publishes an annual referral guide to medical school–affiliated sex dysfunction clinics.
3. Another university source for professionals is a department of psychology with a graduate degree program in

clinical psychology. Many clinical psychology programs have their own training clinics. Although your therapist may be a graduate student, he or she will be closely supervised by a member of the clinic staff. This usually results in good quality, ethical treatment, again at lower fees. To find such a clinic, call the nearest university department of psychology. Ask if they offer sex therapy treatment, or could suggest a referral elsewhere.

4. There are several professional associations of sex therapists. The American Association of Sex Educators, Counselors and Therapists (AASECT) (5010 Wisconsin Avenue, N.W., Suite 304, Washington, D.C. 20016) is one of the most scrupulous. It publishes a directory of members who meet AASECT criteria for sex therapists. Even this society, however, accepts a person with a master's or doctorate degree in a field unrelated to mental health. An AASECT-certified sex therapist does need one hundred hours of individual, supervised sex-therapy training, which is the equivalent of a year's seminar. AASECT has its own code of ethics, a point in its favor.

    A new society with higher standards of admission is the Academy of Psychologists in Marital, Sex, and Family Therapy (246 Virginia Avenue, Fort Lee, New Jersey 07024).

    Although these groups are a good referral source, many fine sex therapists do not belong to either one.

5. Other sources of referrals include city or state psychiatric societies or psychological associations, community mental health centers, directories of psychiatrists or psychologists, or, if all else fails, the phone book. Many phone books, however, do not include a listing for sex therapists or enough information to reveal which mental health professionals specialize in sex therapy.

6. If you do find a therapist, be assertive and check out

her or his background. You have the right to ask about a therapist's training. A psychiatrist should be a Doctor of Medicine who has completed a psychiatric residency and is certified by the American Board of Psychiatry and Neurology. A psychologist should ideally have a Ph.D. from a clinical program that has been approved by the American Psychological Association. He or she should have completed predoctoral and postdoctoral internships. If your state has a licensing law covering psychologists, the psychologist you see should be licensed. A social worker should have a master's degree in social work as well as a license. You can ask the therapist about his or her special training or supervision in sex therapy. A responsible professional is pleased to reveal such credentials.

Some gynecologists and urologists have had special training in sex therapy. My only concern is that their knowledge of individual and marital psychotherapy may not be expert enough to handle more complex sexual problems. This varies with each professional, and depends on the extent of the special training.

Many states also have a license category for marriage and family counselors. These practitioners often have master's degrees in counseling or psychology. Some individuals are very competent therapists, but others are poorly trained. You may want to check out the counselor's reputation in the community, just as you should for any sex therapist.

10

Sexual Enrichment: Revitalizing Your Sex Life

Take a few moments to think about your sex life as it is, and as you would like it to be ideally. If you could change three things about your partner's sexual responses, what would you choose? What three aspects of your own sexual behavior could most improve?

Men often say there is nothing they would like to change, or, if they are having a specific sexual problem, list that alone—"I would like to have better erections." Perhaps you have invested so much caring and effort in your sex life that it has reached its prime, and needs no further cultivation. On the other hand, you may find that with a little weeding or fertilization a few areas could produce a better yield.

I am not suggesting that you start training for the sexual Olympics. In recent years, our society has fostered unreasonable expectations about sexuality. After seeing a few movies or browsing through a bookstore, a man may feel inadequate unless he can last for an hour of acrobatic intercourse and bring his partner to at least five or six earthshaking climaxes. If you wonder whether other people's sex lives are like the novels, remember that the authors of all that steamy prose somehow found time between orgasms to drag themselves out of the bedroom to write.

I also am not saying that "old dogs need to learn new tricks." When I see older men for sex therapy, they sometimes tell me, "You know, you kids think my generation is sexually ignorant. Well, I can tell you that I knew all about oral sex, and group sex, and homosexuality, and the clitoris even when I was back in school." Of course there are no "new tricks." Across the ages of human history, every possible sex act has been tried. Accessible and accurate sex information *is* new, however, even though erotic art from ancient cultures could be used to illustrate a modern sex therapy textbook.

Before World War II, sexual myths and prohibitions were part of growing up in America. In a recent survey of adults over age sixty, about 90 percent recalled hearing negative messages about sex in their childhood. Though some couples have been able to overturn these teachings, many people's sex lives have been sadly limited by their upbringing. One striking fact: the best predictor of a woman's capacity to reach orgasm is not her educational level, social class, age, race, or marital status, but simply her date of birth. The later in the twentieth century that she grew up, the more likely she is to be orgasmic.

The answers do not lie in learning "new tricks" in any case, but in fostering a more open and relaxed sexual climate. For a couple, the novelty of trying a new intercourse position or sharing sexual fantasies can wear off quickly. Lasting changes in a man's sex life can involve creating an atmosphere of tenderness, playfulness, and romance, or gaining confidence that he can trust his partner to listen to his sexual feelings and desires with acceptance.

When older men do reveal the changes they would like in their own or a partner's sexual response, some common goals emerge regarding the quality of the relationship:

"I would like to be able to say, out loud, what I want in bed."

"I would like more variety. Sex has gotten sort of boring."

"I would like to have sex more often. We hardly ever seem to find the time, or our moods don't coincide."

"I wish my wife would try oral sex, or wearing sexy underwear, or even just having sex with the lights on, but I'm afraid to ask her."

"My girlfriend always lets me take the lead in sex. I wish she'd be more aggressive, and even seduce me sometimes."

"I try to show my partner how I like to be touched, but she never seems to get it right."

"I wish I knew what my wife liked in sex. All these years I've had to guess, because she never says anything."

You may have noticed that almost all of these dissatisfactions can be traced to a lack of sexual communication. Current research on older adults shows that a third of couples never discuss their sex lives at all. I will offer suggestions in this chapter to help a couple resolve the silent mysteries and disagreements that can interfere with their sexual pleasure. We will also look at ways to spice up your sexual routine. If you have been having a "meat and potatoes" sex life, why not turn it into boeuf bourguignon, or at least steak and fries? Since the years after fifty should be your sexual prime, you have no more excuses.

FIRST STEPS TO BETTER SEXUAL COMMUNICATION

Irving couldn't decide whether his sixtieth birthday felt like a milestone or a millstone. Although he was really only one day older, it seemed as if the whole weight of his lifetime had dropped onto his shoulders. Perhaps he was more concerned about aging than the average man because his second wife, Jenny, was fourteen years younger. Irving adored Jenny, and often apologized to her for being too tired to go out in the evenings, or for not knowing how to dance to rock music at their friends' parties. Jenny always laughed at Irving's concerns, telling him that she was middle-aged herself, and had two grandchildren.

About the only aspect of his marriage that dissatisfied Irving was his sex life. Although Jenny was affectionate, very attractive, and a skillful hostess, she was almost prudish about sex. She rarely refused to have sexual activity, but her husband always suspected she was responding from a sense of duty rather than out of pure enjoyment. She never took the initiative in suggesting they make love. In bed, Irving had questioned her several times on her preferences, but she always told him she was happy with the ways he touched her. While Irving would have liked to vary their sex life a little, perhaps to try intercourse with Jenny on top, or to include oral sex, he was afraid to ask his wife directly. She might think he was being demanding, or, even worse, would comply just to be a good wife, even though she found these acts distasteful.

On turning sixty, however, Irving felt time slipping through his fingers. One Sunday evening, soon after his birthday, he came up behind Jenny while they were getting ready for bed. She leaned against him as he kissed her neck, but Irving thought he heard her give a small sigh, as if in resignation. Something snapped within him at that moment. "Damn it!" he exclaimed. "If you don't want sex, why don't you just say so!"

Jenny looked at him with hurt surprise. "I'm a little tired, but if you're in the mood for sex, it's really O.K. with me."

"But I don't want it to be just O.K.! I want you to *want* sex."

"Irving, I like having sex with you. Sometimes I'm a little worn out after your kids come for dinner, that's all."

"Well why don't you ever let me know when *you* want sex? Why do I always have to be the aggressor?"

"I don't know. I guess it's a habit. I didn't think you'd want me to ask for sex."

"Well, I do. And it might be nice if you made love to me, for once, instead of lying there like a lump!"

"A lump! Irving, what is the matter with you?"

"What's the matter with *me?* My wife thinks sex equals lying on her back and trying not to fall asleep before it's over, and she wants to know what's wrong with me."

Jenny threw a robe over her nightgown. "If you're that unhappy, maybe you should find a new wife. Or maybe you already have. Is that what this is all about?"

"Jenny! You know I hardly even look at other women."

"I don't know what you do, or don't do, but I can tell you that I'm sleeping in the den tonight."

What did Irving do wrong? His first mistake was to hide his feelings for years, until he could only express them as a volcanic eruption of anger and frustration. One foundation of good sexual communication is to ask for changes from the beginning of a relationship, instead of storing up disappointments.

Men over fifty usually do not have this luxury, however. You may be in a marriage that started when you were too young and shy to talk openly about sex. In order to change things now, you have to fight the inertia of years of silence. Though some men are in newer relationships, each partner has had a long sexual history. Perhaps you had an unhappy first marriage, and so hesitate to spoil things by revealing your sexual dissatisfaction to your current partner. Or maybe you lost a woman whom you loved intensely, and no subsequent lover can ever quite live up to your memories. In any case, you are probably not building your first sexual relationship.

Even though you are not starting from ground zero, there

are some ways to increase sexual communication without putting your partner on the defensive. Another of Irving's errors, for example, was to begin this delicate process when he was feeling tired and rejected. If you want to make some changes in your sex life, the best time to discuss them is when you and your partner are in a calm and intimate mood.

You can plan in advance how to set the scene. What couple activities in your relationship most often lead to a satisfying talk? For some people the best setting is over dessert or a drink in a quiet restaurant. Others feel relaxed after sharing a game of tennis, golf, or bridge. Perhaps your closest time is Saturday night after watching the TV movie, or Sunday morning in bed. Sometimes it is easier to begin discussing sex in a nonsexual situation, however. You may want to choose the living room rather than the bedroom, or a time in the early evening instead of after intercourse, especially if your sexual activity takes place in an atmosphere of tension. Changing your sex life takes work and planning. Things rarely go smoothly and spontaneously at first.

How do you let your mate know that you would like to have a talk about your sexual relationship? It is very easy to set the scene and end up discussing whether to buy a new car or just easing into actually having sex. Bringing up the topic of sex is often the hardest task. You might say, "I'd like to talk a little bit about our sex life," or, "I've been thinking lately about our sexual relationship, and how we might make it even better." Try to get your partner's agreement to listen—"I know it's a little uncomfortable to talk about this, but will you help me try?" "Are you in the mood right now to talk about sex?"

Most of us are somewhat insecure about our attractiveness and our skill as lovers. We did not learn about sex in school, or, indeed, discuss it much in any context, and yet we are supposed to be experts. Each man and woman has "buttons" that get pushed when sex is discussed. If a wife expresses dissatisfaction or disappointment, her husband hears, "You are not good-looking enough, or patient enough, or passionate enough," even if that message was not implied. Before he realizes it, he is either lost in his own self-hatred or busy inwardly blaming it all on her: "She's the one who takes half an hour to reach a climax. I don't know why I even put up with it." In Irving's attempt to talk to Jenny, he was surprised at how quickly each became defensive.

If you ask your partner to change one aspect of her sexual response, let her know that you generally appreciate her as a lover. Then she may feel secure enough to listen calmly to your request. You might start off by listing some of the things you like about her as a sexual partner. For example, Irving could have told Jenny:

"You know I really love your warmth, and the way you just come over and give me a hug sometimes. And you're such a pretty woman. I find myself feeling excited just watching you do something around the house. That's why I'd like to feel more free to be passionate with you, but I have trouble knowing whether you're in the mood for sex."

It is always tempting to start with an accusation. It is easy to self-righteously declare, "You never seem to want sex anymore," or "You always ask for sex when I'm in the middle of reading the paper." "Red flag" words like *ever*, *never*, and *always* should be avoided. Criticism also comes more naturally than praise: "How come you hug all our friends at parties, but you're so cold to me?" or "You're just too inhibited to talk about sex!" When you blame or complain, you automatically put your partner in the wrong.

Try presenting your request in a positive light: "I'd sure like it if you just came up and gave me a kiss on the spur of the moment," or "I know you're a little shy about sex, but I really want to understand your feelings about it. Could we talk a little bit?"

You will have more success in getting through to your partner if you take some of the risks. When you find yourself saying, "You always . . ." or "You never . . ." try changing your statement to reveal some of *your* vulnerabilities. A good way to remind yourself of this tactic is to shape your sentence in the form: "When you do X, I feel Y." The "feel" should describe your emotion, like anger, sadness, or joy. For instance, Irving might have continued:

> "When you pull away from my kisses, I feel like a nervous teenager. I want you, but I also want you to feel as excited as I do. When it seems like you're making love just to please me, I end up feeling rejected."

With this approach he would be much more likely to get his point across to Jenny than he did by telling her that she lies there "like a lump" during sex. Irving's new communication style requires him to reveal his insecurity to Jenny. While showing your feelings may seem "weak," this kind of trust actually takes more courage than the old male approach of being strong and silent.

One pitfall in changing your communication is in hiding behind that word "feel," and yet really expressing only a thought or another criticism. For example, a man might tell his lover, "When you tell me you're too tired for sex, I *feel* you are frigid." Instead of revealing his emotion, however, he is criticizing her. A better communication would be, "When you tell me you're too tired for sex, I get angry. I feel frustrated because I want sex and you don't." Make sure you give your partner a glimpse of what goes on inside of you, rather than commenting only on her shortcomings.

Another way to produce a communication deadlock is to keep bringing up the past. Couples can go on for hours reminding each other: "Last year you told me I was too aggressive, and now you want me to start sex," or "Don't forget that in 1964 you had an affair with our next-door neighbor," or "Last time I tried to talk to you about sex you told me to see a psychiatrist." You and your partner could make an agreement to omit past hurts from your talk. Keep focusing on the changes you want to make *now*.

Sometimes, despite your best effort, your partner does not understand your message. If you can see that the conversation is wandering off target, a helpful way to get back on track is to ask your partner to repeat your communication: "Hey, I think our signals are getting crossed. Could you tell me the message you got from me?" If your partner misunderstood you, restate your message and ask her to summarize again what she is hearing.

JENNY: I don't know how many times I have to tell you that I enjoy sex!

IRVING: It sounds as if you heard me accusing you of being frigid.

JENNY: Yes! That's exactly what I heard.

IRVING: But that's not what I meant. I know you often enjoy sex. What upsets me is to have all of the responsibility for deciding when and how to have sex. I wish you would speak up more, so I don't carry that load all by myself. Do you understand what I'm asking?

JENNY: You'd like me to start sex sometimes, and to let you know more about what I'd like.

IRVING: Yes. That's exactly what I want.

Obviously this whole process is more difficult than it sounds. It takes practice to talk comfortably about sex. For starters, limit your requests to one or two *small* changes in your sexual relationship. One mistake men often make is to floor the gas pedal instead of accelerating gently.

JENNY: Well, what do you want me to do differently?"

IRVING: Let's see . . . I've always liked X-rated movies. Maybe we can go see some together. And how about buying some black lace underwear—you know, the kind with the cutouts. And I want to hear about your fantasies, and what really turns you on. You could even tie me to the bed if you wanted! That's in *The Joy of Sex*. And I'd also like to watch you masturbate, or you could watch me . . . .

JENNY: Wait a minute! I'm your wife, not a porno star.

Irving might get a better response if he began with: "Some time in the next few days, when you're in the mood for sex, could you make the first moves?"

One final suggestion: Do not try to shortcut this talking process by silently giving your partner a sex manual to read. That method of communication is about as caring and mature as the TV commercials in which a bottle of mouthwash is left on a co-worker's desk. The message is: "You have a problem with sex. Maybe reading this book will bring you a little closer to my expert level." No book (including this one) contains the secret of being a good lover. The essence of a good sexual relationship *is* the willingness to communicate. Even if your partner can list and perform an encyclopedia of sexual techniques, she will not know what pleases *you* until you tell her, and vice versa.

PILLOW TALK: GETTING WHAT YOU WANT IN BED

Once you and your partner have agreed that you would like to enrich your sex life, you still need to find words or gestures during sex to let each other know what you want. One common stumbling block is finding comfortable terms to use in referring to the genitals or to certain sexual acts.

Words that enhance a romantic or playful mood in the bedroom may not be the same ones that sound right either in a doctor's office or in the locker room. In the middle of lovemaking, you don't want to sound like an anatomy textbook—"How about orally stimulating my scrotum?"—but some women might be taken aback if you asked, "Honey, could you lick my balls?" Most couples solve this dilemma by using a combination of innocuous words, such as "penis" or "intercourse"; euphemisms like "down there" or "my thing"; slang or pet words, i.e., "John Thomas," "pussy," or "sixty-nine"; or, when words fail, body language. Though many couples have not uttered a peep during sex for thirty years and are perfectly content, it is nice to have a little flexibility. Our capacity for speech is, after all, one of the reasons that humans have such varied sexual repertoires. If you are hesitating about the words to use, you might just try out a few, or check with your lover to see what she prefers.

When you want your partner to change the way she caresses you, there are several helpful guidelines to keep in mind.

1. *Be specific.* Here words can be crucial. Rather than mumbling, "I'd like you to kiss my legs," you may need to state, "It really feels good when you run your lips very lightly across the inside of my thighs." Even more difficult is to ask for a particular kind of genital caress. The most willing partner will be left in the dark by "Please put your mouth on my penis," when you really mean "Would you gently lick my penis just under the head?" If you do not get exactly what you wanted, let your partner know: "That feels great, but I'd like it better if you stroke the shaft a little harder, up and down."

   Sometimes showing your partner how to touch you is worth a thousand words. You can either guide her hand with yours, or if that is awkward, put her hand "piggyback" on top of yours while you touch yourself. This teaches her the kind of motion, pressure, and speed you prefer.

   It is wise to ask for just one or two things on any single occasion. Otherwise, instead of being fun, sex comes to resemble the directions for a complicated model ship —"And now, insert tab D into slot A-2. Apply glue and hold in place for thirty seconds."

2. *Be positive.* Frame your requests in a positive, encouraging way. If you tell your partner "Ouch! that's too hard!" she may feel clumsy and give up. A more successful way to communicate is to say "That's a little hard, but you're touching the right place. Maybe you could try a more circular, almost tickling kind of touch."

3. *Stay in the present.* Avoid criticism and complaints about the past. Not "There you go again. You always want to go on to intercourse before I'm ready," but "I feel like taking my time today. Is it O.K. with you if we just play around for a while longer before we start intercourse?"

4. *Be patient and try, try again.* It may take several tries before your partner gets the hang of what you want. She may also forget your instructions from one night to the next, or your own desires may change. As you practice your communication skills, asking for specific changes in your usual routine should become more natural and less of an effort.

5. *Let your partner know you appreciate the changes she makes.* This is one of the most vital rules of good communication. If you want your partner to stay enthusiastic about your new sexual openness, remember to say "Thank you, that was great!" or "It sure was exciting when you blew in my ear. I never knew I was so sensitive there" or "You really look sexy in your new underwear."

6. *Remember that communication is a two-way street.* Although I have used "he" to identify the communicator and "she" for the partner, your relationship will benefit most if each of you communicates openly. All sugges-

tions in this chapter apply equally to the woman in a couple (or to either partner in a gay couple). Contrary to our tradition that men should be the sexual leaders, both partners can benefit if the woman actively requests her favorite kinds of touching and makes sure her own sexual needs are met.

EXPANDING YOUR PLEASURE WITH TOUCH

A couple can get into a sexual rut. After starting sex in their customary way, they go through a little ritual of "now we rub here, and then on to a few kisses there," always ending in intercourse, a few hugs and yawns, and sleep. Longstanding sexual habits are so comfortable that breaking them is difficult. In fact, you may not want to rock your sexual boat. If you are dissatisfied with a stereotyped routine, however, you may wonder how to alter your patterns. Often men hope that good sex will just happen magically, when a passionate mood hits them —but it does not. Rather than waiting for that thunderbolt from the blue, freshen up your own sex life by declaring a change in the weather.

The series of homework exercises I am about to describe can change the climate in your bedroom. These "sensate focus" sessions are a cornerstone of sex therapy. You are asked to put a high priority on your sex life, to concentrate on sensual pleasure rather than on reaching the goal of erection or orgasm, and to experiment with different kinds of caressing.

Either partner can suggest trying a sensate focus session. The person who starts things, however, should also devise a way to *set the scene*. You should plan on having a whole hour of private, uninterrupted time to try each of these exercises. Leave the phone off the hook, shut the bedroom door, or take other measures to ensure your privacy. Since this will be a special hour that you and your partner dedicate to each other, make the atmosphere particularly pleasant and relaxing. Some couples take a shower or bubble bath together, or spend a few minutes cuddling and talking. You could light the bedroom with candles or put on some soft music. You may want to keep some body lotion or talcum powder by the bed, to use during the touching. It is easiest to do these exercises with your clothes off, but some couples feel more relaxed in their underwear, especially for the first session.

Each sensate focus exercise limits the areas of the body to be touched, or the kinds of sexual activities included. To get the most out of the sessions, you must resist the temptation to slip into your usual sexual routine. A sensate focus exercise should not be a prelude to orgasms or intercourse, but rather a time apart, complete in itself.

If a sexual problem has created tension in your relationship, you may want to put a "ban" on having sex for a few weeks, until you have had a chance to get through this series of exercises. Abstaining from sex may seem like a sacrifice, but learning new and better sexual habits is easiest if you make a break with the past and start again from the beginning. The sensate focus exercises are designed to make this process easier. They are also an enjoyable way to start off on the right foot (or the left earlobe!) with a new sexual partner, or to get your sex life back into gear after an illness.

Exercise I

In this session, you and your partner take turns as the *Giver* and the *Receiver* of touch. The person who starts as Receiver lies face down on the bed. The Giver spends at least fifteen minutes caressing the back of the Receiver's body, and then repeats the process, touching the Receiver's front side for fifteen minutes. In this first exercise, however, the breasts and genital area are off limits for touching. The goal is to enjoy the sensual pleasure of being touched, without worrying about becoming aroused.

As the Receiver, your job is to tune in to your own sensations. Notice where you like to be touched and the kinds of touch that are most pleasurable. You do not need to worry about your partner's feelings. If you find yourself wondering whether your partner is bored or aroused, or if she finds your body attractive, turn your attention back to yourself. See if you can discover something new about your body's responsiveness.

The first time you try a sensate focus exercise, experiencing pleasure is more crucial than communication. Rather than guiding your partner by a word or a gesture, try concentrating quietly on your sensations. If a touch is painful or tickles, you can ask your partner to change to another kind of caress. If you want to give some feedback to your partner, set aside a minute after your turn as Receiver to tell her the three kinds of touch you liked best, and the one that you least preferred. The ratio of three pluses to one minus helps you focus your feedback on pleasure rather than on criticism. As always, be specific in your feedback so that your partner understands exactly what you want.

When you are the Giver, your job is still to focus on your own experience. Notice the different textures and temperatures of your partner's skin. Be as inventive as possible in varying the ways you touch your partner. You can use a light, teasing caress, firmer circular strokes, or massage techniques. You can rub against your partner with your cheek or your hair, or add in a few kisses (but remember to keep it relaxed and sensual rather than sexual). If you like, you can spread some scented oil, body lotion, or dusting powder on your partner's body. Since the aim of the exercise is to experiment, don't limit yourself to the kinds of touching your mate particularly liked in the past.

The time boundaries are suggestions. You do not need to keep a stopwatch by the bed. Most people are tempted as the Giver to spend only five or ten minutes touching each side, but it may take a full half-hour to get over any awkwardness you feel at the start and to give full rein to your creativity in finding new ways to touch.

It makes no difference which partner starts as the Giver. Some couples prefer that the man goes first. Others like the woman to begin the touching. You may want to switch off, letting your partner start as the Receiver on one day and as the Giver the next time.

Couples often find this exercise helps them feel closer and more relaxed. Occasionally, one partner gets very ticklish during his or her turn as Receiver, perhaps reflecting some inner tension. If the Receiver feels ticklish, the Giver can use a firmer touch. Another potential source of conflict occurs if the person who starts as Receiver gets so relaxed that he or she actually falls asleep, or at least is too tired to take a turn as the Giver. The partner who spent all that time doing the caressing may react with resentment. It is best if each partner has a turn before the couple stops.

If the first session went well, you are ready to go on to Exercise II. If you felt a bit awkward or tense, however, give Exercise I another try. Most couples need several experiences with Exercise I to enjoy it fully. If the session was a disaster, this may be a good time to seek some professional help for a sexual dissatisfaction rather than forging ahead on your own.

Exercise II

This session is identical to Exercise I in most respects. Again you begin by setting the scene, spend a half-hour as Giver and then take your turn as Receiver. The breasts and genitals are still off limits. This time, however, the Receiver actively guides the Giver's caresses. The Receiver still concentrates on his or her sensations, but can ask the Giver to touch a certain area or to use a different pressure or type of caress. Remember to be specific and constructive in your feedback rather than merely critical. The Receiver can also guide the Giver's hand, using the techniques discussed on page 185. The Giver should still try a variety of touches, but remain responsive to the Receiver.

After this session, each of you should be more expert in pleasing your partner with touch.

Exercise III

Again you are building on the past exercise. This time, you can add some touching of the breasts and genitals. When these "sexual" areas are included, many couples forget to caress the rest of the body, but you should treat the genital touching as just one small aspect of the exercise.

As the Giver, begin by touching nongenital areas of the Receiver's body. When you do get to her breasts or genitals, use touch that is designed to tease and explore, rather than the rhythmic or high pressure kind of stimulation that usually leads to orgasm. If you get an erection during your turn as Receiver, your partner can switch to touching a nongenital part of your body until the erection goes down. When you are being caressed, pay attention to the sensations in your genitals just as you did to the other areas of your body. Do you learn anything new that you would like to add to your touching during sex? Guide your partner to your most sensitive genital zones. Your practice in using comfortable sexual language can help here. The goal is still to enhance your capacity to enjoy touch, however, rather than to get aroused. Orgasms and intercourse are not part of the exercise.

Exercise IV

In this session the Receiver has the option of asking the Giver to continue the genital caressing to orgasm. If the Receiver does not feel highly aroused, he or she may decide not to try for an orgasm. Remember, though, to include touching of the whole body. Don't just focus on the genital area. Sexual intercourse is still not included as part of the exercise.

This exercise can be especially helpful to older couples in which one partner cannot always have intercourse. Knowing how to satisfy each other without penetration gives you more variety and flexibility in your sex life.

It may take longer for a man or woman to reach orgasm through touching than it does during intercourse. A woman who is used to reaching orgasm through intercourse may need some practice to have an orgasm from your touch or caress. Don't forget some of the suggestions about women from Chapter 4. Since many men over fifty reach orgasm without a full erection, you should not give up on the touching even if your penis remains soft.

Many men and women feel uncomfortable seeing, touching, or tasting semen. It may help to think of semen as very similar to egg white. It is a protein-rich fluid, designed to nourish the sperm cells, and does not normally contain harmful bacteria. You may feel more relaxed, however, if you keep some tissues or a washcloth handy to wipe off the semen after ejaculation.

The second or third time you try this exercise, you may want to experiment with penetration. Since intercourse is really just another variety of touching, you can enhance your sensations during intercourse in the same way that you learned about your other sensual responses. At some point during the session, your partner can sit above you and gently guide your penis into her vagina. You can try penetration without a full erection, just to experience the sensations, and still enjoy the warmth, wetness, and texture of your lover's vagina. (If you have trouble inserting a less than firm erection into your partner's vagina, try using some extra lubrication, and supporting the base of your penis with your hand during penetration.) She can take time to become aware of the shape and feel of your penis, and perhaps try squeezing her vaginal muscles around it. You can either just stop there and disengage or, if you like, each partner may try a few slow thrusting movements. Rather than proceeding to full-scale intercourse, however, return to the usual sensate focus framework and, if you want orgasms, reach them through nonintercourse caressing.

REACHING AN AGREEMENT ON SEXUAL VARIETY

One of the most common sexual conflicts is a disagreement between partners on the kinds of activities they find comfortable. Older adults often feel ambivalent about sexual variety. During their adolescence, the authorities declared that only a few sexual acts were healthy and natural. Nevertheless, in a recent survey, half of men over sixty and a third of women wanted to experiment with new sexual activities. The "sexual revolution" of the 1960s has also influenced older adults, teaching that a wide range of sexual activities are "normal" and almost anything is permissible between consenting adults. Men and women have gotten caught between these extremes. Often two lovers end up at somewhat different places on the attitude spectrum.

Our stereotype is that women are more inhibited about sex. I often see couples who fit this picture.

Bud complained that his wife, Joanne, had not learned anything about sex since their wedding night forty-three years earlier. Joanne preferred to have intercourse in the dark and always wore her nightgown to bed. Although she often did not reach orgasm during intercourse, Joanne moved her husband's hand away if he tried to stroke her genitals.

Bud had always wanted Joanne to stimulate his penis orally, but she told him that she found the idea disgusting. She had trouble understanding why he was dissatisfied when intercourse worked just fine. Joanne believed that she would be equally content, if not happier, if Bud lost his desire for sex. After all, he was approaching sixty-five. She hoped he would soon start to slow down in bed.

It is becoming increasingly frequent, however, for women to express disappointment with their male partner's narrow view of sex.

Wanda married her second husband when they were both in their late sixties. In her first marriage, sex had been one of the most joyful and important parts of the relationship. Although Wanda and her first husband had been virgins when they married, they had learned about sex together, with lots of laughter and experimenting. Over the years they had used many positions for intercourse, as well as spending long periods on foreplay, often including oral and anal caresses.

When Wanda's first husband died of a heart attack, she could not imagine remarrying. Eight years later, however, she wedded her second husband. They had the time and money to live in a warm climate, play golf, and take several trips a year. They were also good companions.

Wanda had been looking forward with delight to having a lover again, but in this department, her new husband was a grave disappointment. For one thing, he rarely touched Wanda except as part of sex. Since Wanda was a very affectionate and cuddly woman, his reserve made her feel rejected and angry. He also was totally silent during sex. When Wanda asked him what he especially liked, he told her "Everything you do is fine."

But everything was obviously not so fine. He seemed to enjoy having Wanda caress his penis orally, but never offered to kiss her genitals. When Wanda suggested that she sit on top during intercourse, he said, "You really are aggressive, aren't you?" Wanda was deeply hurt, although she did not reply. She stopped making any sexual advances, wondering if, indeed, she was abnormal to still have sexual feelings.

If you and your lover disagree on the sexual activities that you enjoy, a calm discussion of the issue may help you reach a compromise. The partner who has been less adventurous must be open to making at least some small changes, however. If you would like to change your mate's attitude from a definite "no" to "let's see how it goes," you may need to understand why she dislikes the idea of a particular sex activity.

Ezra and Bernice had passed their golden anniversary. For a long time, Bernice had wanted their sex life to be a little more romantic. When she was feeling sexy, she always wore satiny nightgowns and left on the bedside lamp. Ezra, however, would flick off the lamp and undress his wife right away, just as a matter of course. When Bernice objected to his brusque approach, he told her she was lucky he could still perform, and not to expect candlelight and valentines after fifty years.

One afternoon, after letting Ezra beat her at dominoes, Bernice took advantage of his good mood. "Ezra, I just want to know one thing. Why do you always like to have sex in the dark?"

"That's the way it's supposed to be."

"Oh come on, honey. You aren't that narrow-minded about other things. I bet you just don't want to look at me because I'm old and wrinkled."

Ezra leaned over and kissed his wife on the cheek. "You're just fishing for compliments."

"No, really, Ezra. I want to know."

"Well . . . maybe I'm a little shy. I guess I was brought up that a man doesn't display himself."

"Really? You really feel embarrassed if I see you naked? Come to think of it, you usually do turn around when you undress."

"Well, you're bound to see me now and then, but we don't have to plan it."

Once you understand your partner's objections to a particular sexual variation, you may be able to think of a way to make the activity more acceptable. Perhaps you can begin by taking some small steps toward the goal you would eventually like to reach.

Bernice moved closer to her husband. "It's not that I want to have sex in front of the neighbors, but I like to see you instead of always being in the dark. You are my husband, after all. You should be glad you still raise my blood pressure after all these years."

"Maybe you need to take more of your pills, then."

"Ezra! Listen, how about if next time I put a candle by the bed. Just one candle. You'll hardly even be able to see."

"I don't know."

"You can keep on your pajamas."

"They just get in the way."

"Then you can close your eyes, instead!"

"You're trying to turn me into one of those dirty old men."

"Oh come on! One candle."

"O.K., but only if you play me another domino game. I'm getting to the age where dominoes are more fun than sex, anyway."

Several types of sexual stimulation commonly become bones of contention in a couple. In the next few sections, you can find some specific suggestions on how to resolve these disagreements.

Genital Touching. If one partner is reluctant to caress the other's genitals with his or her fingers, intercourse may become the be-all and end-all of sex. Not only can intercourse alone be boring, but the lack of other caressing robs the couple of any alternatives to use in coping with a sexual problem. Genital caressing, then, is expecially important to older couples who may not always be able to have intercourse. Yet older men and women often feel shy about noncoital sex.

Usually discomfort at seeing or touching our own or our lover's genitals can be traced to the lessons we learned growing up. The genitals are considered a secret area. Even tropical societies in which little clothing is worn believe in covering the male or female genital area with a small apron or loin cloth. If you walk through an art museum you see paintings and sculpture immortalizing the beauty of faces, breasts, thighs and buttocks, but women are hardly ever shown nude with their legs spread, except in art intended to be erotic. We are a little more liberal in showing penises and testicles without a fig leaf, but rarely does a masterpiece show an erection.

When an area is taboo, it evokes a strong emotional reaction. Many people find their own genitals, or those of the opposite sex, mysterious or even ugly. Yet genitals are just as individual and interesting as the other parts of our bodies. Indeed, artists have often borrowed the phallic shaft or the flowerlike form of a woman's genital lips as a symbol of beauty. We need to reeducate our visual senses to appreciate our "private parts." Looking through books of erotic art or viewing pictures of many different people's genitals can help reshape our attitudes. Since there are so few cultural standards of genital beauty, each of us can make a personal decision about the shapes and sizes we find most appealing.

Looking at your own or your partner's genitals under soft lighting can help you to feel more comfortable. Spend a few minutes identifying the different parts of the genitals and noticing the changes in color, texture, and size as caressing builds sexual excitement. You might try looking at the genital areas as if you were from another planet and had never seen a human being before. Can you guess how humans have sex from looking at their bodies?

Another source of discomfort about the genitals is their physical closeness to the openings that empty our bowels and bladder. We may worry that the genitals are contaminated with urine or feces. Since semen and vaginal lubrication are wet and have a mild odor, we confuse these fluids with the waste products that we have been strongly trained to find disgusting. Actually, when the genitals are clean they harbor far fewer harmful bacteria than are present in the mouth. Diseases that are contagious through genital contact get a lot of publicity, but think how many more illnesses can be caught just through kissing.

Many couples feel more comfortable touching each other's genitals just after a washing. Some lovers make a shower or bubblebath for two a part of their foreplay. To get used to the moist feeling of the genitals, try putting some lubricant (such as K-Y or another water-based gel) on your fingers when you caress your partner. As the lubricant mixes with the body's own fluids, the moisture may seem more natural to you.

At first, spending just a few seconds stroking your partner's genitals and getting used to the sensations may be enough. The sensate focus exercises can provide a good framework for gradually including more genital caressing in your sexual activity. Another way to ease into trying more genital touching is to purchase a vibrator. Using the vibrator to stimulate your partner—or yourself—may help you to feel more comfortable at first. Then you can experiment with using your own fingers to caress the same areas that were most responsive to the vibrator.

Many women, as well as men, get more pleasure out of intercourse and reach orgasm more easily if their genitals are caressed during the thrusting itself. Women often prefer gentle stroking of the area around the clitoris. For men, the testicles and the skin behind the scrotum may be favorite spots for touching.

Oral-Genital Sex. The reasons that inhibit people from touching each other's genitals are even more powerful when applied to oral sex. Although oral sex is an extremely common and normal part of sex play, many couples, particularly older ones, do not feel comfortable with it. Often one partner is more reluctant than the other to try oral sex, which can lead to resentment, especially if one mate expects to get oral stimulation but is unwilling to reciprocate.

Older men who are having mild erection problems often find that oral caressing of the penis produces the fullest erection or is the easiest way to reach orgasm. As an alternative to intercourse, many women prefer oral stimulation to hand stimulation because the area around the clitoris does not become irritated, as it may from rubbing.

Guy credits his second wife, Betty, with curing his erection problem. When the sexual difficulty began, during his first marriage, Guy decided he must be over the hill. A year after his divorce, when he began to date Betty, Guy warned her that he was "impotent." Betty, however, believed in tackling problems "head on." She seduced Guy one evening, and over his objections, began to stimulate his penis orally. To his astonishment, Guy achieved a full erection very rapidly.

The next morning, Guy felt ashamed of himself. He believed that he had taken advantage of Betty's kindness and that a normal man would not need oral sex to get an erection. He had to admit, however, that he had thoroughly enjoyed the experience.

One of Guy's longtime buddies was a doctor. Under the pretense of discussing a "friend's" problem, Guy asked him, "Is it normal to get an erection from oral sex instead of intercourse?"

The doctor shook his head. "Guy, I can't believe you're asking me that. Of course it's normal. Oral sex gives a man even stronger sensations than intercourse does. In fact, when a patient comes to me and complains he can't get it up, I often suggest he try oral sex. He can use it to satisfy his partner too, even if they can't have intercourse. Now is this 'friend' of yours anyone I know?" He winked and Guy, blushing to his somewhat receding hairline, decided not to introduce Betty to the doctor until some time in the distant future.

If you and your partner would like to get more accustomed to oral sex, the key is to approach it gradually. If you have concerns about cleanliness or odor, make sure you wash the genital area beforehand. Rather than trying to bring each other to orgasm with oral caressing, make an agreement the first few times to spend only a minute or two on kissing the genitals. In fact, it may be easiest to confine the first few kisses to the area near, but not directly on, the genitals. If both partners find these caresses pleasurable, you can gradually spend a longer time orally stimulating each other.

Initially, a woman may have some anxiety about her lover ejaculating in her mouth. She may worry that she will choke, that the semen is dirty, or that she will not like the taste. You and your partner may want to discuss these issues before experimenting with oral sex. You could promise to let your partner know when you are close to orgasm, so that she can stop the oral caressing before you ejaculate. Thinking of semen as egg white can also help a woman feel more relaxed about having the fluid in her mouth.

Ideally, there are no "shoulds" that apply to different kinds of sexual play between consenting adults. Just as it is normal to enjoy oral sex, it is also perfectly fine to decide to skip it. If you desire oral sex but your partner remains opposed to it, it is counterproductive to nag, whine, or threaten to find another lover. Perhaps there is something else equally exciting that both of you can enjoy.

Anal Stimulation. Another sexual practice that often causes marital acrimony is anal stimulation. Although not as common as oral sex, anal caressing is far from unusual for American couples. Often men enjoy anal intercourse more than women, perhaps because a woman may find this activity painful if she is tense or her partner forgets to go gently. If you do include some anal stimulation in your sex play, you may want to refer back to Chapter 4 (page 60) for some suggestions on keeping anal sex comfortable and healthy.

There is no "normal" in terms of people's reactions to anal caressing. Some find it highly erotic, while others feel neutral about it. A number of men and women find the whole idea repulsive. The only problematic situation occurs when two partners have differing sexual preferences.

HOW OFTEN SHOULD WE HAVE SEX?

It is rare to find a couple in complete harmony about how often to have sex. Jokes about the wife who has a headache or the husband who falls asleep in front of the TV are staples of comedians' routines.

In couples over fifty, the tug-of-war about how often to have sex may change direction. In young couples, the husband is often the lustier partner, since the wife is worn out by household and child-care tasks. It is not unusual, however, for a husband and wife to switch roles in their middle or later years, with the woman becoming more fond of sex and the man feeling pressured and tired. Menopause may increase a woman's desire, since worries about contraception and pregnancy are forgotten and more leisure time is available. Older men, in contrast, may be distracted from sex by job pressure, or by the depression that often accompanies retirement. Men also fear that they will no longer be able to meet their wives' sexual demands.

On the other hand, some men experience a resurgence of sexual desire in their fifties or sixties. A man may feel satisfied with his career, but wonder what ever happened to the pleasure that he expected from life. As he becomes aware of time getting more finite, he may try to recapture his carefree youth. Though some men use these sexual feelings to refresh their marriage relationship, others turn to midlife extramarital affairs, particularly if the wife has reacted to aging by suppressing her sexuality.

Laura believed that her husband, Ross, had little interest in sex. During their forties, when Laura would have been overjoyed by his attentions, Ross was caught up in expanding his car dealership. After the children left home, Laura occupied herself with community activities and her hobby of needlepoint. Perhaps once every couple of months, the couple would engage in some dutiful lovemaking.

Laura noticed that Ross was taking more care of his appearance, and she was mildly surprised when he chose a sports car to drive as his demo, rather than his usual luxury model. She did not think about the possibility of another woman, however, until one day Ross was rushed from work to the emergency room with a mild heart attack.

Several times at the hospital, Laura answered her husband's phone, only to have the other party hang up. She thought it was a wrong number until the afternoon that she called from home to check on her husband's condition and a nurse told her, "Oh, he's doing just fine. His wife is visiting now. Do you want to speak to her?"

"Excuse me?" Laura said, and then began to put the

clues together. She did not want to upset Ross while he was ill, but over the next week she spoke to several friends, who informed her that Ross's affair with one of the other wives in their social circle was common knowledge.

When Ross recovered, Laura suggested they seek some marriage therapy, to get their communication started again.

Couples coming to my office often ask if their frequency of intercourse is normal for their age. This is a very difficult question to answer, since couples of every age vary so widely in how often they have sex. A more germane question is whether both partners are satisfied. Does the couple agree on how often to have intercourse? Is one person frustrated at a lack of sex or harassed by having intercourse too often?

If partners have different levels of desire, the one who feels reluctant may wish to increase his or her sexual desire to match the mate. Some men or women claim they rarely feel desire. If you pay attention to your sexual thoughts and feelings, however, you often discover you are lustier than you realized.

If you would like to feel in the mood for sex more often, try keeping a "Desire Diary" for a week. Carry a small notebook with you during your daily activities, and if you find yourself having a sexual thought or fantasy or feeling sexually aroused, record this event in your diary. Make a brief note of what occurred, i.e., "felt frustrated because no sex this morning," "sexy feelings watching wife get undressed," or "saw good-looking redhead in the cafeteria at work." You should also note *where* you were, the *time* of day, and *who* was with you. At the end of the week, look back over your diary. Can you see any patterns in the events that put you in a sexy mood? Is there a certain place or time of day that you most often feel sexual desire? Are you most likely to think of sex when you are alone, with your wife or lover, or out with the guys? What can you do to foster a sexual mood?

Some people find that seeing a sexual movie, reading sexy magazines or books, or getting a physical workout (through sports, dancing, or manual labor) helps them feel sexual desire. Couple activities that engender an affectionate closeness—for instance, playing cards, sailing, or just talking together—may also lead to sex. Dressing with special care or wearing something that makes you feel particularly attractive can also help.

It is not always the less lusty partner who needs to change. Sometimes the mate who wants more sex is being unreasonable. If you are frustrated by a lack of sex, is there anything other than intercourse that would ease the situation? Is it actually the sex that you crave? Would you feel satisfied if the two of you spent more time cuddling or exchanging back rubs to provide touching and affection? If your partner made more effort to give you compliments, to say "I love you," or to show caring in other small but thoughtful ways, might you be happier with your current amount of sexual interchange? Sex may be one of the only ways that a couple openly expresses love. Unfulfilled sexual desire may really be a yearning for more caring and attention.

If it is truly the release of orgasm that you miss, you could compromise by masturbating occasionally rather than expecting your partner to equal your desire level. As couples age, there may also be times when one lover would enjoy being caressed to orgasm, even though the other does not feel highly excited or want a "turn." If you are comfortable with non-intercourse touching, you can offer to satisfy each other in this manner.

THE SEXUAL ENVIRONMENT

Even if a couple agrees on how often to have sex, lovers may have different views on when to have it, where to have it, or how to get the whole thing started.

Pat has always been a "morning person" while his wife, Sandra, is a "night owl." Each enjoys sex most at the time when he or she feels refreshed and energetic. Unfortunately, this hour is 7:30 A.M. for Pat, and 11:30 P.M. for Sandra. When their children were young, the couple often bickered over this issue. Pat woke his wife up at sunrise, expecting her to respond to his kisses. She resented losing an extra half-hour of sleep before she had to struggle awake to get the kids off to school. At night, when Sandra was finally ripe for some adult entertainment, Pat was already snoring.

After the children left home to start college or their own families, Pat and Sandra were able to work out some compromises. Sandra knew that if she and her husband made love when he woke early for work, she could go back to sleep for a while. On weekends the couple often had sex in the afternoon, since they no longer had to fight for privacy or tailor their schedule to Little League.

As retirement or children leaving the nest releases time and energy for sex, many couples become aware of a lack of variety in their lovemaking. In addition to expanding their repertoire of caresses, one partner may want to try having sex in a novel location. Again, this can set off a couple disagreement.

Ronald wanted to have sex with his new girlfriend, Dottie, in his backyard. He was sure they would have plenty of privacy, since a solid wood fence surrounded the lot. Dottie objected. What if the neighbors' children climbed the fence, a stray visitor or delivery boy came looking for Ronald, or even a helicopter hovered overhead? Ronald's disappointment made Dottie feel torn, since she really enjoyed dating him. After considering the situation carefully, she offered to cook dinner at Ronald's house and have sex outdoors late in the evening, when she would feel less visible. The occasion ended up to be quite memorable, especially for the local mosquitoes. Dottie, scratching bites in unmentionable locations the next morning, decided she would have preferred helicopters.

If you feel adventurous and decide sex does not just mean "going to bed," plan in advance how to make the new setting comfortable. Try putting a sleeping bag in front of the fireplace, or spreading pillows on the tiled floor—but you had better forgo the kitchen table if your partner has a bad back. If you are an outdoors person, remember the bug spray!

If getting sex started is a problem, you and your mate can clarify the sexual invitations that you would welcome, as well as the ones that make you want to run in the opposite direction.

Stanley's standard opener was to come up behind Rita while she was cooking. Before she had time to turn around, he grabbed her breast or put his hand between her legs. On most of these occasions, Rita gritted her teeth and counted to ten, controlling her impulse to brain Stanley with the frying pan. One morning when Stanley was scrambling eggs, Rita saw her chance to retaliate. She edged closer to Stanley until she was in a good position to get both hands around his crotch. In his astonishment, Stanley splashed hot eggs and butter all over the stove and himself. While he cleaned up, Rita dissolved into giggles. Needless to say, the couple did not have sex after breakfast.

Maria was taught that women should be subtle when they want to have sex. Although she and her husband had been married for thirty years, she never asked him directly if he wanted to make love. When Maria was feeling sexy, she put on some perfume and her favorite robe before she came down to watch the late news with her husband. Sadly enough, Maria was too subtle for her own good. Her husband failed to read her signals and usually fell asleep in the living room viewing the talk shows while his wife tossed and turned in their cold bed.

Many couples get their signals crossed when one partner tries to communicate sexual readiness. If your current method of starting sex leaves something to be desired, how about trying some new strategies? Give yourself the freedom to be creative and even a little silly. The worst that can happen with a loving partner is that you get turned down once in a while.

One night when Maria's husband was oblivious, as usual, to her cologne and peignoir, she decided to do something drastic. She got out a set of black lace underwear that she had bought on sale for a romantic occasion (which never quite arrived). Sneaking down to the hall closet, she put on her raincoat over the lingerie. Maria was afraid her husband would notice that she was up to something, but when she came into the living room his eyes were still glued to the TV. "Hi," she said, to get his attention.

Maria's husband was surprised to see his wife in her raincoat. "Are you going somewhere?" he asked.

"I don't know, am I?" Maria asked, opening her coat.

In the morning, when she woke up next to her gently snoring husband, Maria realized that the TV set was still going strong downstairs.

ENHANCING THE EMOTIONAL QUALITY OF SEX

The actual sexual techniques a couple uses are just one aspect of their experience. Often the crucial ingredient in enriching sex is to change the mood of an encounter. Particularly in long-term relationships, the technical details have often been perfected over the years. Boredom sets in, however, because excitement, romance, and fun are missing.

One of my patients in his seventies described trying to help his wife reach orgasm. The couple used elaborate foreplay, and intercourse itself lasted for fifteen or twenty minutes. It all sounded, however, more like work than recreation. I finally asked, "When was the last time you brought your wife flowers on the spur of the moment, or put candles in the bedroom, or left a love note on her pillow?"

"I can't remember," he replied. "Couples our age don't do that kind of thing. Why, if I tried it, she'd tell me I was nuts!"

Couples who remain content with their sexual relationship continue courting and seducing each other over the years. Letting someone know that he or she is still special can promote the tenderness that turns sex from mechanical to magical. I remember another couple in which the husband wrote his wife more than a thousand love letters in the early years of their marriage, when they were separated by World War II. He still writes her a romantic note, now and then, just to add to her collection.

Though many men have a hard time being openly affectionate, a small gesture can say a lot. One wife recently told me that her husband, who was the silent type, had touched her deeply by calling in the middle of the day, saying "I love you," and hanging up the phone. I teased her that she should have asked, "Who is this?"

Married people often forget to set aside couple recreational time. They go out to dinner with the children and grandchildren, or see a movie with friends, but spend their evenings together reading the paper or doing chores around the house. Perhaps you and your partner can plan to go out on a date. In addition to sharing an enjoyable activity, you can agree to pretend for one whole evening that you are just getting to know each other. See if you can recapture the spirit of courtship.

Feeling closer during sex does not necessarily depend on sentimental greeting cards or gypsy violin music. Another mood that often makes sex richer is playfulness. Many of us tend to take sex much too seriously. Although lovemaking can be beautiful, it also has a healthy potential to be absurd. The freedom to laugh at ourselves, and with each other, is a hallmark of intimacy.

If you would like to allow a more playful feeling to creep into your sex life, consider taking a shower together, having a pillow fight, or starting a wrestling or tickling match. Sound undignified? That is the idea. Books such as *The Joy of Sex* and *More Joy*, both by Alex Comfort, provide some interesting suggestions for expanding your sex play. Not every couple adores burying each other in whipped cream, having the woman answer the door clad only in high heels and an apron, tying one partner to the bed with stockings, or any of the many other variations advocated by the popular press in recent years. However, you may discover a lighthearted idea that each of you would enjoy.

Even if you are hesitant to purchase peekaboo lingerie, you can still experiment with using a fantasy during sex. In a recent survey of adults over age sixty, only 10 percent admitted to having an erotic fantasy during sex. The researchers concluded that older adults believed it was wrong to fantasize in bed with a partner. Yet fantasy is perhaps the easiest way to add variety to your sex life.

Almost everyone has a sexual fantasy now and then, either remembering a favorite past experience, imagining what it would be like to make love with a different partner, or picturing a sexual situation that, in reality, would be much too strange or frightening to try. Just as there is no average in terms of sexual behavior, there is no "normal" fantasy. Having an unusual fantasy does not give the same cause for concern as actually carrying out a sexual act that is risky or harmful to others. If you are curious about the variety of people's sexual fantasies, try reading through a collection of them. In Nancy Friday's books *My Secret Garden* and *Forbidden Flowers* she has collected women's fantasies, and in *Men in Love*, male fantasies. Some men's magazines have a monthly column to which readers contribute their fantasies.

Fantasizing during sex with your lover may help you reach higher peaks of excitement. Some people regard a fantasy as a minor act of unfaithfulness—lusting in the heart. Another perspective is to remember that you are choosing to have sex with your partner, no matter what is in your thoughts. The pleasure your fantasy gives you can enhance the sex you and your partner share together. Some couples enjoy revealing their fantasies, while others prefer to keep them private.

It may take some practice to have a vivid sexual fantasy. Try writing yours down or narrating it into a tape recorder. Imagine your surroundings in detail—the setting, the time of day, season of the year, what you and your partner are wearing and doing, scents, sounds, tastes, etc. If you need inspiration you can base your fantasy on a story or film that you found especially arousing.

A WORD ON PERSPECTIVE

The image of an ideal lover in today's society is the sexual sophisticate, technically polished and without inhibitions. If we are to progress beyond the sexual revolution, however, we need to realize that sexual technique is of minor importance. A man's sexuality is an integral part of his personality and his relationships. Though he may refine the ways he reaches orgasm, the ultimate pleasure of sex lies in the risk of sharing himself with another, so that he feels, momentarily, less alone.

11

Single Again: How to Reenter the Mating Game

An unmarried man over fifty may have special concerns about sexuality. On the positive side, he has the chance to start fresh in a relationship, without the emotional "baggage" of a long-term marriage. On the minus side, however, he faces the anxiety and vulnerability of getting close to a new lover.

How many men are in this situation? Quite a few. According to the 1980 United States Census, about 15 percent of middle-aged men (forty-five to sixty-four years old) are unmarried. After retirement age, the proportion of unmarried men increases to 18 percent, and then rises to 31 percent after age seventy-five. Obviously the issue of being single and no longer young is a major one.

Why do men find themselves single, and how do they adjust sexually? About 5 percent of men choose never to marry. Some have a preference for men as sexual partners, while others simply are not interested in marrying. A majority of bachelors have had a serious dating relationship, however, even if it was not formalized by a marriage ceremony. A number of men are quite content to be single, and by the time they reach middle age, have few worries about dating or sexuality. The great majority of homosexual men over forty, for example, do not fit the stereotype of a lonely and pathetic man mourning his youthfulness. On the contrary most are well adjusted and satisfied with their lifestyle, particularly if they are in a committed sexual relationship.

Some single men, however, reach their middle years and feel that something is missing in their lives.

At age sixty-one, Wendell is contemplating an early retirement from his job as a physicist. He would like to travel and spend more time just socializing. Wendell is not sure exactly why he never married. Although sex has always made Wendell a bit nervous, he enjoys it and has had three fairly long-term dating relationships. Two of these affairs ended when the girlfriend began to pressure Wendell for marriage. The third relationship is still going on. Wendell is not passionate about his current girlfriend, but he feels a real tenderness and affection for her. Wendell is having a hard time giving up his dream of a woman who will sweep him off his feet, but he finds himself thinking about marrying his lover. She would be a very pleasant traveling companion, and her ease with people is something that Wendell admires.

The majority of older unmarried men are single because of divorce or bereavement. Each married man runs a fair risk of seeing his relationship end during his lifetime. For instance, if you were born between 1900 and 1914, by age seventy-five you would have had a 15 percent chance of being divorced and a 15 percent chance of being widowed.

While the likelihood of bereavement has been stable in recent years, the rate of divorce has been steadily increasing. In 1970, less than 6 percent of ever-married men aged forty-five to fifty-four were divorced, but in 1980, that figure was up to 10 percent. These statistics may seem more real to you if you consider that a quarter of all couples who married in the year 1950 were divorced before reaching their silver wedding anniversary.

There also seems to be a trend for longer-lasting marriages to break up. About a third of divorces occur after more than ten years of togetherness. Some factors that may lead to divorce after twenty or thirty years of marriage include the "empty nest" syndrome, i.e., the loss of a common purpose when the children leave home; the recent focus on putting one's own life goals before duty to the family; and women's new economic and emotional independence.

Whatever the cause of a divorce, the results are usually traumatic, particularly for men who have never really lived alone before.

Marv's wife left after thirty-two years of marriage. Although the couple had not spent much time together since their courtship, Marv had been relatively content. He was absorbed in his job as a mechanic and in his hobby of rebuilding antique cars. When the children were in high school, his wife had returned to her career as a nurse. The couple's sex life had been unexciting, but it had satisfied Marv's needs. His wife, however, told him before she left that she had never been happy with him as a lover and saw him as a selfish and cold person.

Two years after his divorce, Marv has learned to cook a few dishes besides scrambled eggs and hamburgers and is considering selling his house and moving to a condominium in an all-adult complex. He is reluctant to give up his yard and workshop, however. Marv has had a few dates, some involving casual sex, but he did not enjoy any of the women very much. Most were a good ten or fifteen years younger than Marv, who found himself impatient with their young children and at a loss for topics of conversation. He shamefacedly admits, however, that he does not find women his own age sexually attractive.

Marv has adjusted to single life by working overtime and drinking more than he knows is healthy. He is not sure what he wants for the future, except somehow to re-create the comfortable past.

In addition to its emotional strain, divorce exacts measurable costs in terms of health. It seems that for men in particular being married is good medicine. Men who are divorced or widowed, and to a lesser extent men who remain single from choice, have strikingly higher rates of psychological disorders, suicide, physical illness, alcoholism, as well as death from auto accidents, homicide, heart attacks, and some types of cancer.

Why do married men have better health? When a man's emotional needs for warmth and intimacy are met, he tends to take better care of himself. A married man has his family's support in coping with the stress of daily living. After a man loses the woman he loves, either through death or as a relationship sours, he seems to care less about his fate, even taking unnecessary risks with his health and safety.

A "nagging" wife can also be an important health asset. Women have been raised to take care of their men, in sickness as well as in health. In my work with cancer patients, I am amazed at how often the wife has to coax her husband to see a doctor when he begins to have symptoms. Wives can actually reduce cancer deaths in married men, since the earlier cancer is diagnosed, the more successfully it can be treated. The moral, if you are single, is not necessarily to marry, but to invest extra effort in maintaining your own health.

There has never been a good study of sexual problems in unmarried men. I suspect, however, that men who are widowed and divorced are at higher risk for difficulties with sexual desire and erections. Increased use of alcohol and tobacco, heart disease, high blood pressure, and cancer can all interfere with sexual function—and all are more common in bachelors and in men who are divorced or widowed. If you are a single man with a sexual problem, the suggestions in previous chapters on getting good sexual health care apply to you.

Men who are divorced or widowed should also be forewarned of some unique patterns of emotional stress that may interfere with their sex lives. Although the medical causes of sexual problems are similar in widowed and divorced men, psychological factors affecting sexuality differ for the two groups.

Men who go through a divorce lose their relationship through choice, either their own or their wife's. Often sexual dissatisfaction plays a role in that decision. If a man feels rejected by his wife, particularly if she has criticized his sexual prowess, after the divorce he brings his resulting insecurity and anger to his new dating relationships.

When Lou's youngest daughter started high school, his wife, Andrea, went into partnership with two other women in their neighborhood, opening a swimwear shop. The success of this business seemed to change Andrea's whole personality. She criticized Lou's handling of their finances, went out at night without him if he said he was too tired, and hired a cleaning woman to do the housework. At about this time, Lou became sexually involved with one of the receptionists at work. One of Andrea's friends saw Lou and his girlfriend having dinner at a restaurant on an evening when he had told his wife he would be working late. The friend called Andrea, who confronted Lou with her wish for a divorce.

Although Lou offered to give up his affair, and even to try marital counseling, Andrea would not change her mind. Lou complained that she was using his one mistake as an excuse to end a marriage that she no longer needed financially. To make things worse, Andrea's lawyers used Lou's adultery to force him to move out of the house and give his wife a very favorable settlement. Lou's children were embarrassed by the gossip in their suburb and refused to visit their father in his new apartment. Lou's girlfriend kept hinting that she would like to move in with him.

When the new couple did have sex, Lou could not stop thinking about Andrea and the contempt in her voice when she had told him, "Your little girlfriend is welcome to you." Lou found that he could rarely get an erection anymore with his girlfriend, and within a few weeks they broke up, much to Lou's relief.

Even if a man has made the decision to leave an unhappy marriage, he may feel ill at ease with the prospect of dating again. In the past ten or fifteen years, women have become more forward in asking men out. This new female assertiveness can be disconcerting to men who were used to the dating rules that prevailed before "women's liberation."

When Jeff and his wife separated, he was stunned by his sudden popularity. It seemed as though every other weekend he was invited to a friend's house and provided with a single, female dinner partner. One divorced friend persuaded Jeff to accompany him to a meeting of Parents Without Partners. Within two hours, Jeff was handed three women's phone numbers.

Jeff did not really feel like dating yet, but when several of his new acquaintances called, he did not have the heart to say no. He was even more taken aback, however, by his dates' sexual invitations. While Jeff was debating whether a goodnight kiss was in order, one woman started unbuttoning his shirt. On another occasion, he went along with his date's advances, but felt very nervous and awkward. When they had intercourse, Jeff ejaculated almost immediately. Although the woman said she understood, he could tell that she was disappointed. Jeff had never imagined a need to set limits on sex before, but now he decided to put a moratorium on dating until he met someone who really attracted him.

On the other hand, many divorced men approach the dating scene with high expectations. They have read and heard about the new sexual freedom and hope to become a part of it all. They may look forward to having lovers who are younger, more attractive, or just different from their wives. Often they begin dating with enthusiasm, looking forward to casual sex, no commitments, and lots of fun. Since the ratio of single men to single women is increasingly in men's favor as they get older, these close encounters may not be hard to find. After age sixty-five, for example, there are three unmarried women for each single man. Many of these women would jump at the chance to have some affection, companionship, and sexual pleasure. After the initial excitement wears off, however, a divorced man may find that dating is not all that he dreamed.

Larry, an assembly-line worker, went to singles' bars and dances in the first year after his divorce. However, he is now living with a woman who is about three years younger than he is. This is what Larry had to say about his dating experiences:

"I'm naturally sort of shy, even though I joke around a lot. At bars, I usually just sat around, waiting to see if a woman would talk to me. Sometimes it happened, and sometimes I'd go home alone. I never went with anyone who wasn't clean and nice-looking, and I've never had to pay for sex, if you know what I mean. Some of the guys think I'm crazy because they've seen me turn down a woman who wanted to come home with me. I guess a man is supposed to be able to have sex with anyone, but there must be something wrong with me. I'm just not made that way.

"I met the gal I date now at a party. She wouldn't go to bars, because she's not the type. Her first husband treated her pretty badly, and she likes me because I'm good to her. Sex is better with her too, because there's some loving to it. With most of those other women, it was fun while it lasted, but I felt lonely afterward. I just wanted them to leave. Toward the end, before I met my girlfriend, sometimes I couldn't even get it up unless I'd known the woman for a while. That's the most embarrassing thing, when you can't perform."

Widowers have a different problem. Their marriages did not end by choice, but because they lost a spouse to death. Even more than a divorced man, a widower often goes through a period of major depression, in which he feels helpless and immobilized. A divorced man can feel justifiably furious at his ex-wife. As he expresses his rage and hurt, it gradually fades with time. A widower often feels angry too—after all, his wife has also left him—but where should he direct his anger? In the great majority of cases, his wife did not want to die and there is rarely anyone he can blame for her death. If he is religious, he is not comforted by being angry with God.

In default of a better target, he may turn his anger back on himself. He blames himself for not taking better care of his wife or somehow preventing her death. He remembers all the times he fell short of being the perfect husband. He dwells on the words of love or farewell that were left unsaid. These feelings of guilt and unrecognized anger can prolong a man's period of mourning beyond healthy limits.

Difficulty in resuming sex after a bereavement is so common that a "widower's syndrome" has been identified by sex therapists. In the classic picture, the wife has a lingering final illness, so that the couple is unable to have sex together for a number of months or even years. The husband becomes his wife's nurse and emotional supporter. Since he realizes that her illness is terminal, he has a chance to come to terms with her death. By the time she does reach the end of her life, the husband often experiences relief, which may make him feel guilty. A few months after the death, the widower begins to date again. He may even become engaged or remarry. When he tries to have sex, however, he discovers he can no longer get or keep a good erection.

Sex therapists assume that the widower's problem is caused by anxiety at being with a new partner after a long marriage, or to unresolved mourning for the deceased wife. Many widowers find that they do feel nervous with a new partner, or that they are having thoughts about their former wife during sex. It is almost impossible, at first, to avoid making comparisons.

Walter waited a good six months to start dating after his wife's death from uterine cancer. Even then he chose carefully—an attractive and soft-spoken widow who had been a customer at his jewelry store for several years. The couple had dinner together a number of times before they began to have a sexual relationship. Walter was delighted to find that he could still enjoy sex, because it had been three years since he and his wife had been able to make love together. In the forty-four years of his marriage, he had never slept with another woman.

The third evening that Walter and his lady friend tried having sex, the setting was Walter's bedroom. This was their first visit to Walter's home, and he had looked forward to showing his new lover how he lived. He found himself feeling a little uncomfortable, however, as if an invisible audience were watching. When the couple went into the bedroom, Walter's lady friend commented on the fact that he still kept his wife's perfume bottles on the dresser.

"You know, I never felt I was over my husband's death until I cleaned out his closet," she told Walter. Walter agreed that he probably should give away his wife's things. He found himself feeling distant and annoyed, however, and was unable to get sexually aroused. He kept remembering a newspaper article on being widowed, which was illustrated by a photo of a double bed, with one side rumpled and the other looking as if it had just been made. "This was our bed," he thought to himself, "and I never should have brought her here."

When a man is first widowed, he may tell himself that he could never look at another woman. In the lonelinesss after his wife's death, however, he realizes he needs to make new ties. Widowers often worry that to date is to be unfaithful to their wife's memory. The wife's own attitude as she was dying may be an important factor in the widower's adjustment. Many wives, while they are ill, suggest that their husband find a new love if he is widowed. A few, however, ask the husband not to date or remarry. This latter situation can really set a man up to feel guilty, as in this example from a recent "Dear Abby" column:

DEAR ABBY: My wife of many years died recently. She made a peculiar request before she passed on. She asked me to have her cremated, then mix her ashes in a can of white paint and paint the bedroom ceiling with this mixture.

This understandably creates a difficult dilemma for me. I certainly want her near me, but not necessarily when I'm entertaining in the bedroom.

—PEELING PAINT IN DAYTON

DEAR PEELING: I don't foresee much datin' in Dayton with the ashes of your dear departed mate on the bedroom ceiling. Honor her request, but entertain elsewhere.

In my own research, I found the widower's syndrome of erection problems to be even more common in men whose wives died suddenly, rather than after a long illness. If death occurs in an accident or from an unexpected heart attack or stroke, there is no opportunity for a man to prepare himself or to say goodbye. The tasks of mourning and going on with life then become even more difficult. In terms of sex, a man may not wish to get close to a new partner, since he is still coping with the shock of losing his dependable and beloved wife.

Whether a man is widowed or divorced, some psychological counseling can help him deal with his anger and grief and regain sexual fulfillment. Sometimes, however, the psychological fact of a divorce or bereavement makes a man or his doctors overlook a physical problem that could be interfering with sexual function. My research with widowers revealed that many of their erection problems had a medical basis. This is why it is just as important for a single as for a married man to have a thorough medical evaluation of a sexual problem.

HEALTHY SINGLEHOOD

Whether a man is a lifelong bachelor, divorced, or widowed, he may wonder how to have a happy sex life as a single man over fifty. All of the guidelines that you have read about sexual function and aging, sexual communication, and sexual health care are relevant for the single man. In addition, however, the unmarried man should consider some specific issues:

1. *A period of celibacy can help you recover from the pain of a breakup or bereavement.*

When a relationship has ended, only you can judge when you are ready to seek a new one. Other people's opinions about the proper length of time before dating after a breakup, divorce, or a wife's death are truly not important. If your marriage ended after years of nasty fights or your wife died after an illness of several years, you may feel released from pain and ready to begin a new love life. On the other hand, if the ending of a marriage, or even a fairly casual dating relationship, was sudden and traumatic, you need time to rest and recuperate.

As you will recall from Chapter 3, a period of celibacy should not prove harmful to your sexual response. After the loss of a mate, you may feel little, if any, sexual desire for several months. As your sexual feelings return, you can give yourself permission to try masturbating to achieve some pleasure and release. Use your sexual fantasies to "rehearse" how you will meet and interact with a new lover when you feel ready. Imagine the kind of woman you will find attractive, where you will meet, and how you would like sex to be.

2. *When you do begin to date, take things slowly and try not to exceed your comfort level.*

Older men who reenter the dating scene often put pressure on themselves to act like nineteen-year-olds. They believe they should be ready for sex at any time with anyone. Unlike a teenager with his first car, you should know better than to outdrive your headlights on a dark highway. This is a time in your life to learn to slow down and even to say "no." Setting a sexual speed limit for yourself may be particularly important in a world where women have learned to take the initiative.

You need to accept that you will not feel attracted to every woman who is interested in you. It will do neither partner any good to try to force yourself into sex. In fact, you would be setting the scene for an erection problem. Even if you do find a woman sexy, you may need a longer acquaintance period than she does before starting a sexual relationship, especially if she has not gone through a recent loss.

Sometimes a woman is surprised when a man says "no" to a sexual invitation. Her first thought is that the man finds her unattractive. If you are dating someone you like, but you are not yet ready for a sexual relationship, why not explain your thinking to her? You can say, "I'm really enjoying spending time with you and I think you're very attractive, but I want to take things slowly as far as sex is concerned." If a woman really wants you, she should be willing to wait a while.

Rather than jumping right into dating or setting yourself a goal of resuming sex, concentrate at first on increasing your social life in general. After a divorce or bereavement, a man often feels lonely or sad if he socializes in the same settings as he did with his wife. Now he is no longer one half of a couple. Lifelong bachelors also often have narrow social circles and could use a wider network of friends.

Taking a leisure class in art, cooking, a foreign language, or a sport is one way to meet people who share an interest with you. Churches and senior citizens' centers also have social groups for older single people. Men are welcomed with open arms to these heavily female environments. Women, as well as men, make good friends and companions, even if you are not in the market for a lover. If you later decide to renew your sex life, you may feel closer to someone who started out as your buddy than to a stranger you meet on a blind date or at a bar.

When you try your first sexual activity after a dry spell, start with a few kissing sessions rather than going from the first embrace to intercourse in one date. The sensate focus touching exercises from Chapter 10 can provide a good beginning for a new sexual partnership. You can let your partner know that you would enjoy taking time to explore sensual pleasure together. Go ahead and tell her that you have not had sex for a while. She will probably be complimented that you have chosen her as your first new partner. Women usually enjoy being the "giver" and helping their lover feel more relaxed. Revealing your nervousness, as well as your attraction, can make a woman feel needed and valued.

If you are still living in the home where your last relationship took place, choose a room for your first sexual experiences that does not remind you of your former wife or lover. Nothing throws cold water on your sexual desire as effectively as memories of the past. Try to find a setting where you feel relaxed and ready to enter a totally new phase of your sex life. Alternatives might include your girlfriend's house, a weekend resort, the room that used to be your den, or your redecorated bedroom.

3. *If you have trouble getting or keeping an erection, do not panic.*

Minor sexual difficulties are so common when starting a new relationship that you really should expect them as a rule, rather than as the exception. Most often, with some time and patience the problems resolve themselves. Your partner's body feels more familiar, you get used to her touch, you are more confident of each other's affection, the past fades, and your sexual responses return to normal.

If you have an erection problem with a new partner, think of it as a cue to slow down. Give each other back rubs, or spend a while kissing and touching, instead of aiming for intercourse. When you are relaxed enough to appreciate the pleasure you get from touching and you feel ready for a more intense kind of closeness, you can move on toward intercourse, perhaps using the steps outlined in the sensate focus exercises.

If you had an erection problem with your last partner and are starting over with someone new, telling her about your sexual difficulty can help you relax. If all goes well, she will be pleasantly surprised. If you have an erection problem again, however, she will be prepared to sympathize and help. If your erections do not improve or if other sexual difficulties are causing tension, sexual counseling and a physical examination may be in order.

Neal had had erection problems in all three of his dating relationships since his wife's death. Neal was very lonely and wanted to marry his current woman friend. He was afraid to make that commitment, however, unless the couple had a satisfying sex life. He sought help from one psychologist, who told him that the erection problem was due to unfinished grief over his bereavement. She said that the "widower's syndrome" could last for one to three years and Neal should just wait it out.

Unsatisfied with this advice, Neal went to a clinic that specialized in treating sexual problems. A thorough physical exam and health history did not suggest any medical cause for the sexual problem. Before putting Neal through more specialized tests, it was decided to try some brief sex therapy. His lover was willing to work with Neal, so the couple had ten sessions together, with homework assignments in between. Neal spent some time alone with the therapist, as well, to discuss his adjustment to being widowed. At the end of the treatment, Neal was having good erections and also felt more at peace with himself and the memory of his wife.

SHOULD I REMARRY?

The issue of remarriage for older men is really too complex to handle in a book focusing on sex. I can offer some interesting statistics and observations, however.

The rates of remarriage for divorced and widowed Americans over fifty have remained stable during the past twenty years. Men are much more likely than women to remarry, because older men have so many more potential mates. Not only are there more single women than men, but men often marry younger women, while the reverse situation is still considered unusual. For both men and women, the South and West are the regions of America where most retirement-age remarriages occur. The divorced are also more apt to remarry than the widowed.

The remarriage most likely to succeed is one in which the bride and groom have known each other for a reasonable length of time, the couple is living in a new home rather than in one that previously belonged to either partner, their income is adequate, and the children approve of the relationship. This last factor is a sad reversal of the usual parent-child roles. Many senior citizens' children try to regulate their parents' sex lives. Adult offspring are often ashamed that their parents still dare to be sexual people, not to mention their fears of losing part of an inheritance to Mom or Dad's new spouse.

When older men and women live in nursing or retirement homes, their children often pressure the staff to forbid sexual relationships between residents. In some settings, even married couples are not allowed to share a room. Hopefully our growing awareness of the healthiness of sexual feelings for people of all ages will put an end to this puritanical bullying! Some of the best nursing homes set aside rooms where dating couples can spend some time alone together; in others, residents are encouraged to put a "do not disturb" sign on their door when they want some privacy.

Older couples frequently live together rather than marrying. Often a marriage would cause one partner to lose retirement or reduce Social Security benefits, or the couple deems it unnecessary to formalize a love relationship when the childbearing era is past. According to the 1980 census, 230,000 American men aged forty-five to sixty-four and 99,000 men sixty-five and over are living with a companion outside of marriage. In a recent survey of older adults, an overwhelming 91 percent approved of unmarried couples living together.

What is the importance of sex in remarriage? In the survey just mentioned, 98 percent of adults over sixty believed that sex plays at least some role in the decision to marry in later life. When men and women compared sex in their current marriage to an earlier one, about 30 percent said lovemaking was better now and 56 percent said it was just as good as in the past. Only 13 percent found sex to be worse in their current relationship.

In my practice I have seen a number of men who wished to remarry or at least to find a caring relationship, but hesitated because of an erection problem. Some of these men wanted desperately to have penile prosthesis surgery. Although sex is one important part of marriage, penis-in-vagina intercourse on the wedding night is not a prerequisite for a true emotional and spiritual commitment. By all means seek help for a sexual problem, but do not let a limp penis keep you sitting at home alone. Pay attention to the sixty-odd inches of your body that still work, rather than to the six inches that are temporarily out of commission.

The statistics tell us that being part of a couple is good for our health, both mental and physical. There is nothing magic, however, about marriage per se. The key to well-being is taking care of your body and making the effort to put some caring into your life. Sex is one type of caring, but many men find that the love shared with a good friend, a grandchild, or even a pet makes living worthwhile.

12

And Now It's Up to You!

Now that you have read this whole book, you can consider yourself well versed on the sexual health of men over fifty. You know that there is no male menopause, but that a man's sexual desire after age fifty depends on his lifelong sexual patterns and on the general state of his health. You have been alerted to some common changes that a man may notice in his erection response as he grows older—an increase in the time it takes to get a full erection, a need for direct caressing of his penis, and a greater tendency to lose erections. You know that these changes, far from being catastrophic, can inspire a couple to add a new richness and sensuality to their sex life. And don't forget that older men can make intercourse, as well as foreplay, last longer!

You now have a better understanding of women's sexuality as well. You know that menopause does not signal the end of sex and that women appreciate a man's tenderness as much as, or more than, his penis. You also have an idea of how that penis functions and the causes of erection problems in older men. You are aware that your mind, as well as your body, can influence your sexual function.

You also can tell the difference between good sexual health care and the miracle pills offered by quacks as sexual remedies. You have a clear idea of the impact of ill health on your sex life and are familiar with exams available to find the cause of a sexual problem. You have some strategies for approaching your family doctor about a sexual problem and even for finding the right kind of specialist. If you have been hesitating about getting help for a sexual problem, this information about the medical, surgical, and counseling treatments available should help you decide whether to invest your energy in finding a solution.

Even if your sexual relationship has been running smoothly you now possess techniques to increase your communication, enhance your pleasure in touching, and inject some extra romance and fun into your lovemaking. If you are unmarried, you are aware of some of the pitfalls in starting a new sexual relationship and how to avoid them.

What then will you do with all this book learning? If you do not put your knowledge to use, this book's value is reduced to a collection of ink marks on pressed sawdust. The fate of the printed page is not the issue—you can give this book to your mate to read, return it to the library, put it on the shelf for future reference, or consign it to your wastebasket.

This book will have succeeded, however, if it leads you to enhance even one aspect of your sex life. Depending on your current needs, that could mean trying one of the touching exercises, asking your partner to leave on the lights, making a doctor's appointment to find out why you are having trouble with erections, experimenting with masturbation for the first time in years, spinning a sexual fantasy, telling your daughter to stop criticizing you for dating "at your age," or even telling your partner "Not tonight, honey."

The crucial factor in any positive step is your willingness to take action. Though your lover, your doctor, your sex therapist, or this book can help, the choices are yours.

Sexual health is a matter of common sense: Understand your body, take care of your general health, stay as physically fit as possible, put a high priority on your intimate relationships, and take the risk of asking your lover for what you want. The needs for touching, affection, and sexual pleasure are lifelong. May each year after fifty be the most memorable of your sex life.

REFERENCE NOTES

page
2

**1: You as a Lover: Are You Getting Better
or Just Older?**

Patterns of sexual interest and intercourse: L.K. George and S. J. Weiler, "Sexuality in Middle and Late Life: The Effects of Age, Cohort, and Gender," *Archives of General Psychiatry* 38 (1981): 919–23.

2–3

A discussion of the causes of erection problems can be found in G. Wagner and R. Green, *Impotence: Physiological, Psychological, Surgical Diagnosis and Treatment* (New York: Plenum Press, 1981), 37–88, 149–54.

page
9–10

2: Is There a Male Menopause?

Effects of testosterone are discussed in R. C. Kolodny, W. H. Masters, and V. E. Johnson, *Textbook of Sexual Medicine* (Boston: Little, Brown, & Co., 1979), 107–08, 19–22.

10

Theories of male menopause are from S. M. Harman, "Clinical Aspects of Aging of the Male Reproductive System," in *The Aging Reproductive System*, ed. E. L. Schneider (New York: Raven Press, 1978), 29–58.

10   Information on female menopause is from Kolodny, Masters, and Johnson, *Textbook of Sexual Medicine*, 103–06.

11–12   The evolution of menopause is discussed in D. P. Barash, *Sociobiology and Behavior* (New York: Elsevier, 1977), 291–92.

12   For hormones and aging, see S. M. Harman and P. D. Tsitouras, "Reproductive Hormones in Aging Men. I. Measurement of Sex Steroids, Basal Luteinizing Hormone, and Leydig Cell Response to Human Chorionic Gonadotropin," *Journal of Clinical Endocrinology and Metabolism* 51 (1980):35–40.

12   testosterone levels do not change with age: F. E. Purifoy, L. H. Koopmans, and D. M. Mayes, "Age Differences in Serum Androgen Levels in Normal Adult Males," *Human Biology* 53 (1981):499–511.

12   One recent study of men over sixty: P. D. Tsitouras, C. E. Martin, and S. M. Harman, "Relationship of Serum Testosterone to Sexual Activity in Healthy Elderly Men," *Journal of Gerontology* 37 (1982):288–93.

13   hormone levels and homosexuality: H. F. L. Meyer-Bahlburg, "Sex Hormones and Male Homosexuality in Comparative Perspective," *Archives of Sexual Behavior* 6 (1977):297–325.

13   Theories on hormones and aging are in Harman, "Clinical Aspects of Aging," 39–45.

14   Alfred Kinsey's sex studies: A. C. Kinsey et al., *Sexual Behavior in the Human Male* (Philadelphia: W. B. Saunders, 1948), 218–62.

14–15   The Duke studies are summarized and reinterpreted in L. K. George and S. J. Weiler, "Sexuality in Middle and Late Life: The Effects of Age, Cohort, and Gender," *Archives of General Psychiatry* 38 (1981): 919–23.

17   In 106 cultures: R. L. Winn and N. Newton, "Sexuality in Aging: A Study of 106 Cultures," *Archives of Sexual Behavior* 11 (1982):283–98.

18–19   Men's characteristic sexual interest levels are discussed in C. E. Martin, "Factors Affecting Sexual Functioning in

	60–79-Year-Old Married Males," *Archives of Sexual Behavior* 10 (1981):399–420.
20	Detailed information on sexual desire problems is found in H. S. Kaplan, *Disorders of Sexual Desire* (New York: Brunner/Mazel, 1979).
20	The Coolidge Effect is discussed in E. Walster and G. W. Walster, *A New Look at Love* (Reading, Mass.: Addison-Wesley, 1978), 75–76.

page   **3: When Mystery Is Not Romantic: The Sexual**
25–28   **Response and Aging**

25–28	The sexual response cycle is described in detail in H. S. Kaplan, *Disorders of Sexual Desire* (New York: Brunner/Mazel, 1979), 9–21.
28–30	The effects of aging on the sex response cycle are discussed in W. H. Masters and V. E. Johnson, *Human Sexual Response* (Boston: Little, Brown & Co., 1966), 245–66.
31	In one large survey: B. D. Starr and M. B. Weiner, *The Starr-Weiner Report on Sex and Sexuality in the Mature Years* (New York: Stein & Day, 1981), 253.
31–32	Facts on NPT are summarized in I. Karacan, "Clinical Value of Nocturnal Erection in the Prognosis and Diagnosis of Impotence," *Medical Aspects of Human Sexuality* 4 (1970):25–34.
32	Testosterone and NPT have been studied by R. C. Schiavi et al., "Hormonal Variations During Sleep in Men with Erectile Dysfunction and Normal Controls," *Archives of Sexual Behavior* 11 (1982):189–200.
33	Aging and NPT have been studied by E. Kahn and C. Fisher, "REM Sleep and Sexuality in the Aged," *Journal of Geriatric Psychiatry* 2 (1969):181–99; and I. Karacan et al., "Sleep-Related Penile Tumescence as a Function of Age," *American Journal of Psychiatry* 132 (1975):932–37.
34	In a recent survey: Starr and Weiner, *The Starr-Weiner Report*, 38.
35–36	On obesity and sex, see R. C. Kolodny, W. H. Masters, and

V. E. Johnson, *Textbook of Sexual Medicine* (Boston: Little, Brown, & Co., 1979), 249–53.

36   The discussion of fitness and sex is based on L. Remes, K. Kuoppasalmi, and H. Aldercreutz, "Effect of Long-Term Physical Training on Plasma Testosterone, Androstenedione, Luteinizing Hormone, and Sex-Hormone-Binding Globulin Capacity," *Scandinavian Journal of Clinical Laboratory Investigation* 39 (1979):743–49; and R. J. Young and A. H. Ismail, "Ability of Biochemical and Personality Variables in Discriminating Between High and Low Physical Fitness Levels," *Journal of Psychosomatic Research* 22 (1978):193–99.

36–37   relationship between alcohol use and sex: P. D. Tsitouras, C. E. Martin, and S. M. Harman, "Relationship of Serum Testosterone to Sexual Activity in Healthy Elderly Men," *Journal of Gerontology,* 37 (1982):288–93.

36   alcohol use can damage a man's hormonal balance: G. Wagner and R. Green, *Impotence: Physiological, Psychological, Surgical Diagnosis and Treatment.* (New York: Plenum Press, 1981), 81–88.

37   heavy smokers also may have sexual problems: L. Forsberg et al., "Impotence, Smoking and Beta-Blocking Drugs," *Fertility and Sterility* 31 (1979):589–91; and A. G. Keresteci et al., "The Vasculogenic Etiology of Erectile Impotence" (paper presented at the meeting of the American Urological Association, Kansas City, Mo., April 1982), 174.

37   The study on quitting smoking and erection problems is by W. D. Jarman, M. Edson, and J. Elist, "A Clinical Study of the Medical Management of Impotence" (paper presented at the meeting of the American Urological Association, Kansas City, Mo., April 1982), 190.

38   "use it or lose it": W. H. Masters and V. E. Johnson, "Sex and the Aging Process," *Journal of the American Geriatrics Society* 29 (1981):385–90.

38   My own research: L. R. Schover, I. Karacan, and K. M. Hartse, "The Widower's Syndrome: Organic or Psychogenic Erectile Dysfunction?" (paper presented at the meeting

of the Association for the Psychophysiological Study of Sleep, San Antonio, Texas, June 1982).

38   testosterone levels in . . . monks: A. A. A. Ismail et al., "Assessment of Gonadal Function in Impotent Men," in *Reproductive Endocrinology*, ed. W. J. Irvine (Edinburgh: Livingston, 1970).

39   The Kinsey studies: A. C. Kinsey et al., *Sexual Behavior in the Human Male* (Philadelphia: W. B. Saunders, 1948), 499.

39   The Starr-Weiner survey: Starr and Weiner, *The Starr-Weiner Report*, 57.

39   A very fine discussion: B. Zilbergeld, *Male Sexuality*, (New York: Bantam Books, 1978), 160–76.

42   For decreased genital sensation with age, see N. Corby and R. L. Solnick, "Psychosocial and Physiological Influences on Sexuality in the Older Adult," in *Handbook of Mental Health and Aging*, ed. J. E. Birren and R. B. Sloane (Englewood Cliffs, N.J.: Prentice-Hall, 1980), 896.

page   **4: What Do Women Really Want?**
44   Female masturbation was studied in A. C. Kinsey et al., *Sexual Behavior in the Human Female* (Philadelphia: W. B. Saunders, 1953), 130–32.

49–50   Myths about penis size are discussed in W. H. Masters and V. E. Johnson, *Human Sexual Response* (Boston: Little, Brown, & Co., 1966), 191–95.

50   a spot on the front wall: A. K. Ladas, B. Whipple, and J. D. Perry, *The G Spot* (New York: Holt, Rinehart and Winston, 1982), 20–29.

52   Women's difficulty reaching orgasm during intercourse is discussed in L. Barbach, *For Each Other* (New York: Anchor Press/Doubleday, 1982); and in S. Hite, *The Hite Report* (New York: Macmillan, 1976).

52   According to Kinsey: P. H. Gebhard, "Factors in Marital Orgasm," *The Journal of Social Issues* 22 (1966):95.

52   " 'Look Ma—no hands!' ": Barbach, *For Each Other*, 27.

53   Masters and Johnson actually observed women: Masters and Johnson, *Human Sexual Response*, 127–40.

58–61   The discussion of female anatomy and sexual response is based on ibid., 37–99.

58   a small zone on the front wall: Ladas, Whipple, and Perry, *The G Spot*, 30–58.

61   A recent survey of older men: B. D. Starr and M. B. Weiner, *The Starr-Weiner Report on Sex and Sexuality in the Mature Years* (New York: Stein & Day, 1981), 86.

61–62   For psychological aspects of menopause, see L. B. Rubin, "Sex and Sexuality: Women at Midlife," in *Women's Sexual Experience: Explorations of the Dark Continent*, ed. M. Kirkpatrick (New York: Plenum Press, 1982), 61–82.

62–64   physical aspects of menopause: S. R. Leiblum, "Researcher: Vaginal Atrophy Linked to Sexual Inactivity in Older Women," *Sexuality Today* 6 (Number 23): 1–3; and R. Kolodny, W. H. Masters, and V. E. Johnson, *Textbook of Sexual Medicine* (Boston: Little, Brown, & Co., 1979) 103–06.

63   one study of women over sixty: Starr and Weiner, *The Starr-Weiner Report*, 86.

63–64   Women often hesitate: *Post-menopausal Estrogen Therapy* (New York: American Council on Science and Health, 1983).

65   For hysterectomies and sex, see L. Dennerstein, C. Wood, and G. D. Burrows, *Hysterectomy: How to Deal with the Physical and Emotional Aspects* (Melbourne: Oxford University Press, 1982); and Kolodny, Masters, and Johnson, *Textbook of Sexual Medicine*, 198–201.

page   **5: Middle Age Is the First Time You Can't Do It Twice.**
67   **Old Age Is the Second Time You Can't Do It Once!**
         interviewing men in the 1940s: A. C. Kinsey et al., *Sexual Behavior in the Human Male* (Philadelphia: W. B. Saunders, 1948), 235–38.

67   interviews in the 1970s: C. E. Martin, "Factors Affecting Sexual Functioning in 60–79-Year-Old Married Males," *Archives of Sexual Behavior* 10 (1981): 399–420.

68–70   A detailed discussion of the anatomy of erections can be found in G. Wagner and R. Green, *Impotence: Physiologi-*

cal, Psychological, Surgical Diagnosis and Treatment (New York: Plenum Press, 1981), 7–36.

72   "spectatoring": W. H. Masters and V. E. Johnson, *Human Sexual Inadequacy* (Boston: Little, Brown, & Co., 1970), 191.

72   men raped by women: P. Sarrel and W. H. Masters, "Sexual Molestation of Men by Women," *Archives of Sexual Behavior* 11 (1982):117–32.

72–73   laboratory test of "erections on demand": D. H. Barlow, D. K. Sakheim, and J. G. Beck, "Anxiety Increases Sexual Arousal," *Journal of Abnormal Psychology* 92 (1983):49–54.

81–83   A complete discussion of medical causes for erection problems can be found in G. Wagner, "Organic Causes of Impotence: Medical," in *Management of Male Impotence*, ed. A. H. Bennett (Baltimore: Williams & Wilkins, 1982), 128–34.

page   **6: Sexual Health Hazards: Some Diseases of Aging**

86   If an illness is prolonged: L. Leiber et al., "The Communication of Affection Between Cancer Patients and Their Spouses," *Psychosomatic Medicine* 38 (1976):379–89.

91–92   The role of arteriosclerosis in erection problems is discussed in a variety of sources, including A. G. Keresteci et al., "The Vasculogenic Etiology of Erectile Impotence" (paper presented at the annual meeting of the American Urologic Association, Kansas City, Mo., April 1982), 174; V. Michal and V. Ruzbarsky, "Morphologic Changes in the Arterial Bed of the Penis with Aging: Relationship to the Pathogenesis of Impotence," *Investigative Urology* 15 (1977): 194–99; R. Virag, "Arterial and Venous Hemodynamics in Male Impotence," in *Management of Male Impotence*, ed. A. H. Bennett (Baltimore: Williams & Wilkins, 1982), 108–27; G. Wagner, "Organic Causes of Impotence: Medical," in *Management of Male Impotence*, ed. A. H. Bennett (Baltimore: Williams & Wilkins, 1982), 128–34; and G. Wagner and R. Green, *Impotence: Physiological, Psychological, Surgical Diagnosis and Treatment* (New York: Plenum Press, 1981), 63–72.

92   surgeons can sometimes improve a man's erections: D. P. Flanigan et al., "Elimination of Iatrogenic Impotence and Improvement of Sexual Function After Aortoiliac Revascularization," *Archives of Surgery* 117 (1982):544–50.

92   "pelvic steal syndrome": I. Goldstein et al., "Vasculogenic Impotence: Role of the Pelvic Steal Test," *Journal of Urology* 128 (1982):300–305.

92   "vasodilators": W. D. Jarman, M. Edson, and J. Elist, "A Clinical Study of the Medical Management of Impotence" (paper presented at the meeting of the American Urologic Association, Kansas City, Mo., April 1982), 190.

93   Surgical cures for erectile dysfunction are reviewed in Wagner and Green, *Impotence*, 155–66.

93   For antihypertensives and sex, see J. Buffum et al., "Drugs and Sexual Function," in *Sexual Problems in Medical Practice*, ed. H. I. Lief (Monroe, Wis.: American Medical Association, 1981), 211–42; R. C. Kolodny, W. H. Masters, and V. E. Johnson, *Textbook of Sexual Medicine* (Boston: Little, Brown, & Co., 1979), 321–28; and H. B. Moss and W. R. Procci, "Sexual Dysfunction Associated with Oral Antihypertensive Medication: A Critical Survey of the Literature," *General Hospital Psychiatry* 4 (1982): 121–29.

95   A group of British researchers: S. Mann et al., "Coital Blood Pressure in Hypertensives: Cephalgia, Syncope, and the Effects of Beta-Blockade," *British Heart Journal* 47 (1982):84–89.

95   Survey of information from physicians on sex for cardiac patients is from T. Kavanaugh and R. J. Shepherd, "Sexual Activity After Myocardial Infarction," *Canadian Medical Journal* 116 (1977):1250–53.

95   50 to 75 percent of cardiac patients: Kolodny, Masters, and Johnson, *Textbook of Sexual Medicine*, 169–82; and C. Papadapoulos, "A Survey of Sexual Activity After Myocardial Infarction," *Cardiovascular Medicine* 3 (1978):821–26.

95–96   For coital death, see L. R. Derogatis and K. M. King, "The Coital Coronary: A Reassessment of the Concept," *Archives of Sexual Behavior* 4 (1981):325–35; and M. Ueno,

"The So-called Coition Death," *Japanese Journal of Legal Medicine* 17 (1963):333–37.

96   Studies on the safety of sexual activity for cardiac patients are reviewed in J. Friedman, "Sexual Adjustment of the Postcoronary Male," in *Handbook of Sex Therapy*, ed. J. LoPiccolo and L. LoPiccolo (New York: Plenum Press, 1979), 373–86.

96–97   For angina and sex, see G. Jackson, "Sexual Intercourse and Angina Pectoris," *International Rehabilitation Medicine* 3 (1981):205–08.

97   For arrythmias and sex, see Derogatis and King, "The Coital Coronary," 119–20.

97   Cardiac Rehabilitation Program: C. M. Cole, et al., "Brief Sexual Counseling During Cardiac Rehabilitation," *Heart and Lung* 8 (1979):124–29; see also J. D. Sanders and D. H. Sprenkle, "Sexual Therapy for the Post Coronary Patient," *Journal of Sex and Marital Therapy* 6 (1980):174–86.

98   Diabetes and sexuality is discussed in S. B. Jensen, "Diabetic Sexual Dysfunction: A Comparative Study of 160 Insulin Treated Diabetic Men and Women and an Age-Matched Control Group," *Archives of Sexual Behavior* 10 (1981):493–504; and Kolodny, Masters, and Johnson, *Textbook of Sexual Medicine*, 128–42.

98–99   counseling to treat diabetic men: D. C. Renshaw, "Impotence in Diabetics," in *Handbook of Sex Therapy*, ed. LoPiccolo and LoPiccolo, 433–40.

99   a recent study of forty-seven diabetic men: M. J. Jevtich, "Vascular Factor in Erectile Failure Among Diabetics," *Urology* 19 (1982):163–68.

99–100 Diabetic side effects and erection problems are discussed in Jensen, "Diabetic Sexual Dysfunction," 493–504.

100–104 Sexuality and cancer is discussed in Kolodny, Masters, and Johnson, *Textbook of Sexual Medicine*, 273–98; A. C. von Eschenbach and D. B. Rodriguez, *Sexual Rehabilitation of the Urologic Cancer Patient* (Boston: G. K. Hall, 1981); and L. R. Schover and A. C. von Eschenbach, "Sexual Rehabilitation of the Urologic Cancer Patient," *Medical Aspects of Human Sexuality* 17 (1983):172–85.

102   cancer of the penis and cervical cancer: S. Graham et al., "Genital Cancer in Wives of Penile Cancer Patients," *Cancer* 44 (1979):1870–74; and P. G. Smith et al., "Mortality of Wives of Men Dying with Cancer of the Penis," *British Journal of Cancer* 41 (1980):422–28.

102   Researchers are speculating: R. E. Stahl et al., "Immunologic Abnormalities in Homosexual Men: Relationship to Kaposi's Sarcoma," *The American Journal of Medicine* 73 (1982):171–78.

103   radiation to the pelvis: I. Goldstein et al., "Radiation-Induced Impotence: A Clinical Study" (paper presented at the meeting of the American Urologic Association, Kansas City, Mo., April 1982), 174.

104–05   For sexuality and lung disease, see E. C. Fletcher and R. J. Martin, "Sexual Dysfunction and Erectile Impotence in Chronic Obstructive Pulmonary Disease," *Chest* 4 (1981):413–21; and Kolodny, Masters, and Johnson, *Textbook of Sexual Medicine*, 263–65.

105   For alcoholism and sexuality, see Kolodny, Masters, and Johnson, *Textbook of Sexual Medicine*, 239–44; and Wagner and Green, *Impotence*, 81–82.

106–07   For BPH and sexuality, see D. Brandes and R. G. Garcia-Bunuel, "Aging of the Male Sex Accessory Organs," in *The Aging Reproductive System*, ed. E. L. Schneider (New York: Raven Press, 1978), 127–57; and Kolodny, Masters, and Johnson, *Textbook of Sexual Medicine*, 215–19.

106–07   For effects of TURP on sexual function, see E. P. So et al., "Erectile Impotence Associated with Transurethral Prostatectomy," *Urology* 19 (1982):259–62.

107–08   For Peyronie's disease, see Kolodny, Masters, and Johnson, *Textbook of Sexual Medicine*, 219; and J. P. Pryor and O. Kahn, "Beta Blockers and Peyronie's Disease," *Lancet* 8111 (1979):331.

page   **7 : You and Your Doctor: Your Right to Sexual Health**
110   For deficits in physicians' sex education, see, H. I. Lief and A. Karlen, *Sex Education in Medicine* (New York: Spectrum Publications, 1976).

114–20   Physical exams for erection problems are summarized in D.
K. Montague, "The Evaluation of the Impotent Male," in
Management of Male Impotence, ed. A. H. Bennett (Balti-
more: Williams & Wilkins, 1982), 52–61; and G. Wagner
and R. Green, *Impotence: Physiological, Psychological,
Surgical Diagnosis and Treatment* (New York: Plenum
Press, 1981), 89–130.

116   For X rays of the pelvic circulatory system, see C. M.
Juhan, G. Padula, and J. H. Huguet, "Angiography in
Male Impotence," in *Management of Male Impotence*, ed.
A. H. Bennett (Baltimore: Williams & Wilkins, 1982), 73–
107.

118–19   The value of NPT in diagnosing erection problems is dis-
cussed in I. Karacan and C. A. Moore, "Nocturnal Penile
Tumescence: An Objective Diagnostic Aid for Erectile Dys-
function," in ibid., 62–72; and P. Marshall, A. Morales, and
D. Surridge, "Diagnostic Significance of Penile Erections
During Sleep," *Urology* 20 (1982):1–6.

119   The new take-home gauge is described in A. Ek, W. Brad-
ley, and R. J. Krane, "A New Concept in the Measurement
of Penile Rigidity" (paper presented at the meeting of the
American Urologic Association, Kansas City, Mo., April
1982), 175.

120   do-it-yourself method: J. M. Barry, B. Blank, and M. Boi-
leau, "Nocturnal Penile Tumescence Monitoring with
Stamps," *Urology* 15 (1980):171–72.

121   One respected urologist: A. L. Finkle, "Genitourinary Disorders of Old Age: Therapeutic Considerations Including
Counseling for Sexual Dysfunction," *Journal of the American Geriatrics Society* 10 (1978):453–58.

121–22   A German research group: O. Benkert et al., "Effects of
Testosterone Undecanoate on Sexual Potency and the Hypothalamic-Pituitary-Gonadal Axis of Impotent Males," *Archives of Sexual Behavior* 8 (1979):471–79.

122   For testosterone therapy side effects, see R. C. Kolodny,
W. H. Masters, and V. E. Johnson, *Textbook of Sexual
Medicine* (Boston: Little, Brown, & Co., 1979), 328.

122   yohimbine: A. Morales et al., "Nonhormonal Pharmacologi-

cal Treatment of Organic Impotence," *Journal of Urology* 128 (1982):45–47.

122–23 vasodilator: W. D. Jarman, M. Edson, and J. Elist, "A Clinical Study of the Medical Management of Impotence" (paper presented at the meeting of the American Urologic Association, Kansas City, Mo., April 1982), 190.

page **8: Medical Treatments for Sexual Problems**

125–26 Testosterone therapy is discussed in S. B. Streem, "The Endocrinology of Impotence," in *Management of Male Impotence*, ed. A. H. Bennett (Baltimore: Williams & Wilkins, 1982), 26–45.

126 high levels of prolactin: M. F. Schwartz, J. E. Baumann, and W. E. Masters, "Hyperprolactinemia and Sexual Disorders in Men," *Biological Psychiatry* 17 (1982):861–76.

126 recent report from Harvard Medical School: R. F. Spark, R. A. White, and P. B. Connolly, "Impotence Is Not Always Psychogenic: Newer Insights into Hypothalamic-Pituitary-Gonadal Dysfunction," *Journal of the American Medical Association* 243 (1980):750–55.

126–27 Fourteen out of sixteen men: P. Salmimies et al., "Effects of Testosterone Replacement on Sexual Behavior in Hypogonadal Men," *Archives of Sexual Behavior* 11 (1982):345–54.

127–29 Vascular surgery to correct erection problems is discussed in R. Virag, "Revascularization of the Penis," in *Management of Male Impotence*, ed. A. H. Bennett (Baltimore: Williams & Wilkins, 1982), 219–33; G. Wagner and R. Green, *Impotence: Physiological, Psychological, Surgical Diagnosis and Treatment* (New York: Plenum Press, 1981), 161–64; and A. W. Zorgniotti, "An Appraisal of Penile Revascularization," in *Management of Male Impotence*, ed. A. H. Bennett (Baltimore: Williams & Wilkins, 1982), 234–36.

128 For aortoiliac surgery, see D. P. Flanigan et al., "Elimination of Iatrogenic Impotence and Improvement of Sexual Function After Aortoiliac Revascularization," *Archives of Surgery* 117 (1982):544–50; and L. Forsberg, A. M. Olsson,

and P. Neglen, "Erectile Function Before and After Aorto-Iliac Reconstruction: A Comparison Between Measurements of Doppler Acceleration Ratio, Blood Pressure and Angiography," *Journal of Urology* 127 (1982):379–82.

130–43   The types of penile prosthesis, and patient satisfaction with them, are reviewed in R. S. Beaser et al., "Experience with Penile Prostheses in the Treatment of Impotence in Diabetic Men," *Journal of the American Medical Association* 248 (1982):943–48; A. H. Bennett, "The Inflatable and Malleable Penile Prosthesis," in *Management of Male Impotence*, ed. A. H. Bennett (Baltimore: Williams & Wilkins, 1982), 210–18; R. P. Finney, "Rigid and Semirigid Penile Prostheses," in *Management of Male Impotence*, ed. A. H. Bennett (Baltimore: Williams & Wilkins, 1982), 198–209; and Wagner and Green, *Impotence*, 155–61.

143   The two new inflatable models are presented in R. P. Finney, "New Totally Intra-Penile Inflatable Prosthesis for Impotence" (paper presented at the annual meeting of the American Urologic Association, Las Vegas, Nev., April 1983), 219; and F. B. Scott, "Experience with a New Inflatable Penile Prosthesis" (paper presented at the annual meeting of the American Urologic Association, Las Vegas, Nev., April 1983), 220.

page
160

9: Sex Therapy: Or It's Not So Crazy to Get Some Counseling

specialists at the University of Chicago: H. W. Schoenberg, C. K. Zarins, and R. T. Segraves, "Analysis of 122 Unselected Impotent Men Subjected to Multidisciplinary Evaluation," *Journal of Urology* 127 (1982):445–47.

162   "sexual history": W. E. Masters and V. E. Johnson, *Human Sexual Inadequacy* (Boston: Little, Brown, & Co., 1970), 330–34.

162–63   The principles of sex therapy were first set out in ibid. More recent references include H. S. Kaplan, *The New Sex Therapy* (New York: Brunner/Mazel, 1979); and J. LoPiccolo and L. LoPiccolo, eds., *Handbook of Sex Therapy* (New York: Plenum Press, 1978).

166–67   sexual surrogates: Masters and Johnson, *Human Sexual Inadequacy*, 146–54; and L. Wolfe, "The Question of Surrogates in Sex Therapy," in *Handbook of Sex Therapy* ed. J. LoPiccolo and L. LoPiccolo (New York: Plenum Press, 1978), 491–98.

168   Sexual function after penectomy is discussed in M. H. Witkin and H. S. Kaplan, "Sex Therapy and Penectomy," *Journal of Sex and Marital Therapy* 8 (1982):209–21.

169   In one clinic: J. G. Blaivas et al., "The Diagnosis and Treatment of Erectile Dysfunction" (paper presented at the meeting of the American Urologic Association, Kansas City, Mo., April 1982), 175.

page   **10: Sexual Enrichment: Revitalizing Your Sex Life**
176   negative messages about sex: B. D. Starr and M. B. Weiner, *The Starr-Weiner Report on Sex and Sexuality in the Mature Years* (New York: Stein & Day, 1981), 283.

176   the best predictor of a woman's capacity: P. Morokoff, "Determinants of Female Orgasm," in *Handbook of Sex Therapy*, ed. J. LoPiccolo and L. LoPiccolo (New York: Plenum Press, 1978), 147–66.

177   a third of couples never discuss: Starr and Weiner, *The Starr-Weiner Report*, 140.

187–93   The sensate focus exercises are modified versions of those described in H. S. Kaplan, *The Illustrated Manual of Sex Therapy* (New York: Quadrangle, 1975), 29–59; and W. H. Masters and V. E. Johnson, *Human Sexual Inadequacy* (Boston: Little, Brown, & Co., 1970), 67–91.

193   half of men over sixty: Starr and Weiner, *The Starr-Weiner Report*, 110.

193–210   Some techniques that sex therapists use to help a couple enrich their sex life are described in L. R. Schover, "Enhancing Sexual Intimacy," in *Innovations in Clinical Practice: A Source Book*, ed. P. A. Keller and L. G. Ritt (Sarasota, Fla.: Professional Resource Exchange, Inc., 1982), 53–66.

197   For genital taboos in tropical societies, see C. S. Ford and

F. Beach, *Patterns of Sexual Behavior* (New York: Harper Torchbooks, 1951), 93–95.

197   For the female genitals as art, see T. Corinne, *Labia Flowers* (New York: Naiad Press, 1981); and B. Dodson, *Liberating Masturbation* (New York: Body Sex Designs, 1974).

197   A discussion of genital esthetics can be found in L. Barbach, *For Each Other* (New York: Anchor Press/Doubleday, 1982), 51–54.

209   Alex Comfort: A. Comfort, *The Joy of Sex* (New York: Crown, 1972); and A. Comfort, *More Joy* (New York: Crown, 1974).

209   The survey on fantasy in older adults was in Starr and Weiner, *The Starr-Weiner Report*, 125–26.

210   Nancy Friday's books: N. Friday, *My Secret Garden* (New York: Simon & Schuster, 1975); and N. Friday, *Forbidden Flowers* (New York: Simon & Schuster, 1976); and N. Friday, *Men in Love* (New York: Delacorte, 1980).

page   **11: Single Again: How to Reenter the Mating Game**

211   Statistics on marital status are from Bureau of the Census, *Statistical Abstract of the United States* (Washington: U.S. Department of Commerce, 1981), 37–40.

212   The great majority of homosexual men: R. M. Berger, "Psychological Adaptation of the Older Homosexual Male," *Journal of Homosexuality* 5 (1980):161–75.

212–13   Divorce statistics are from Bureau of the Census, *Statistical Abstract of the United States*, 37–40; and R. B. Stuart, *Helping Couples Change: A Social Learning Approach to Marital Therapy* (New York: The Guilford Press, 1980), 1–8.

214–15   For marital status and health, see Stuart, *Helping Couples Change*, 8–13; and L. M. Verbrugge, "Marital Status and Health," *Journal of Marriage and the Family* 41 (1979):267–85.

217   three unmarried women: J. Treas and A. Van Hilst, "Marriage and Remarriage Rates Among Older Americans," *The Gerontologist* 16 (1976):132–36.

218–20 "widower's syndrome": M. W. Hengeveld and A. Korzec, "Mourner's Impotence," in *Medical Sexology*, ed. R. Forleo and W. Pasini (Littleton, Mass.: John Wright–P.S.G., Inc., 1980), 243–48; and R. C. Kolodny, W. H. Masters, and V. E. Johnson, *Textbook of Sexual Medicine* (Boston: Little, Brown, & Co., 1979), 512–13.

220–21 "DEAR ABBY . . .": *Houston Post*, February 13, 1983, p. 15G.

221 In my own research: L. R. Schover, I. Karacan, and K. M. Hartse, "The Widower's Syndrome: Psychogenic or Organic Erectile Dysfunction?" (paper presented at the meeting of the Association for the Psychophysiological Study of Sleep, San Antonio, Tex., June, 1982).

221–23 Celibacy and a man's right to say "no" to sex are discussed in B. Zilbergeld, Male Sexuality (New York: Bantam Books, 1978), 177–224.

225–26 For marriage for older adults, see W. C. McKain, "A New Look at Older Marriages," Family Coordinator 21 (1972):61–69; and Treas and Van Hilst, "Marriage and Remarriage Rates," 132–36.

226 Sex in nursing homes was studied by M. Wasow and M. B. Loeb, "Sexuality in Nursing Homes," in *Sexuality and Aging*, ed. R. L. Solnick (Los Angeles: University of Southern California Press, 1978), 154–62.

226 According to the 1980 census: Bureau of the Census, Statistical Abstract of the United States, 41.

226–27 In a recent survey of older adults: B. D. Starr and M. B. Weiner, The Starr-Weiner Report on Sex and Sexuality in the Mature Years (New York: Stein & Day, 1981), 260–61.

INDEX

Women (*cont'd*)
  as "insatiable," 56–57
  menopause of, 10–11, 61–64
  older, sexuality of, 61–65
  sexual needs and preferences
     of, 43–65
  sexual responses of, 58–61

X rays, 116–17

Yohimbine, 122

Zilbergeld, Bernie: *Male Sexuality*, 39